Trust Is a Double-Edged Sword

Trust Me

Waywill

Copyright © 2022 by Waywill.

Library of Congress Control Number:	2022902380
ISBN: Hardcover	978-1-6698-1026-1
Softcover	978-1-6698-1025-4
eBook	978-1-6698-1024-7

All rights reserved. No part of this book may be reproduced or transmitted in any form or by any means, electronic or mechanical, including photocopying, recording, or by any information storage and retrieval system, without permission in writing from the copyright owner.

Any people depicted in stock imagery provided by Getty Images are models, and such images are being used for illustrative purposes only.
Certain stock imagery © Getty Images.

Print information available on the last page.

Rev. date: 09/28/2022

To order additional copies of this book, contact:
Xlibris
844-714-8691
www.Xlibris.com
Orders@Xlibris.com
828661

CONTENTS

Introduction v

Chapter 1	Trust Me (Until You Distrust Me)	1
Chapter 2	Should You Buy What You Are Being Sold?	28
Chapter 3	A Friend in Need Is a Friend Indeed	64
Chapter 4	Do You Trust Yourself?	81
Chapter 5	Whom Are You Fooling?	102
Chapter 6	Maybe My Brain Needs to Be Smarter	119
Chapter 7	Until Death Do Us Part	135
Chapter 8	Thirty Plus: Happily Ever After	157
Chapter 9	Should I, or Shouldn't I?	165
Chapter 10	Trusting Too Much Can Put You in Harm's Way	174
Chapter 11	What Happened to the Humans?	186
Chapter 12	How Can We Believe the Numbers?	198
Chapter 13	Political and Judicial System Trust: What an Oxymoron	210
Chapter 14	Trust Starts in Childhood	229
Chapter 15	Beauty Is in the Eye of the Beholder	248
Chapter 16	Ego: How Dangerous Is It?	256
Chapter 17	Ask Yourself These Questions	267
Chapter 18	Conclusion	272

Appendix A: The Ten Commandments of Trust 275
Appendix B: Trust 911: Trust Warning Signals 279
Appendix C: Trust Triage: How to Recover When Your Trust Is Violated 281
Index 283

INTRODUCTION

TRUST IS A double-edged sword. What does trust really mean to you? Do you trust your partner? Do you trust what you are being sold? Do you trust your own decisions? Do you trust what others tell you? Trust means vulnerability—it means accepting the sincerity and truth of what someone says, whether spouse, friend, business partner, boss, salesman, colleague, or even offspring.

If you trust a person, you can close your eyes and believe that that person will guide you safely in the dark. A trusting relationship is open and reciprocal; both parties meet on a field of transparency, mutual aid, and informed choice.

When any of those factors is violated, either unilaterally or by both parties, trust is destroyed. The contention of this book is that your trust—and maybe the trust others place in you—can be betrayed more often than any of us would like to believe. In order to successfully navigate life, in business and intimacy, you must become aware of the dangers and possibilities that are present when you are called to trust, as all of us are almost constantly.

I want you to consider the myriad aspects of what trust means in your life and how everything you do, think about, and live with is fortified or weakened by the way in which you place trust in others.

I started out thinking that this book isn't about me, but in fact, it is. I wrote it because of what happened to me, which you will learn in the next chapter. More importantly, though, it really is about you. It is about all of us. It is about self-awareness, truth, humility, and objectivity. Please acknowledge that we all are the same. We get up every day and live our lives. Our hearts beat; our emotions flare up based on memories or interactions. We love, crave, and desire sincere companionship, best friends, great partners, and implicit allies. Sadly, we often suffer disappointment and injury on our journeys. Some of this is inevitable; life is a mixture of tragedy and joy. But a good deal of our suffering arises because we misplace our trust. The hard truth is that most of us trust too easily. Some of this is due to lazy thinking and mental shortcuts. Clearly, there is no educational program on the subject of trust; we have to rely on life experiences—ours and those of others. Perhaps it is human nature to impulsively wish to trust. It is something we think we are supposed to do. I now realize that I am that way. But I have also made too many mistakes trusting people too easily. Painful lessons have taught me the pitfalls of misplaced trust and the error of giving my trust too easily.

Have you learned this yet? How many times have you been hurt because you naively trusted someone? Even after getting burned, many of us make the same mistakes again. Why do we do that?

Again, I ask you to consider: what does trust really mean to you? How have you been impacted by relying on trust? Do you consider trust instinctive? Or is it something that must be earned by facts and actions?

Is your trust guided by a whim or a researched reality? What has occurred when you trusted others?

Can we ever—and forever—really trust someone?

Does self-interest always take over and destroy the trust that we once considered sacrosanct?

Think hard about these questions and be entirely honest as you consider them. I am asking you to consider not only whether you are able to trust others but also whether they should trust you. What we observe in others also exists in ourselves. If you need to, put down this book and really consider these questions. Maybe you've never been willing to face them before. Share your feelings with yourself and be as objective and unsparing as possible.

You picked up this book for a good reason. You probably wouldn't be reading these words if you did not have a sense that trust in your life isn't what you would like it to be. Maybe you have suffered betrayal or committed acts of betrayal yourself. Hence, I am asking you to pause and think about the question of how you trust others and what you expect in return. This isn't a rhetorical question. This question is relevant for all of us.

You must be more aware of the impact of trust within your relationships and throughout your life. Your future happiness could depend on your willingness to consider these questions. You may be getting agitated by what I am stating—and if you are, *good*. It means that what I am saying is finding its mark. If you are not reacting, then you are avoiding. I want you to ponder the word *trust* and what it means to you. I do not care what it says in a dictionary; I want to know what it means to you. In fact, trust isn't just a word. It is a "something," an essence that reverberates through our consciousness and dictates our feelings, thoughts, and behaviors. It is the foundation of our relationships. It is everything in our lives. Trust figures into every kind of relationship and venture. It is the determining factor that ultimately brings joy or sorrow, at least within those circumstances that we can select. Because it is the pivotal point of all relationships, trust is the core of life. It is the law of being.

Before continuing with this book, please take a moment to reflect on what you've just read, even if you think you know your feelings about trust. Consider the basic fact that trust commences at the beginning of your life—trust in your parents—and is supposed to extend to all the key relationships that later emerge. But consider this: Is this ideal just a fantasy? A falsehood? Is trust ever possible, if only because those whom you trust are influenced by their own self-interest? Trust is earned. Do you trust your financial adviser, your spouse or mate, your boss or coworkers, your friends, your doctor, or even your children? Go through the list and think about it. When something happens that you know is wrong—such as someone breaking his or her word—do you just avoid it? What and how do you feel? Perhaps what you wish to be truly isn't, and you make excuses to yourself to avoid that reality. The simple truth is that real trust is earned. Otherwise, there is only blind faith. And blind faith will burn you sooner or later. For babies and children, trust is implicit. It is absolute.

We want to believe that we can trust the people in our lives who raise us and teach us. Our survival is in their hands. To not trust would be too terrifying to contemplate (although some children obviously are forced into that crisis). All of us want to feel and believe that our parents love us implicitly and that they are dedicated to do everything to nourish, empower, and most importantly, protect us. The ideal is that their deep love for us means that they put us ahead of themselves and that they innately wish for our well-being because we are an extension of them. At least, this is how it should be.

Unfortunately, there are negative aberrations at this early stage of life, especially when parents think solely about themselves. I have heard too many stories about young children being used as pawns when their parents were getting divorced. I have witnessed, as you probably have, mothers or fathers who forsake this implicit trust and intrinsic obligation and see their children as tools of self-interest. This occurs whenever a parent places his or her self-interest ahead of the children's emotional well-being. The potential scars and psychological damage inflicted on these children could impact their lives on many levels well into adulthood. In that sense, who and what we are is determined by trust at the most rudimentary and formative stages of our lives.

I consider and reflect on my own life experiences in this regard. I was born in New York City. My parents, without question, loved me. I grew up an only child, so perhaps I got more attention than many children receive. This was accentuated by the tragedy of my older sister dying at nine months old due to an allergic reaction to an injection. This occurred before I was born. My mother never emotionally recovered and became an alcoholic. My dad was a working man. He owned a gas station in Queens and was a tough guy. That said, he always loved me and took real pride in my accomplishments. As a child, however, I noticed and felt significant dysfunction in their relationship. I didn't realize that something was wrong because I knew nothing else. I accepted it as a norm. Now, as an adult, I reflect on this and realize that, if you do not know something is bad, it becomes acceptable and natural. This is why children copy our best and our worst traits. Their trust in us is implicit. Consider how important that is.

The phrase "perception of self" relates to this. I do not mean how you see yourself; rather, I mean how others perceive you. Do you care? You may not, but you ought to. If someone is jealous of you, he or she doesn't count. But consider how other people see you. Do you do the right things in their eyes? Do you treat people respectfully? Are you responsible and honest? Do you treat others the way you would like to be treated? Can you be trusted?

My parents fought a lot and showed no warmth toward each other. Again, that was my norm. They got divorced when I was five years old. They then remarried each other when I was fifteen years old and got divorced again when I was twenty-five years old! (I am not making this up.) So, you can trust me when I tell you that I grew up in a dysfunctional setting. I had no role models to demonstrate the importance of a loving and lasting relationship or the importance of trust in maintaining a relationship. I am not complaining, but I have become aware of this, not because of what happened then, but more so because of my life now.

Now is today and tomorrow. How important is trust in that? For me, it is my strength and my weakness. I have learned the hard way how trust works, and I want to share my mistakes and help you not to make the same ones. I am sure that by this point in *Trust Is a Double-Edged Sword*, you are reflecting on your life, and you are replaying errors in judgment and the disappointment and hurt that misplaced trust has caused you.

This book isn't about self-help per se. It is about self-awareness. Self-awareness is a responsibility to ourselves and a discipline that requires work. In effect, self-awareness is a mindset. It is also a secret weapon. Self-awareness underpins nearly every other skill you possess. If you are self-aware, you can grow, improve, learn, and get better. If you are not self-aware, you will probably plateau and end up stuck. Sun Tzu's ancient treatise, *The Art of War*, teaches that, if you know your enemy and know yourself, you need not fear the result of a battle. If you know yourself but do not know your enemy, every victory will be accompanied by a commensurate defeat. And if you know neither the enemy nor yourself, you will lose every battle.

This book can help you in both endeavors: knowing yourself and knowing a (potential) adversary. The point is not to replay the tape of your life and grow emotional over the past or to ruminate on imagined future outcomes; rather, focus on appreciating your failings and strengths in matters of trust and acting on them.

Whom Do You Trust the Least?

When it comes to honesty in the workplace, some professions have a better reputation than others. For example, some people might question a contractor who surpasses his quoted price. Or some people might blame a salesperson when a newly purchased used car breaks down after twenty miles. That begs the question, what professions do Americans trust the most? In 2019, American analytics company, Gallup, Inc., delved into the issue and released the results of an interesting poll about honesty and ethical standards: Nurses are top of the honesty league and have been there for eighteen years in succession. The public has a high level of trust in medical professionals in general, and 84 percent of Americans assess nurses' honesty and ethical standards as *high* or *very high*. Doctors and pharmacists also ranked highly in the honesty category, with 67 and 66 percent trusting each profession respectively. Despite controversy over police shootings and heavy-handed law enforcement, 54 percent of Americans continued to view police officers as *honest* and *ethical* while 13 percent gave them a low rating. Members of Congress rank at the bottom of the honesty scale, with 58 percent of the public claiming they have *poor* or *extremely low* levels of honesty and ethical standards. Car salespeople are also one of the least-trusted professionals in America today with only 8 percent of people viewing them as *honest* and *ethical*.[1]

We all can think of people whom we don't trust. This feeling, unfortunately, isn't an anomaly. We have all had bad experiences in which trust was breached. Trust is and always has been at the core of all personal and business relationships.

Recently, these issues have played out on a global scale. In spring 2020, the world changed, and people everywhere experienced an unprecedented upheaval from the coronavirus disease (COVID-19) pandemic. In the short span of about six weeks, our way of life was upended as we were subjected to quarantine mandates, face masks, social distancing, and an all-but-shattered economy.

Every day, we were barraged by news reports. The US President either misrepresented the facts or blamed others for what happened after earlier downplaying the severity of the virus. It seemed difficult to trust anyone. We saw every stranger on the street as a carrier. We were warned to remain at least six feet away from one another. Fear abounded.

How did this happen? Who was responsible?

---

[1] RJ Reinhart, "Nurses Continue to Rate Highest in Honesty, Ethics," *Gallup*, January 6, 2020. https://news.gallup.com/poll/274673/nurses-continue-rate-highest-honesty-ethics.aspx.

In December 2019, the United States and China agreed on a Phase One trade bill that included a commitment by China to make substantial purchases of US goods and services in coming years. Six weeks later, the trade truce agreement between the United States and China was signed. China, however, slipped in an "out clause" that stipulated they didn't have to make good on what they committed to buy from the United States if there was an act of nature or a pandemic. Within days, China announced the emergence of the coronavirus. The Chinese government knew in late November of the coronavirus through cases being reported in the city of Wuhan in Hubei Province. The first Wuhan doctors who reported the outbreak were arrested and accused of spreading harmful rumors. By enforcing their silence, China may have intentionally exacerbated the pandemic. This is criminal because we know that unfettered travel and trade made the disease a global phenomenon that was impossible to contain.

In January and February 2020, we heard some news about Wuhan, yet few alarms were sounded. In fact, President Trump repeatedly downplayed the severity of the virus. On February 27, Trump said the outbreak would be temporary: "It's going to disappear. One day, it's like a miracle—it will disappear."[2] The head of the National Institute of Allergy and Infectious Diseases, Anthony Fauci, MD, advised a few days later that he was concerned about the situation, "As the next week or two or three go by, we're going to see a lot more community-related cases."[3] On March 6, President Trump said, "Anybody that needs a test, gets a test. We, they're there. They have the tests. And the tests are beautiful."[2] The truth is that the country's testing capabilities were severely limited. Many states experienced a shortage of testing kits, as was widely reported. Indeed, Trump made his claim one day after

---

[2] Stephen Collinson, "Trump seeks a 'miracle' as virus fears mount," *CNN*, February 28, 2020. https://www.cnn.com/2020/02/28/politics/donald-trump-coronavirus-miracle-stock-markets/index.html.

[3] Christian Paz, "All the President's Lies About the Coronavirus," *The Atlantic*, November 2, 2020. https://www.theatlantic.com/politics/archive/2020/11/trumps-lies-about-coronavirus/608647/.

his own vice president, Mike Pence, confessed that "we don't have enough tests today to meet what we anticipate will be the demand going forward."[4] Trump stated on March 17, "I've always known this is a real—that this is a pandemic. I felt it was a pandemic long before it was called a pandemic…I've always viewed it as very serious."[5] Yet Trump repeatedly downplayed the significance of the coronavirus even as outbreaks began nationwide.

A Pandemic Era Lesson Learned

One big lesson that leaders should heed is based on the pandemic that killed at least fifty million people worldwide from 1918 to 1920. And that lesson is: Tell the truth. In 1918, we were at war, and the government lied about the severity of the pandemic because officials didn't want to upend the war effort. Similar lies were repeated a century later. Following such events—the consequences of which are still unfolding as I write these words—how do we trust our leaders in times of crisis? Or even every day?

Writing this book became a mission for me. I realized that trust is at the core of everything in our lives, and the breadth of its violations affect us in profound ways. My goal is to increase your awareness of the importance and risks of trust, and my reward will be making a difference in your life.

---

[4] BBC, "Coronavirus: White House concedes US lacks enough test kits." *BBC.com*, March 6, 2020. https://www.bbc.com/news/world-us-canada-51761435.
[5] Quint Forgey, "Trump, who downplayed pandemic threat, says he 'always viewed it as very serious'," *Politico*, March 17, 2020. https://www.politico.com/news/2020/03/17/trump-shifting-coronavirus-tone-134100.

CHAPTER 1

Trust Me (Until You Distrust Me)

IT CAN TAKE years to create trust, seconds to shatter it, and a lifetime to rebuild it. Imagine that, if you are not careful when you are making love to your partner, you could be poisoned or impaled. The mating dance of scorpions has always fascinated entomologists. To watch male and female scorpions perform their special choreography before mating is a terrifying spectacle. They have to be extra vigilant and careful not to inject each other with the poison at the end of their tails. Without sexual intercourse, that species would obviously have become extinct eons ago. Yet they have reproduced abundantly and occupy an important place in the animal kingdom. Trust prevails between these lovers, so their "lovemaking" will not turn into a bloodbath. Porcupines also mate carefully, cautiously experiencing intimacy without impaling each other in their embrace.

Trust is a fundamental prerequisite to their union. Thus, trust exists and thrives throughout nature. We humans should be aware that trust is a vital factor in the processes of life. Trust is not a human invention that we designed only when we became civilized; it originated in early human culture. Trust can vanish or diminish in many relationships and often does. Something happens—inconsistent behavior, a bad act, the wrong thing said, the development of a visceral sense—that causes discomfort that swells into doubt. This is called "distrust".

As I am writing this book, I find myself incessantly discussing the topic with friends, acquaintances, and even strangers. This helps me consider the myriad ways in which trust is at the core of everything in life. There are several reasons for my discussions and comparisons.

First, I am obviously passionate about the subject. My intention is to stimulate readers' thoughts and bring to the forefront an essential awareness, which we often don't like to think about. I have discovered that, by sharing my objectives, I sometimes evoke meaningful reactions and hear stories that are relevant, including personal examples of trust violations and their impact. It seems that everybody has had a bad breach-of-trust experience. Some of the stories I hear are truly moving and have traumatized the people involved.

Recently, I attended a real estate trade show and started to converse with someone who was standing next to me during the networking break. After some introductory conversation, we started to talk about what we do. I mentioned my real estate endeavors and then started to talk about my new book and the horrible experience I'd had with a crooked, sociopathic partner. (This experience was the catalyst that inspired me to write *Trust Is a Double-Edged Sword*, and I will explain the situation in this chapter.)

My new acquaintance's face became ashen, and he told me he'd had a bad experience as well, and he shared it with me. This fellow was in a real estate service business. He was having a conversation with the senior partner of the firm regarding a bill that had been paid by a big client that had included a significant erroneous overcharge that client was not aware of. The senior partner told my acquaintance not to worry about it because the client would never notice it. This gentleman told me that he felt very uncomfortable about the senior partner's decision, but he nonetheless went along with it. What he didn't consciously realize was that he had just shifted from trusting his partner to mistrusting him in all other contexts. He said that, as time passed, other things occurred that exacerbated his mistrust. Then the senior partner took a bonus on a transaction that he did not procure, and for my new acquaintance, that had been the final straw. He had been, in fact, the source of the business, but he had been cheated out of the compensation.

What would you do in a circumstance like this? How would you continue to work under such circumstances? Maybe you'd be stuck, and you'd need the salary and wouldn't be able to afford to move on and try to find a new job. In this case, my new acquaintance ultimately resigned from his position.

Sometimes, distrust exists immediately with no interaction. There doesn't have to be a specific reason; nothing needs to have happened. It isn't unusual for people to feel uncomfortable or to distrust other people who are different from themselves. These differences, fairly or not, can cause discomfort, disinterest, insensitivity, and distrust. To be honest, I have at times been guilty of these types of feelings. It is not intentional; neither do I consciously think about it. But in truth, I sometimes do feel nonaligned and uninterested toward someone who appears different from me. I think it is best described almost like a "feeling of no feeling." The perceived lack of commonality almost makes such a person exist only figuratively on an emotional level. Unfortunately, I think most of us are this way, at least in some of our initial interactions.

Sometimes, events occur that immediately change these biases. Degrees of trust and comfort can elevate very quickly in the face of unexpected or bonding events. A classic example is the terrorist attack on the World Trade Center on September 11, 2001. On that day, the world was upended and instantly changed. In the face of that tragedy, New Yorkers and all Americans were united and trusting regardless of our differences. As a result of the terrorists' acts that day, security measures were strengthened throughout the United States. Today in New York City, you cannot enter an office building without going through security and presenting your credentials. We encounter this in many areas of life. I personally consider the security procedures at El Al airlines over the top. I will not fly El Al, Israel's airline, because the security measures passengers have to go through are beyond invasive. If your last name sounds Arabic, you're under suspicion and almost always ostracized. In some cases, terrorism has escalated distrust to such a level that daily life and routines are affected. Hence, we can see how crises both build and erode trust.

History tells us so much about trust and betrayal of trust. Strife is the mother of nature and civilization, indeed. Here are a few examples:

- Mark Antony loved and trusted Cleopatra implicitly. But when the sea battle of Actium occurred with the Roman fleet of Octavian, Cleopatra had a change of heart and ordered the retreat of her fleet. The withdrawal proved devastating, and it caused the complete defeat of Mark Antony, who witnessed the betrayal of his lover and military ally. Neville Chamberlain, the English prime minister, trusted Hitler as they both signed the Munich Agreement, which allowed Hitler to seize the Sudetenland. Chamberlain's gullibility had an enormous impact on Hitler, who felt empowered and emboldened to continue his world conquest. Churchill tried to influence Chamberlain because he knew the führer could not be trusted, but Churchill couldn't act on that insight because his party wasn't in power.

- During World War II, if you were Japanese and lived in the United States, there was a high probability that you would wind up in an internment camp even if you were a United States citizen. In light of the attack on Pearl Harbor, all Japanese people in the United States were hated and distrusted.

These are just a few examples of how trust in a leader or nation can be routinely violated. The actions mirror our more familiar experiences, including our association with technology. Tech and trust. It is incredible what the Internet and cell phones enable, no less all the other technologies that enhance our lives and grant unprecedented access to information and communication. But with all great things come some severe downsides. I, for one, am nervous about online banking. I know it is easier, but there is a caveat. Has your account been hacked? What about social media? I am mindful of never posting anything too personal.

Today, if you are unhappily married or going through a divorce, it's so easy for an innocent picture to become the basis for accusations. Worse is when a post isn't so innocent and becomes potentially incriminating.

When a matrimonial attorney considers representing a new client, one of the first things he or she does is an online search of the prospective new client and then that client's spouse. This valuable tool has supplanted the need for private detectives. Facebook, with over a billion members, has become a reliable resource for damaging evidence during divorce proceedings. Eighty-one percent of members of the American Academy of Matrimonial Attorneys have used or encountered evidence that appeared on social media.[6] Sixty-four percent of attorneys cited Match.com as the primary source for online dating evidence. As of this writing, there are more than 2,500 online dating services in the United States alone, and a thousand new online dating services open worldwide every year.[7] Some estimates say there are eight thousand competitors worldwide. All these sites are sources for evidence that may be used against a spouse.

Mark Helweil, who is my matrimonial attorney, shared a story in which the use of social media had a great impact on one of his cases. He was representing a man who was in a post-judgment custody dispute and seeking custody of his son. After the divorce, the man discovered that his ex-wife was publishing a blog that exposed all her thoughts and feelings. During cross-examination, the attorney was able to use statements from the blog as primary evidence for the court to grant final custody to the father. The attorney diffused the wife's efforts to sabotage the relationship between the child and the father. In the judge's final decision, she explained how material from the blog influenced

---

[6] The National Law Review, "Family Law: Social Media Evidence In Divorce Cases," February 14, 2019. https://www.natlawreview.com/article/family-law-social-media-evidence-divorce-cases.

[7] Haley Matthews, "27 Online Dating Statistics & What They Mean for the Future of Dating," June 15, 2018. https://www.datingnews.com/industry-trends/online-dating-statistics-what-they-mean-for-future/.

her decision to award custody to the father. This is a great example of the double-edged sword of the Internet. Remarkably, 30 percent of users of the local dating site Tinder are married. Sites like Ashley Madison (which has been hacked) cater to married people seeking affairs, and more than 130 million people worldwide visit this site each month.[8] These statistics highlight the problems that run throughout many relationships. They also highlight the commonality of infidelity.

Consider how exposed you are when pursuing relationships online. Be especially aware of the risk of digital photos. A good friend of mine found himself in a very awkward predicament because of them. He is a prominent investment banker, and during his divorce, he began dating a successful attorney who was a partner at a prominent law firm. Playfully, he took nude pictures of her on his cell phone. His girlfriend wasn't bothered that he did it at that time, but several days after the photos were taken, she asked him to remove the pictures from his phone because she was concerned about the possibility that he might lose his phone and the nude pictures might be exposed. He understood her concerns; he knew how her reputation and business career could be impacted if the photos got out. He took them off his phone and put them on his home computer.

The man has twins who, at that time, were ten years old, a boy and a girl. His daughter was just beginning to get into social media, exploring the associated websites through which she and her friends could share their lives. One of the sites she liked required photos, but she didn't have any photos of herself that she was able to download. Apparently, on a weekend when she was staying with her father, she decided to log on to his computer to find a picture of herself. In doing so, she came across the naked photos. She didn't say anything to her dad, but she did tell her mother.

---

[8] Blair Shiff, "One-third of Tinder users are married, research says," *13 News Now*, May 18, 2015. https://www.13newsnow.com/article/life/one-third-of-tinder-users-are-married-research-says/291-221912793#:~:text=Tinder%2C%20the%20popular%20dating%20app,percent%20were%20in%20a%20relationship.

This is another example of how your actions you believe to be secret can come back to bite you. Rather than reacting appropriately to the news, his wife's rage overwhelmed good judgment, and this triggered a series of events that caused significant legal intervention. His wife instructed her ten-year-old daughter to download the nude pictures onto a flash drive the next time she stayed at her father's house. Consider how inappropriate this is—a mother using a young child to extract naked pictures from her dad's computer. As instructed, the child delivered the flash drive to her mother. My friend found out about it afterward. He was driving in the car with his son, who told him that his sister had downloaded the photos. My friend almost got into an accident. He immediately called his attorney, who reacted in dismay. What happened next is a spot-on example how ridiculous actions exacerbate the issues associated with divorce.

His attorney immediately called a criminal attorney who was associated with his firm. The mother's action was clearly criminal and could be prosecuted as a felony. My friend's attorney reached out to the opposing counsel. My friend, at this point, was feeling massive distress, knowing he had to tell his girlfriend what had happened. It isn't surprising that she reacted poorly, and their relationship quickly soured. She, in fact, became threatening and irrational. The situation began to snowball. At first, his wife's counsel was unresponsive, but then matters got worse. When my friend confronted his wife, she became belligerent and said she was going to post the pictures publicly to embarrass him and his girlfriend. The criminal attorney notified local authorities what had happened and started the process of having the wife arrested. In addition, his matrimonial attorney reached out to child services to alert them of alleged child abuse. This incident was now creating all sorts of reactions and ramifications, all of which caused legal intervention. His wife's matrimonial counsel reacted by getting her representation by her own criminal attorney, who then reacted. Eventually, the matter reached the point at which the police were going to arrest my friend's wife. Worse yet, the children were in the middle of all this. His wife's attorney filed an emergency motion to get in front of the matrimonial judge in an attempt to derail her arrest. The judge did intervene and required the wife to bring the flash drive to court. During the hearing, the judge asked to see the pictures in the chambers. My friend almost had a heart attack, and his attorney jumped up and asked the judge not to view the pictures. In the end, the judge asked the wife to turn over the flash drive to the court; the judge then ordered the flash drive destroyed. In addition to all the emotional duress, the nude pictures on his computer cost him $70,000 in legal fees.

Be careful what you post and be mindful of taking pictures and saving them. Always remember you cannot fully trust tech or more specifically, those who may use it against you.

It can be dangerous to give away your trust. I will soon share with you one of the key episodes in my life that drove me to write this book. I had a partner who turned out to be a thief and a sociopath. He put me in harm's way, and I have had to deal with the ramifications of his heinous acts. On some level, I feel like a fool because there were signs—odd behavior and inconsistencies. I accepted some of these; I choose to look away from others. I am guilty of this both on a business and personal level. I will tell you that it hurts, and it caused me significant financial and emotional damage.

Being truly honest, I must say I am guilty of being lazy. I should have taken seriously what I sensed a lot earlier, and I should have reacted much sooner than I did. What do you do when you discover that a trusted partner has violated your trust? When the shit hits the fan, so to speak, sadly, we all react differently, and generally not too well. In my case, the breadth of my ex-partner's duplicitous acts affected many people in many ways. The circumstances that enabled this to happen were all rooted in a foolish sense of implicit trust.

Before I share that story, however, I first want to note how financial frauds play out. On a much larger scale, I remember vividly the respect and admiration showered on Bernie Madoff. He was a financial superhero, revered by all, and someone who was thought to outperform the smartest investors. The trust he engendered almost made it seem as if he walked on water.

His investors were too lazy to verify the facts. The reality is that he stole and squandered an estimated $65 billion. The numbers are calculable, but the damage he caused is not. As reported by CNBC[9], an investor burned by Bernie Madoff even jumped to his death from a New York City hotel. How did Madoff live with himself? The truth is, Bernie Madoff was a sociopath and had no empathy or sense of guilt for what he did. If you look at the news footage at the time, you will see that he was stoic and expressionless; his eyes were vacuous. In a rare conversation with Madoff in prison in 2011, Barbara Walters discovered he was irritated at being viewed as a criminal character. He informed her, "The average person thinks I robbed widows and orphans. I made wealthy people wealthier."

New York Times financial writer Diana Henriques interviewed Bernie Madoff for her book, *The Wizard of Lies*, which eventually became an HBO film. Madoff told Henriques, "People are greedy."[10]

What motivated Madoff to start the plan, and what did he expect to happen? "Somehow, I assumed it would work out." He informed he said to her. "It was almost like—it sounds horrible to say it now—but I just wanted the world to come to an end. When 9/11 happened, I thought that would be the only way out—the world would come to an end, and I'd be dead, and everyone would be gone."[11]

---

[9] Andrew Ross Sorkin, "Bernie Madoff: His Life and Crimes," *CNBC*. https://www.cnbc.com/bernie-madoff-his-life-and-crimes/.

[10] Bloomberg, "Book Review: The Wizard of Lies: Bernie Madoff and the Death of Trust by Diana B. Henriques," May 5, 2011. https://www.bloomberg.com/news/articles/2011-05-05/book-review-the-wizard-of-lies-bernie-madoff-and-the-death-of-trust-by-diana-b-henriques

[11] Kaitlin Menza, "How Bernie Madoff Took His Family Down," *Town & Country*, April 14, 2021. https://www.townandcountrymag.com/society/money-and-power/a9656715/bernie-madoff-ponzi-scheme-scandal-story-and-aftermath/.

Madoff outlived his sons although he passed away in 2021. Mark committed suicide in 2010, and Andrew died of cancer recurrence in 2014. Madoff's wife, Ruth, visited her husband in jail and spoke with him on a regular basis until Mark committed suicide. She did not visit after that.

The Madoffs have five grandkids, all of whom have changed their last names in the hopes of avoiding the family's humiliation. Stephanie, Mark's widow, agreed to an interview immediately after her husband's death in 2011. She cried as she stated, "I hate Bernie Madoff." She stated with tears, "If I saw Bernie Madoff right now, I would tell him I hold him fully responsible for killing my husband. And I'd spit in his face."[11]

There is no shortage of Wall Street crimes. Enron was a Wall Street darling. The story of Enron Corporation depicts a company that reached dramatic heights only to face a dizzying fall. The feted company's collapse affected thousands of employees and shook Wall Street to its core. Enron's stock was valued $90.75 at its height, but it was valued at just $0.26 when the company declared bankruptcy on December 2, 2001.[12] Many people are still perplexed as to how such a formidable company, formerly one of the largest in the United States, could crumble practically overnight. It's also difficult to comprehend how its executives were able to deceive authorities for so long using fictitious holdings and off-the-books bookkeeping. Enron used special-purpose vehicles (SPVs) and special-purpose entities (SPEs) to conceal mountains of debt and toxic assets from investors and creditors.

The underlying fact is that money, wealth, and recognition are often the driving forces behind illicit acts. If you rewind the tape to late 2007 when the mortgage crisis occurred, you can see how unbridled trust in Wall Street and the banking world helped facilitate the financial debacle now called the "Great Recession" (2007 to 2009). I am assuming that

---

[12] History.com Editors, "Enron files for bankruptcy," *HISTORY,* December 3, 2021. https://www.history.com/this-day-in-history/enron-files-for-bankruptcy

most of you have either read the book or seen the movie, *The Big Short*. If you haven't, I recommend them both.

Wall Street is the tail that wags the dog. It is all about making money—*big money*. Unfortunately, integrity and virtue come second. Before the Great Recession, how many of you could define credit-default swap or collateralized debt obligation (CDO) or understand the ramifications of these financially engineered products? My guess is very few of us had a clue other than those who conceived and traded them. *The Big Short* vividly recounts what happened, and the movie dumbs down the explanation of the catastrophe so those of us who are not financially sophisticated can understand it. The movie features a scene in a casino in which people are playing blackjack. A crowd of onlookers behind them are conversing. One player is on a winning streak and holds a jack and an eight of diamonds. The player feels confident she is going to win the hand again.

The player next to her says, "I will bet you will lose this hand, and I will give you three-to-one odds." Being on a winning streak, the player takes the bet. Two bystanders directly behind the player make a bet that the nonplaying bettor is going to win the bet. One onlooker says to the other, "I will bet you that she wins, and I will give you five-to-one odds." The second bystander takes the bet. Standing by those bystanders are two more bystanders who heard their bet. One tells the other, "I bet you the first bystander who bet that the player would win loses, and I will give you twenty-to-one odds." The second bystander says, "You have a bet." And so on.

This example demonstrates how much leveraged and unsecured debt Wall Street manufactured—and trusting buyers invested in. In the real world, the product was called synthetic CDOs. They acquired and then repackaged subprime mortgages. These loans were as high as 95 percent loan-to-value (LTV). The mortgage holders, most of whom had low credit scores, put down very little money; and the interest rates were adjustable after a low-rate teaser period. The mortgages were commingled to create bonds. These synthetic CDOs also made bets that the bonds would perform; these bets were unsecured and didn't have mortgages as assets. Financially, these synthetic instruments created twenty-to-one leverage. One CDO that had $50 million worth of bonds created financial bets of $1 billion. When it became clear that the CDOs were filled with bad mortgages, the collapse played out like dominoes—everything fell. One group of investors prevailed. Credit default swaps were another kind of bet that these CDOs and mortgage market would fail. When they did, some rather astute investors made billions while the economy collapsed.

Try to imagine that, at that time, there was a product actually marketed to the public called "liar loans". These were loans for which a borrower did not furnish accurate income documentation. This was an example of the incredible audacity and lack of regard that pervaded the financial markets. Even worse, there existed a product called a NINJA loan (no income, no job, and no assets). For these loans, lenders were required to make little or no effort to verify the borrower's capacity to repay the debt. This isn't bullshit—it actually occurred. With such loose guidelines, borrowers could take out mortgages with no ability to repay it and could even lie about their income and assets.

Another classic scene in the movie took place in a strip club. Some very smart investors early on started to see the meltdown that was coming. These savvy few started to dig in and figure out how bad it would be when it all blew up. One of these investors was doing due diligence on the mortgage market in Florida and met with two cocky mortgage brokers who bragged about how much money they were making with subprime mortgages. They said they made five times more than normal by selling subprime mortgages to people who couldn't afford a mortgage. One of the brokers said he had a lot of clients who were strippers. The investor asked if he could meet one of them. At the strip club, while she was dancing for him, he kept drilling her about her mortgage. Shocked, he discovered she had five mortgages, which covered 95 percent of her purchase price, and each was an adjustable-rate mortgage (ARM). The stripper was oblivious to all this. She was shocked to learn that, when the teaser low-entry rate expired, her rate would shoot up 200 percent. She gasped and told him she couldn't afford that.

One of my businesses is real estate lending. I am a bridge lender, which means I provide short-term loans. Another aspect of my business is buying distressed loans. Over the years, I have done this mostly when things go badly for the borrower, which often happens in a recession. In 2010, as the meltdown was in full force, I was getting opportunities from many brokers who sent me a plethora of defaulted mortgages. If a mortgage looked compelling, I would jump in my car and go visit the encumbered property.

The story that stands out to me is about an apartment I went to see in Key Biscayne, Florida. Key Biscayne is a beautiful island connected to Miami. It is surrounded by the ocean on all sides. The defaulted mortgage had a principal balance of $325,000 (that is, before all interest owed on the default). My sense or hope was that this was a valuable apartment, at least worth what was owed. As I approached the street where the apartment building stood, I passed the Ritz-Carlton. (By the way, one of my favorite Ritz-Carltons. It is awesome!) I was enthused by the possibilities of the area. I drove down the street and saw the apartment building. It was a two-story catwalk building; the second floor was accessed by a flight of stairs that led to an outdoor walkway from which the units were accessed. Instantly, I was disappointed. I knew there was no way this apartment could be worth $350,000. Even the best unit in the building couldn't possibly have that value. I got out of the car and went to meet Steve, the agent who was going to show me the unit. He greeted me and motioned me toward the stairs. I said to myself, *At least the unit is on the second floor. Maybe it will be a nicer unit and will have more value.* When we got to the stairs, Steve went along to another set of stairs going down. I stopped and asked, "Where are we going?" "To the apartment," Steve replied. The apartment was the superintendent's unit. It was below grade. Small, slanted windows looked out onto the sidewalk. The apartment was a studio. I was shocked. It was maybe six hundred square feet. The apartment wasn't even worth $40,000 let alone $350,000. Some institution made this loan, and Wall Street securitized it and sold it off to trusting investors. As you may guess, I didn't buy the mortgage.

You might ask how all of this happened. Aren't there checks and balances? There are supposed to be, but they were forsaken. What made this scam even more outrageous was the fact that these mortgage pools were well rated by qualified rating agencies such as Moody's Corp. These ratings created a positive perception, making the investments seem safe. It was a sham. The rating agencies were more concerned with collecting their fees than they were about the quality and merit of the ratings they were giving. In fact, these mortgage pools should have been rated at lowest possible level.

The 2008 financial crisis caused six million people to file bankruptcy and eight million people to lose their homes. Credibility is one of the many foundations of trust. I guess this is an obvious statement but consider how fast credibility can disappear. Bernie Madoff consistently generated 12 percent returns over many years, even in adverse or bad markets. No one questioned his prowess or legitimacy—except Harry Markopolos. As early as 1999, Harry Markopolos, a certified fraud examiner, documented allegations of fraud against Madoff Investment Securities, LLC, to the Securities Exchange Commission (SEC). In one of his written communications to the SEC from November 7, 2005, Markopolos detailed no less than thirteen red flags related to the legitimacy and legality of Madoff Securities's investment scheme. He concluded, "Madoff Securities is the world's largest Ponzi scheme."[13] His warnings fell on deaf ears. Unfortunately, ethics run second to earning or stealing money.

What happens when you are a victim of a breach of trust? How do feel? What do you do? How angry are you? How do you maintain

---

[13] SEC Office of Inspector General Report of Investigation: Case No. OIG-509, "Executive Summary." https://www.sec.gov/files/oig-509-exec-summary.pdf

control and keep from doing something stupid? This may or may not be hypothetical for you.

Fast-forward to today and the preceding decade. We now are experiencing the subsidy bubble. Companies such as WeWork, Uber, and Lyft are among the companies that are losing billions of dollars—yet have absurd high valuations. In the third quarter of 2019, Uber reported revenues of $3.16 billion on losses of $5.2 billion. WeWork, at its peak valuation, was $47 billion.[14] The valuation collapsed when the initial public offering (IPO) debacle occurred, and it was revealed that the business was subsidized to grow while it was hemorrhaging cash.

There was a time when value had a direct correlation to earnings. The bottom line is that these companies are all losing money in vast amounts. Thanks to Wall Street, however, private equity funds and investors keep investing in these companies, subsidizing their losses, and with each round, they are increasing in valuation.

Discounts and freebies to customers enable many tech startups to lure in new customers. These include free lunch delivery, $3 beauty products, and bargain rides. Still, these goodies have fallen out of favor with investors who are losing patience with the failure of these companies to turn a profit. This is a much smaller example of what transpired in 2008 with the implosion of the mortgage market and banking system.

Caveat emptor is Latin for "let the buyer beware." It is in our nature to want to buy. We want to believe and trust and to reap the benefits. I trusted—and I got burned. I promised to tell you my story. Sadly, being screwed by someone isn't hypothetical for me. What I am about to describe was the catalyst that inspired me to write and share my story. As you learn the details. be objective and think about your own experiences. Acknowledge your own mistakes in judgment. In order to

---

[14] Matt Rosoff and Sally Shin, "WeWork tells investors it lost $1.25 billion in the third quarter," *CNBC*, November 13, 2019. https://www.cnbc.com/2019/11/13/wework-q3-2019-earnings-lost-1point25-billion-on-934-million-in-revenue.html.

do that, we must be willing to open up and be honest. If I can do it, so can you!

"The best way to find out if you can trust somebody is to trust them," Ernest Hemingway wrote. I learned this the hard way. About twenty years ago, I met D through a friend. (I will be using initials in this story rather than full names.) He was moving back to New York from California and was looking for an opportunity to get into the real estate business. My partner, M, and I met him and brought him into our company to assist us. Our business was multidimensional; we had a division that originated short-term bridge loans secured by real estate and another division through which we managed properties that we owned. Initially, D worked with M overseeing day-to-day operations of the properties. Eventually, he entered a new role assisting me on the lending side.

In 2007, my partner, M, and I decided to split up. It wasn't a pleasant breakup because M had surreptitiously cut a deal with someone I had brought in as a client to replace me as the funding source. I had spent most of my time procuring new investors to fund our transactions. He did this because he was capturing more equity with this new partner. When I found out, I was blown away. I had met M on my first day of college. He became my best friend. We did everything together. After twenty years of friendship, this breakup was happening. I couldn't believe at the time that it was real. I had trusted him implicitly. That said, we had been having some issues, and I did feel we were growing apart. But I didn't expect him to do what he did. Behind my back, he and his new partner arranged a $100 million credit line with WestLB, a German bank. Once the credit line was approved, M made his move. He called me into his office and announced our breakup. The issues that we had been having had made me feel that, ultimately, we would break up; I just didn't expect it to happen then. I was in the middle of a god-awful divorce and on the brink of going to trial. In addition, my mother had passed away a week before. I looked at M and said, "Okay, but I can't handle two divorces simultaneously." I asked him to let me just get my marital divorce over first. "No, we have to break up now," he said. I was dismayed to put it mildly and walked out of the office. When I returned, M, without consulting me, informed all the employees we were breaking up. I was furious. M had thought that he would make me an offer, and I would simply leave. It didn't end that way. I felt terribly violated and couldn't believe this was happening. Enter D.

At that point, D had been with us eight years and was a partner in some of the buildings we had acquired. D wound up aligning with me and significantly helped me wrestle control of the company. In the end, M left, and D and I took over the firm and its portfolio. I was totally indebted to D and grew to trust him implicitly. My divorce proceedings escalated, so D thankfully oversaw all day-to-day operations. He was watching my back. Until he wasn't.

After M left, we started our new company and became partners in our endeavors. Shortly thereafter, we experienced the Great Recession of 2008, and we dealt with defaults and foreclosures. Life was very stressful. Some strange things started to happen, but I essentially disregarded them. Objectively, I was avoiding confrontation and not recognizing that, where there is smoke, there is fire.

During the fallout we experienced while dealing with the defaults caused by the collapse of the mortgage market, D got in trouble through bizarre circumstances. D's son was not getting enough playing time on his basketball team. He was in high school at the time. D had some negative interaction with the coach. I don't know all the facts, but then something bad happened. D and his wife, N, got arrested. D had set up a surreptitious email account and sent threatening emails to the basketball coach and his wife. He then sent slanderous emails to the school that employed the coach. His goal was to get the coach fired. The coach panicked and went to the police. The police were able to trace the emails and found that they were coming from D's residence. This outrageous act drew media attention and was even discussed on a morning talk show.

When I found out, I was in disbelief. I approached D. He denied the allegations. Initially, I believed him, but it turned out he was lying. My investors and business associates saw the articles, and I found myself no longer believing D. This event combined with other anomalies. They were signals that I just didn't know how to deal with. What type of person does something like this? The answer, as I eventually learned, is a *sociopath*.

I started to hear stories about other people in Cresskill and Alpine, New Jersey, who were receiving derisive, unsigned letters or were being maligned. One story involved our investor, C, who was also D's best friend. Correction: once upon a time, he was his best friend. They were members of the same country club, played golf, traveled with their wives, and were generally inseparable.

In 2008, because of the financial meltdown, we got hurt in some transactions, and investors incurred losses. D's best friend sued our company and us individually. Before this happened, I had spoken to C only on a superficial level, extending pleasantries at D's family events. During the fallout from the 2008 collapse, C called me aside a few times. He was infuriated, and he exuded frustration based on what D was telling him. Before C commenced his lawsuit, he came to our offices and taped his meeting with D. C explicitly went through his portfolio, asking D detailed questions.

When I listened to the tape, I grimaced several times. D had answered C's questions with lies. I also recall that in one of the few calls I received from C, he asked me about a specific transaction. When I answered him, he said, "That isn't what D told me." "What I am telling you is the correct answer," I replied. The lawsuit was bad—not that any lawsuit is good, but the animus C had for D was way over the top. I wound up resolving the lawsuit and met with C. At that meeting, he said, "Waywill, I feel sorry for you. D is a sociopath." I thought that he was just venting out of frustration. Now I know he was spot-on.

In May 2018, a bizarre thing happened to me. My girlfriend at the time had cosmetic surgery on her breasts. She was going to stay with me during her recovery. The day she was due to come home, I decided to go online and buy a cake from the erotic bakery. This is an example of my sense of humor, and yes, it was a boob cake. The purveyor sent me a bill online; the bill included a drawing of the cake, and the drawing included the words I had asked him to write on the cake. He told me that I had to sign the bill ASAP so he could deliver the cake to my residence in a timely way. Oddly, I was unable to print the bill from my desktop, so I forwarded the bill to my receptionist and asked her to print it so I could sign it and email it back to the purveyor. I told her what it was, and she smiled and agreed. (Our receptionist had worked for us over ten years.) This event happened on a Thursday. The following Monday morning, D came flying into my office, screaming, "What did you do? What did you do?" In his hand, he had a copy of the receipt for the boob cake. He contended that our receptionist gave it to him and told him that she had saved the receipt for a rainy day. I looked up in disbelief and said, "What are you talking about?" "This is sexual harassment and is subject to the Me-Too movement. We are all going to get sued. I am calling our lawyer."

I ignored his tirade. D then went to our other partner and falsified what had happened, trying to get him nervous as well. D called our attorney, a real estate attorney, who suddenly became an authority on labor law. Brian, our attorney, came to our offices and sat down with the three of us and explained how low the bar is regarding the Me-Too movement.

I had no patience for this, and I walked out of the meeting. Without my consent, D had our real estate attorney sit down and interview our receptionist and all the other employees.

This was Monday, May 1, 2018. The next day, a letter on our company's stationery was hand delivered to several boards of companies that I have a business relationship with. The letter listed my various positions and then stated I was under investigation for pervasive hostile work conditions and for sexual harassment. The letter listed five employees who had been affected—with the memo that I had been asked not to return to our offices until the formal investigation was completed. It said the investigation was being led by our real estate attorney and listed his name. The letter was unsigned. I am not making this up. This actually happened. I found out about it a couple of days after the letter was delivered. I was shocked. I couldn't fathom who would do such a terrible thing. I was sickened by this horrible act at first and didn't know who had done it. I didn't know what to do.

Fortunately, the letter didn't cause the extent of damage that the writer intended it to, although I did resign from one organization because they were making a big deal of the allegations. I didn't go to my office from May to September during working hours because I felt so angered, and I didn't know who had orchestrated the attack on me. I decided to reach out to C, D's former best friend. He had warned me about D, and when I told him what had happened, he asked me to send him the letter, which I did. After reviewing the letter, he called me and said that D definitely had sent it. He told me that, when he sued us, a letter had been sent to the president of the company where C's son just started his first job after finishing college. The letter stated his son was being accused of sexual harassment and that a prominent law firm in New York had been hired, and there would be an article in *The Wall Street Journal*. That letter, too, was unsigned. His son almost lost his job, but fortunately, he did not. C then noticed how the word *harassment* had been misspelled in my letter—it was similarly misspelled in the letter about his son. I heard other stories similar in gravity, which had happened to other people who lived in the same neighborhood as D. What type of person does something like this? C had said he was a sociopath. I think he is worse.

He is a psychopath.

When I returned to my office, the employees had heard about the letter, and they were shocked. I met with all of them, and they assured me that they would never believe such a thing. Our bookkeeper told my other partner, W, that we didn't know who D really was. When I discussed this matter with D, he blamed our loan originator and named him as the guilty party. He was lying.

The work environment became more and more toxic. In October, I discovered that D had added his three kids to the company payroll. An employee had spotted a check made out to one of D's kids and informed me. I went right to my other partner and asked him if he knew about this. The answer was, of course, *no*. When I approached our bookkeeper, she revealed that D told her that W and I knew that his kids were on the payroll and that it was okay with us. I asked whether she found it odd that D's kids were on the payroll and neither W's nor my kids weren't. She kicked the can on the answer. I asked her not to say anything to D until I could figure out how to handle the situation. Unfortunately, she didn't follow my request.

The next day, I went into D's office and said, "D, I need to talk to you. I'm not sure how to address this because it is unbelievable to me. Did you put your kids on the company payroll?" It was now October. It had started in January. He replied, "Oh, I had to—they're taking classes at Syracuse that require them to be on a company payroll, but I paid the money back." I stared at him in disbelief. I couldn't believe he would make up such a ridiculous justification for this lie. It turned out that after our bookkeeper disclosed that I was aware of the money paid to his kids, D paid back 25 percent of what he had taken. Again, he lied. I obviously would check to see if he had legitimately paid the money back.

W and I both felt great discomfort. The problem was exacerbated because D ran operations and oversaw property management. I became really concerned. I had implicitly trusted D. I had known him for twenty years, and he had always claimed he was "watching my back." In retrospect, when someone says that to you, you should have the same reaction you have when someone says, "Trust me."

I found myself in an excruciating position. D handled so much, and both W and I were unaware of his improprieties. In fact, I discovered that he had lied to us about many important business matters. I started digging. I went to the bank and pulled bank statements and checks on various accounts going back five years. Shockingly, I found thievery. We owned a building in Long Island City. D managed day-to-day operations, and every month he made distributions. There were three partners: D, my ex-partner M, and myself. D would orally update me regularly on what was going on, and I stupidly never looked over his shoulder. It turns out that the rent collected was almost twice as much as he represented to M and me. In addition, the rent he stole was being paid to one of his entities, the name of which was an acronym of his kids' names—"Lubajari". I also discovered many checks made out to cash and wires sent to Syracuse University to pay his kids' tuition. I couldn't believe what I discovered. In that instant, I called M, and he and I went out to the property and took control, cutting D off from all authority. M promptly filed a lawsuit, and the story was picked up in the April 10, 2019, edition of *Real Deal*. Shortly thereafter, I also filed a lawsuit against D.

Unfortunately, what I ascertained was only the surface. Needless to say, things got a lot worse. I discovered more theft alongside forgeries of my signature on checks and important documents.

In 2019, W and I decided to close down our company (Paradigm Capital). I took control of operations and all the portfolio assets. D was shut off from having any control or access to bank accounts and was no longer able to make any decisions. I discovered crazy things and matters got worse. If you saw me in 2019, you would have noticed that my hands were shaking because my blood pressure was affected.

One of many examples was that we owned an office building in East Orange, New Jersey, which had issues and was in bankruptcy due to a large real estate tax lien we inherited when we took over ownership. I brought in a professional property manager and reached out to our bankruptcy attorney. I had never spoken to him before this point in time. He told me we were in real trouble. The judge couldn't stand D, and he told me D would lie and provide misleading information to the court. The judge decided to convert our Chapter 11 filing into a Chapter 7 bankruptcy, which is essentially an order for a foreclosure sale. Our attorney informed me we had two weeks to pay off the tax lien or we would lose the building and all of our investment. He also shared that D received a loan commitment from a local bridge lender and the loan commitment was submitted to the court, but the lender backed out because according to D, the lender's wife died in a car accident in Italy, and he wasn't making loans anymore. "I will send you all the documents," he said. I was flabbergasted. Neither W nor I knew anything about this. D would tell us everything was fine and moving along. In contrast, I now had two weeks to come up with $2,000,000, or we were toast. While I was reviewing the files, W called me and asked if I saw the loan commitment from the bridge lender who had backed out. I said I didn't look at it because it was a dead deal. I was focusing on how to come up with the money in two weeks. W said to look at the loan commitment because it was our (Paradigm's) loan commitment with another company's name on it. I took a look and couldn't believe it. He was right; it was our document. I Googled the company and the signatory on the commitment and couldn't find anything. The only thing I had was their office address on the top of the commitment. They were located in Alpine, New Jersey. My assistant lived in Fort Lee, and I asked him to go over to the building to see if he could find the company. The address was the Alpine police headquarters building. D submitted a fake loan commitment to the bankruptcy court and was intentionally shoving us in a position to lose the building. The signatory on the loan commitment was "Peter Frank", a fake name. This really happened. By the way, I did wind up coming up with the $2,000,000 and saved the building. Peter Frank was the name of the villain in the movie, *Thunderball*. To date, I know of four different fake names that D has used to either defame or swindle. One of them was "Richard Hanson", a serial killer. D was trying to belittle me by sending derisive messages to investors, representing that he was the son-in-law of an investor and was representing him. I was watching a movie called *Frozen Ground* with Nicholas Cage, and the killer in the film was Richard Hanson. When I reached out to all the investors in that transaction asking could the father-in-law of Richard Hanson please identify himself, no one responded. Thereafter, the maligning messages stopped.

In March of 2022, D's wife allegedly committed suicide by jumping off a terrace from their apartment in Boca Raton, Florida. She had three kids. Some of her friends that I know are convinced that there is no way that she would commit suicide, no less jump off a terrace. This is an unbelievable tragedy. Some people who know that I wrote this book because of D surmise this story is also the next Netflix series.

Stay tuned!

Here is a stunning statistic from a UC Berkeley study: one out of seven US public companies commits fraud every year.[15] This is not petty fraud. This is based on a study of detected and undetected fraud, and it costs shareholders about $380 billion a year. Fraud has become a feature and not a bug of the financial services industry. Sadly, when it comes to money, there are too many instances of fraud and thievery. We all must always have our guard up. Consider yourself very lucky if someone earns your trust. Earned trust is truly sacrosanct. Unfortunately, the previous stories typify the sad reality of breaches of trust.

Trust brings us a special sense of comfort and security. Remarkably, in today's world, there are encouraging, outlier stories that are hard to believe, considering what I have just illustrated. Have you ever experienced something that is completely contrary to the way things are?

---

[15] Sara Zaske, "Big name corporations more likely to commit fraud," *WSU News*, February 2, 2021. https://news.wsu.edu/press-release/2021/02/02/big-name-corporations-likely-commit-fraud/.

For part of my childhood, I grew up in the rural suburb of Millbrook, New York. For years, I continued to go there on weekends, and I still go up for an occasional trip. About two years ago, I was driving on a country road when I saw a meat and produce store out in front of a farm. I pulled the car over, and my girlfriend got out and walked around the property, passing the store without going in. I entered the store and noticed there was no employee there. There was no one to pay for items if I wanted to buy something. The owners operated the business on a trust system. They had all types of meats in the freezers, and each item had a price on it. If you wanted something, you just took it. Whatever the price was, you were expected to put money in a box on the counter. You bagged your own food and just left. I was really taken by this. Are they getting ripped off? Maybe not. I picked out a couple of items and put the cash in the box, but I still couldn't believe the business model. I stopped, paused, and said to myself, *There must be cameras at least watching us.* I scanned the store and amazingly saw no cameras. Then I thought to myself, *Even if they had cameras, what good would they do? I'd be long gone before anyone got there.* I got in my car, and we drove off. The house was directly across the road. Would someone come out to chase people stealing their meat? And if, in fact, there were no cameras, how would they even know if people stole from them? I couldn't believe any business would display this level of trust.

This happened 2017. While I was writing this book, I realized that the experience was so relevant, I never forgot it. It kept coming back to me. So, in August 2019, I returned to the store in Clinton Corners, New York. I was hopeful that nothing had changed, as I wanted to learn more about this business. I pulled up in front. Sure enough, nothing had changed. The doors to the store were wide open, and no one was there. I was with my girlfriend, Nicole. I had told her the story. We both got out of the car. Suddenly, a pickup truck came out of an adjacent field and stopped near the store. I walked over and introduced myself. I asked the driver if he owned this business. "Yes," he said. I told him I had been there two years before and had been taken by the degree of trust he demonstrated. I asked if he worried that people would steal things or leave less money than they should. He said he was not worried. He explained that he was from Colorado and had worked on several farms. Out there, nobody locked their doors, and all the farms did business that way. I told him about this book and said I wanted to mention him and his business. I told him I would send him a copy when it was published. He became excited and quickly ran to his pickup, retrieved his card, and then offered it to me, along with two giant tomatoes from his stand, which he insisted that I take for free.

The next morning, Nicole and I went to a local breakfast place that was right out of a Norman Rockwell painting. It was clear this was a family business, and my visceral sense was that it had been there for a long time. It was one of those little roadside country restaurants. We ordered breakfast, and the woman asked if I wanted to pay now or when the food was ready. I responded by asking if I could pay her on Tuesday. (It was Sunday, and I was joking.) She said "okay", smiled, and then I paid her. I shared the scenario with Nicole and said I was going to go back and tell the woman about this book. I asked her a question: "If I was serious about paying on Tuesday, would you have trusted me to return even though you didn't know me?" Undaunted and smiling, she said, "Yes, we do that all the time." Wow. Could you even fantasize that your business could operate like that?

Distrust is the rusted side of the double-edged sword. Trust is the gilded side of the sword. I don't think I will ever fall into the camp of total distrust, but I am wiser and much more aware now. I am also glad to know that there are people in our world whom you can trust and who trust you.

CHAPTER 2

Should You Buy What You Are Being Sold?

LET'S OPEN THIS chapter with a ridiculous, irreverent, rhetorical, and maybe even comical question: Have you ever thought about what cavemen wanted or desired and what products they used or trusted? My guess is probably not! The term *products* may be inappropriate here considering that, during prehistoric times, there were no products or manufacturers promoting their wares.

The fact is, humans really weren't very dimensional back then; neither did they have a lot of options or choices to consider or experience. For the most part, humans were outright instinctual and urge oriented. They wanted what they wanted when they wanted it. It is probable that early humans were not very respectful or considerate, especially to one another. I am guessing about this, but human nature validates the assumption. In fact, their needs and wants were rudimentary, instinctive, and all about eating, safety, and inconsiderate immediate fulfillment. These visceral or undeveloped urges and thoughts dictated their behavior, actions, and trust decisions.

But their safety was clearly reliant and dependent on a weapon of choice, sometimes a club to wield to fend others off or to use to hunt to get food. Can you visualize a large man with poor posture wearing an animal skin garment trudging along, carrying a tree limb, grunting to intimidate? Who among the tribe and fellow cavemen had a better club and was respected and feared the most? That product, limb, or device didn't have a reputation or brand that made it stand out. There was no marketing or promoting. The respect came from the recognition of fear that each caveman mandated with a bellow or a hand-waving scream. Probably assuming a subliminal reaction, I guess the key attribute was that big was good, and that was intimidating.

Now imagine if we could go back in time and come up with a name, a marketing plan, and a brand for the club. The intention, of course, is to capture the market and get customers and create a trust that the club you have is the best club. You are the cool caveman, and you stand out. How about we call the killer club the Whacker? It could be the Rolls-Royce of the time. What is your first reaction? I am thinking there may be a concern at least by modern mores. Let's consider the marketing ramifications. Do you think cavewomen would be attracted to cavemen who strutted around waving the biggest Whacker? No, seriously. This was then, not now. Did the Whacker have sustenance from a branding perspective and evoke trust that it does what we think it does? Hold on, maybe not. The killer club—the Whacker—may be perceived negatively by cavewomen. Even then, maybe the Whacker might seem crude as a name. Perhaps cavewomen were not so different then from the way women are today.

Let's move forward to modern times and the way we think today. Let's refine the branding to create the product with recognition and acceptance. Okay, "The Whacker will make you stand out and get you dinner with one swipe." Even better, "Your Whacker will be the biggest, and it will always be up for the occasion." What do you think? Okay, come on! It is important to have a sense of humor. All kidding aside, however, there is an absolute correlation among brand recognition, product reputation, belief, and what ultimately gains trust. The branding and marketing of products are intended to create trust in the claims made in the promoting of the product.

We Buy Based on Perception

A product's reputation and its representations affect our buying habits in so many ways. We buy everything we consume based on our perception of quality, safety, usefulness, and in many cases, our own manipulated recognition of these factors. Consumerism is as American as apple pie. Our society devours material products. Captains of industry have long known that they can amp up our longing for things and gratify our wants (at least temporarily) with great marketing and the creation of belief in the quality of what we purchase and consume. The CEOs who run these multinational companies want to seduce us. They realize that they need the power of glorified advertising to hustle their products and build want and intended perception.

Volvo is one of the most ambitious car manufacturers, and focus has been on safety as far back as I can remember. They targeted families with promises of protecting them, especially their children, from accidents. They branded themselves as family friendly. The old Volvos looked like boxes on wheels, but it didn't matter because they saved lives after all. I remember ads showing cars rolling over without the cabin collapsing. The company was believed and trusted. Volvo still boasts that they have more safety systems on board than other manufacturers. But are they sincere in that promotion?

Things changed significantly when the Ford Motor Company bought the Swedish car manufacturer in 1999. The interests and motivations of protecting the family had been the brand's prime association, but after the acquisition, the brand's profile changed direction. Volvo became more concerned with making cool-looking cars. While safety had been the main concern and was the quintessential branding image of the company through its history, style stepped to the forefront. Part of the motivation for change was production costs. Steel is expensive, and maximizing collision safety decreases affordability. Management had to consider other options to keep their product price competitive with other cars. They continued to emphasize that their cars are safe, and they are, but the focus somewhat pivoted.

Auto industry pundits and gurus issue reports on marketing representations. The most widely regarded authority is *Car and Driver* magazine, which rates cars in many categories. A recent list of the top ten safest cars ranked Genesis G80 (manufactured by Genesis in Korea) at the top of the list; Volvo received no ranking at all.

TP Dilemma

Nothing is worse than toilet paper that feels rough and falls apart when you use it, but the last thing you want to do is flush money down the toilet by splurging on pricy rolls. How many of you remember the ads in which Mr. Whipple jumped out of an aisle in a supermarket telling shoppers not to squeeze the Charmin? These ads appeared for over twenty years, and Charmin claimed their toilet paper was so soft it was irresistible, and you couldn't help but squeeze it. As effective as their campaign was, I never once had the urge to squeeze Charmin toilet paper. My guess is neither have you. However, the brilliance of their marketing campaign was such that everybody recognized the claim, and many believed it. Procter & Gamble, the owner of the Charmin product line, has gone all out marketing and selling its products and subliminally making us believe their representations that their toilet paper is softer than all their competitors.

Today, the lineup of Charmin toilet paper choices is quite long:

- Ultra Soft Mega Roll
- Ultra Soft Super Mega Roll
- Charmin Forever Roll
- Ultra Strong Mega Roll
- Ultra Gentle Mega Roll
- Charmin Essential Soft Mega Roll
- Charmin Essential Soft Strong Mega Roll

I am now thinking about this superfluous variety and their catchy names. Why are there so many choices? This is a perfect example of a form of hypnosis that overwhelms and confuses buyers with an abundance of clever stimuli, thus overloading their cerebral circuits. People's brains download these abundant choices. This manipulates decision making and causes people to buy the product or products. I go to Costco every few weeks, and recently, I walked down the paper goods aisle. I did notice that there were several choices of Charmin toilet paper. I guess writing this book is making me more conscious of everything. Next time I go to Costco, I am going to see if the choices are priced differently. What is the difference between them? The labels don't tell us. Is Ultra Soft Mega Roll of lesser quality than the Ultra Soft Super Mega Roll? This is a rhetorical question, but on some level, it's funny—or is it? What is the truth? What marketing can we believe?

Bottom line (pun intended): the twenty-four pack of soft and absorbent toilet paper is a user favorite, and it remains affordable. Pros: This toilet paper is nice to touch but sturdy enough not to tear easily while in use. The thickness of the paper determines how long a roll will last. Because the paper is absorbent, you won't need to use as many squares during each bathroom visit. Cons: Rolls are so large that they may not fit on all holders.'

Okay, the consumer has been influenced and may believe that Charmin is the softest toilet paper. My experience is that the women I know like only Charmin and react negatively if I have another brand in my house. I personally am into longevity, and I tell them that length of the roll is more compelling to me. For that reason, I prefer Scott. Well, I decided to Google it: who makes the softest toilet paper? I found a rating that did rank Ultra Super Mega as number one. Okay, I guess I am a believer now, but I still like Scott toilet paper.

Pass the Sunscreen Please

On a more serious note, what about products that we buy every day that can impact our health? I am speaking about products we apply to our skin or ingest. Are you a consumer who actually takes the time to read the labels that list the ingredients on food products or cosmetics? I was remiss about doing this for most of my life; in fact, I almost never thought about it. Since I started doing this research, however, I have become more aware and, in some cases, have been astounded by what is in front of my eyes. This sudden awareness, combined with my girlfriend cajoling me to skim what appears on labels, has altered my shopping patterns. I suggest you do the same and become conscious, responsible, and much more vigilant about what you consume or apply.

Did you know?

- The last time Congress passed a law regulating the cosmetics industry was 1938.[16]
- Twenty-six seconds is all it takes for the chemicals in skincare products to enter your bloodstream.[16]
- Only eleven ingredients that used to be used in skincare and cosmetics are currently banned or restricted by the US Food and Drug Administration. The European Union, on the other hand, has prohibited 1,328 chemicals that are known or suspected of causing cancer, genetic mutations, reproductive damage, or birth defects.[16]
- Researchers found 287 harmful synthetic compounds used in skincare and cosmetic items in the umbilical cord of infants.[17]

---

[16] Scott Faber, "80 Years Later, Cosmetics Chemicals Still Unregulated," *EWG*, June 25, 2018. https://www.ewg.org/news-insights/news/80-years-later-cosmetics-chemicals-still-unregulated#:~:text=It's%20been%2080%20years%20since,168%20different%20ingredients%20every%20day.

[17] EWG, "Body Burden: The Pollution in Newborns," *EWG*, July 14, 2005. https://www.ewg.org/research/body-burden-pollution-newborns

The Environmental Working Group (EWG) is the go-to resource if you want to learn about the products and ingredients. I am astonished at what I have learned on their site. You can research specific ingredients and determine whether they are safe. EWG's mission is to help people to live healthier lives in a healthier environment. Through breakthrough research and education, EWG's goal is for consumers to have a choice and be able to take civic action. They are a nonprofit, nonpartisan organization devoted to protecting human health and the environment.

EWG's revolutionary research has changed the argument over environmental health. EWG's group of scientists, lawyers, policy experts, and programmers work hard to make sure someone is standing up for public health when industry and government will not. Through their online databases, communication campaigns, apps, and reports, EWG are empowering and educating consumers to make informed and safer decisions about the products they are buying and the companies they support. In response to consumer pressure, these companies are now improving their practices and removing potentially dangerous chemical ingredients in their products, and here's an example. What do we know about suntan lotion?

An article written by Leah Zerbe, MS, NASM-CPT, NASMCES, published in a 2019 EWG report, disclosed that nearly two-thirds of all sunscreens either don't provide protection against ultraviolet rays or contain questionable ingredients that are absorbed by the human body. Sunscreen chemicals hit our bloodstream within hours. Half of these products being sold and displayed in the US would not be allowed in European market because they provide inadequate protection.

"Sunscreen is unique compared to many other personal care products," Zerbe writes, "because we apply it thickly on our skin multiple times a day. We do not really get that hours-long skin absorbing exposure like shampoo you quickly wash off."[18] You can find the worst and best sunscreens for yourself and your kids and learn more by reading the EWG's 2019 report that explains the ingredients and labeling claims of more than 1,300 products with SPF. Find the resource at https://www.ewg.org/sunscreen/. It's a reader-friendly article, and I encourage you to see it for yourself. With that in mind, let me quote some high points, which are captivating on their own but will also make you think about how your consumer trust is abused. Key findings in EWG's sunscreen report are as follows:

- About one-half of the sunscreen products sold in the United States would not pass the stricter European standards because they do not filter enough ultraviolet rays.
- Although strong proofs show sunscreens can even prevent skin cancer, it is still legal for most sunscreens to make cancer-prevention claims.
- Nearly 67 percent of sunscreen products that have been reviewed either did not adequately protect from ultraviolet rays or contained dangerous ingredients. Some of the most worrying ingredients include oxybenzone, known as endocrine disruptors, and retinyl palmitate, a form of vitamin A that may damage skin and can possibly lead to skin tumors.
- Oxybenzone is extensively used in American chemical-based sunscreens. Lab testing shows skin penetration rates of 1 to 9 percent. That's worrying, given that the agent acts like an estrogen in our body, and it is linked endometriosis in studies of women and abnormal sperm function in animal studies. Oxybenzone acts as a skin allergen in a good number of people, and so does methylisothiazolinone, which is a common sunscreen preservative found in most products. Gratefully, Hawaii laws call for a ban on oxybenzone in sunscreen because it can bleach and kill coral reefs.

---

[18] Leah Zerbe, "The Best Sunscreens of 2019," Katy Birth Center, June 13, 2019. https://katybirthcenter.com/natural-birth-learnings/the-best-sunscreens-of-2019-and-toxic-ones-to-avoid/

- From 2007 to 2018, there has been a 41 percent rise in mineral sunscreens in the US. These sunscreens tend to block ultraviolet better than chemical sunscreen ingredients, and they are rated safer on EWG's sunscreen database.
- EWG's 2010 review indicated that about 40 percent of sunscreens contain vitamin A ingredients. These can react with ultraviolet rays and increase the risk of skin tumors.
- Scientists do not know for sure if sunscreen helps prevent melanoma. In fact, as EWG documents in its summary of the sunscreen guide, "Sun exposure appears to play a role in melanoma, but it is a complicated disease for which many questions remain unanswered. One puzzling fact is that melanomas do not usually appear on parts of our body that get sun exposure in a daily basis."[18]
- Be cautious of ultrahigh SPF claims. There are more of them today than there were years ago. The United States has not permitted modern sunscreen ingredients that do a better job of broad-spectrum protection. Because of this, ultraviolet protection is often lacking in SPF 70+ products. In other established countries, SPF is usually capped at 50.
- Stay away from spray sunscreen. It's difficult to apply because thickness provides adequate protection. Additionally, the spray delivery increases the risk that you and those around you are drawing the chemicals directly into your lungs.
- Nearly 30 percent of sunscreens tested in 2018were spray sunscreens, up from about 20 percent in year 2007. As noted, these sunscreen sprays pose inhalation risk and are difficult to apply correctly. Even the Food and Drug Administration raised concerns about spray sunscreens, although the agency hasn't banned them yet.
- The Food and Drug Administration banned the use of misleading sunscreen product claims like "waterproof" and "sweatproof" in 2011, but other misleading marketing terminologies remain in use like "sun shield" and "age shield."

- Avoid the sun and get your vitamin D levels checked by your doctor. A growing number of the world's population is now deficient in vitamin D because of sunscreens and spending more time indoors. The good news is that you can get vitamin D and protect yourself from burns without turning to sunscreen.

I was telling a friend about the EWG report on suntan lotion. He proudly said he uses Neutrogena brand; he obviously buys into their branding claims of quality. I showed him the report, which stated that Neutrogena has been rated as one of the worst products. You should have seen his face. He was shocked. An informed consumer is an anomaly. Most consumers have no idea what they are using.

Trust becomes faith in the companies that sell products. Regrettably, there's no monitoring agency that is vigilant in addressing the use of these questionable products and/or confronts the management of the manufacturers. In essence, the public becomes a target until there is a breaking point.

Take Your Vitamins

In another example of misplaced consumer trust, many of us ingest vitamins and herbal supplements every morning that we think are good for us. Unfortunately, we are being sold a bill of goods. Shockingly, yet predictably, there is very little oversight of companies that sell vitamins and supplements. The bottles are emblazoned with marketing promises. The yellow ones will make you stronger. The red ones will increase your energy levels. The purple ones will heal your scars. It's a veritable rainbow of cures. They offer quick and easy solutions.

Most medicine is bound by evidence. Most supplements are not. The FDA is not authorized to evaluate a supplement's efficacy or safety. It's up to the manufacturer alone to make sure their products are safe and as effective as they claim. How many manufacturers do you think routinely check the quality and contents of their supply chains of raw ingredients, which are sold on the world market and may not even contain the ingredients that are identified on the labels and may also contain harmful metals or pesticides?

One disastrous and scandalous analysis of supplements sold at GNC, Target, Walgreens, and Walmart found that four out of five products didn't contain the ingredients they claimed.[19] The United States Pharmacopeial Convention runs a voluntary testing program for supplements to ensure they contain what they claim to in the amounts listed. Moreover, they test to make sure the products are contaminant-free and made with clean, safe manufacturing practices. They maintain a list of all the supplements that are certified on their website (https://www.usp.org/reference-standards/reference-standards-catalog), and it contains shockingly few brands. Now there are supplement companies that sell products that have merit and integrity in their representations.

Drink Your Greens

I recently interviewed Marc Wachler, CEO and founder of Live Ultimate. Marc is an authority about wellness. His passion originated from deciding to take care of himself and learn about the best things to eat from a health and wellness perspective. What we consume is life or death, and being aware is essential. Marc, after doing extensive research, always bought dark greens because of their nutritional value. He didn't know the science, but he always wanted to look and feel his best. At the age of thirty, he went to Hawaii to a Tony Robbins and Deepak Chopra event called Life Mastery. He was there for ten days, and he learned so much. The importance of having an alkali diet was paramount. So many things in life are out of our control, but what we ingest isn't. All

---

[19] Sarah Kaplan, "GNC, Target, Wal-Mart, Walgreens accused of selling adulterated 'herbals'," *The Washington Post*, February 3, 2015. https://www.washingtonpost.com/news/morning-mix/wp/2015/02/03/gnc-target-wal-mart-walgreens-accused-of-selling-fake-herbals/

of us can start every morning with a green drink. We know that deep-dark greens are the foods that contain the most alkali. Most people have acidic diets. They consume meats, coffee, dairy, alcohol, sugar, etc.

Marc left the conference and started to have a dark-green drink every day. He noticed he had more energy, became leaner, had better digestion, and looked better. For the next several years, he became a student and researched the best superfoods, trying different brands and learning about the sources. At forty, he went for a blood test, and his results were extraordinary. His testosterone levels were like those of a twenty-five-year-old. His doctor was taken aback and asked him if he was taking human growth hormones. Marc told him about his diet, and the doctor told him to keep doing what he was doing. The National Institute of Health attests that an alkaline diet consisting of deep-dark-green vegetables increases growth hormones, and that is really the fountain of youth. Marc then went on a mission to find the best sources of organic superfoods on the planet for himself, and then he decided he wanted to share his passion. He founded and launched Live Ultimate to create a coveted brand and business with the highest accreditation. It wasn't easy to learn about sourcing ingredients. The challenges and the lack of transparency were daunting. The labs would push back, saying not to worry about it. It is about marketing. Nobody does these extra things because it is too laborious. It didn't make sense to Marc, but it was clear that the labs didn't want to do the extra work. It was all about making profits, and that was a lot easier than raising standards.

Watch What You Put on Your Skin

When Marc and his wife decided to start a family, he looked at her skin-care products and noticed the chemicals on the label. After doing some research, he realized how toxic some skin-care products were. If you simply Google two words—*cosmetics* and *cancer*—you will find pages of research that prove that what we put on our skin is absorbed into our bloodstream, potentially causing serious health issues and cancer.

In fact, EWG, the most respected nonprofit, nonpartisan organization, did a big study in which they tested umbilical cords of newborns and found two hundred different chemicals in the bloodstream linked to skin-care products the mother used, and many of those ingredients are known to cause cancer.

Marc decided to develop a skin-care line under the strictest standards. His goal—and what he has accomplished—is that his products are EWG verified. EWG verified is the highest recognition of safety, and it is a painstaking process to achieve. EWG reviews all the ingredients in a product but also the source of origin of each ingredient. If a product is EWG certified and carries their seal of recognition, you will know the product is safe to use or consume. When it comes to skin care, you should go to EWG.org/skindeep and type in the ingredients that are on your product label to ascertain their safety. EWG provides a safety rating one to nine—one being the safest, and nines the most toxic. You will be shocked to learn that some of the most trusted brands are using toxic chemicals.

Live Ultimate's mission is to provide the highest-quality, pure, and sustainable superfood ingredients from the most respected organic farmers. Their products lock in the nutrition and benefits nature intended to profoundly improve the quality of people's health and appearance and overall well-being.

Trust and Advertising

You might be surprised to discover how marketing affects not only our perception of health but also, some of our most widespread culture perceptions as well. In 1931, Coca-Cola was in financial duress. Its sales were slumping due to a federal mandate that forced the company to remove cocaine from its soda and replace it with caffeine. Yes, Coca-Cola used to contain cocaine! The government realized that addiction has immense health and commercial implications. Coca-Cola realized it had to recreate demand without the euphoric feeling created by the narcotic. The research and development department of Coca-Cola desperately needed an innovative advertising campaign. How could they restore the sparkle associated with that essential but now missing ingredient? As a solution, the soft-drink giant hired Swedish American artist Haddon Sundblom to create a jolly, ruddy Coke-drinking Santa Claus. Sundblom modeled Santa on his friend Lou Prentiss, whom he chose because he was chubby and cheerful and had a ruddy face and a white beard. Coca-Cola insisted that Santa wear a bright-red suit—Coca-Cola red.

The Santa Claus that we know today actually began as a branding strategy to resurrect sales of Coca-Cola. The 1800s Santa Claus looked totally different. He appeared either in bishop's robes or wearing a pointed hat, long coat, and straight beard. It wasn't uncommon to see Santa drawn as quite tall and gaunt. In European tradition, Santa often wore a black suit. Today, however, the bright, ruddy, roundish Santa we are familiar with is based on the drawings of Sundblom.

This story illustrates the seductive power of advertising to reshape not only our perception of a product but also of a ubiquitous cultural icon. Meanwhile, the lure of the color red, which is a vivid and energizing hue, restored to the drink the zest, vigor intensity, and vibrancy once associated with cocaine.

Myth plays such an important role in how we perceive products and ourselves. Remember the once-vaunted ties between coconut oil and health? Just a couple of short years ago, a national advertising campaign promised that coconut oil could do no wrong. Practically out of nowhere, it was being touted as a superfood, thanks to claims that it helps burn fat and curbs hunger among other impressive feats. Just recently, however, a Harvard professor fired the metaphorical shot heard around the world, saying that coconut oil is pure poison. This report came not too long after the American Heart Association (AMA) urged people to steer clear of saturated fatty acids, among them coconut oil. It is a frightening fact that 17.3 million people die of cardiovascular disease every year, according to World Health Organization.

Johnson & Johnson is a company that boasts a perception of quality and trust. Founded in 1885, Johnson & Johnson is actually a holding company for 265 individual companies. It sells products that we all use like baby powder, baby shampoo, and baby lotion. Its branded products include Listerine mouthwash, Tylenol pain reliever, Rogaine hair loss treatment, Band-Aid bandages, Aveeno face washes, Neutrogena skin care, Lubriderm skin care, Bengay muscle relaxer, Neosporin disinfectant, Pepcid heartburn relief, Nicorette nicotine gum, Motrin, Benadryl, Sudafed, Mylanta, Visine eye drops, and Acuvue contact lenses to name a few.

Johnson & Johnson faced more than a hundred thousand lawsuits in March 2018 alone over claims that its products are defective.[20] Lawsuits point to internal documents showing that J&J and its subsidiaries knew about problems with their products but sold them anyway.

Pending lawsuits against J&J:

- DePuy ASR acetabular system and DePuy ASR hip resurfacing system. Number of lawsuits: more than 1,650. Injuries: dislocation, loosening, metallosis (metal poisoning), revision surgeries.
- Pinnacle acetabular cup (device used in hip replacement). Number of lawsuits: more than 9,400. Injuries: dislocation, loosening, metal poisoning, revision surgeries.
- Pelvic (transvaginal) mesh (device used in treatment of pelvic organ prolapse). Number of lawsuits: more than 24,000. Injuries: erosion, infection pain, urinary problems, recurring prolapse, recurring incontinence.

---

[20] Drugwatch, "Johnson & Johnson." https://www.drugwatch.com/manufacturers/johnson-and-johnson/

- Risperdal (drug used in treatment of mental disorders). Number of lawsuits: 18,500. Injuries: enlargement of male breasts, surgery to remove male breasts, emotional injuries, diminished quality of life.
- Xarelto (drug used to thin blood). Number of lawsuits: more than 20,300. Injuries: severe, sometimes deadly, bleeding events, blood clots, wound leaks, infection.
- Johnson's talcum powder. Number of lawsuits: more than 6,550. Injuries: ovarian cancer, mesothelioma cancer.
- Opioids. Number of lawsuits: more than 430. Injuries: addiction, overdose, respiratory depression, respiratory failure, death.

Seven of the top ten healthcare-related verdicts in 2017 featured J&J.

- J&J was part of the US Department of Justice's third-largest pharmaceutical settlement. J&J paid the Justice Department about $2.2 billion in 2013. Manufacturers of Risperdal, Invega, and Natrecor all agreed to settle civil and criminal accusations.
- A jury in Missouri ordered J&J to pay $72 million in a Johnson baby powder case in February 2016. The verdict was overruled by an appeals court in 2017.
- In May 2017, a jury in Missouri awarded a lady $110.5 million after she acquired ovarian cancer after using Johnson's baby powder and Shower to Shower talcum powder.
- J&J paid $33 million to the majority of US states and the District of Columbia in May 2017. J&J was accused by the states of misrepresenting the manufacturing methods of some medicines. Motrin goods were included in this. These items were eventually recalled.
- A California jury ordered J&J to pay $617 million to six patients in a Johnson's baby powder case in August 2017. The decision was reversed by a trial judge in October 2017.[21]

---

[21] Jen Christensen, "Johnson & Johnson ordered to pay $417 million in talcum powder case," CNN, August 22, 2017. https://www.cnn.com/2017/08/21/health/johnson-and-johnson-talc-verdict/index.html.

Trust and Internet Consumerism

Technology has exponentially broadened our scope of trust and vulnerability. The limitations of traditional logistics and distribution are being replaced by the development of cloud-based services and digital content. In addition, the fuel that enables a lot of this change is empowered by collaborative consumption. The creative endeavor of selling a collaborative system is the governance that is building trust among strangers and facilitating meaningful connections. The gamut of businesses using these advancements is limitless.

Airbnb has grown to a multibillion-dollar enterprise creating a marketplace that never existed before. It is fueled by a trust network in which ratings provide confidence and credibility among members and users.

E-commerce powerhouses like Amazon, eBay, and ASOS expose us to new economic modalities on an almost daily basis, redefining, narrowing, and in some cases, obliterating connections between suppliers, manufacturers, wholesalers, retailers, and consumers. This process is called *disintermediation*, and it has traditionally been defined the "removal of intermediaries from the supply chain" or, in more familiar terms, "cutting out the middleman."

There are almost eight thousand dating sites in the world, and about one thousand new sites are launched every year. Human matchmakers are becoming obsolete. Meeting potential social friends or sexual partners the old-fashioned way through social events, parties, bars, dance halls, and personal or family introductions is being replaced by more dynamic dating sites sensitive to our social, economic, racial, cultural, gender, and sexual preferences.

eBay has created a marketplace for almost everything. Products can be bought for less, and a rating system creates either trust or distrust of both sellers and buyers. I always log on to eBay as I like to find items of interest for low prices. Recently, I tried on a pair of sunglasses in the Los Angeles John Varvatos store. I really liked them. I sat down on the couch in the store and searched John Varvatos sunglasses on eBay. I found the exact same pair for $120 less than the store price. I bought them. I have to be honest—I felt a sense of satisfaction sitting on the couch buying the glasses on eBay. Everybody likes getting a deal.

Groupon enables us to eat, shop, travel, and enjoy services at discount prices. There are countless other sites and apps that also offer shoppers benefits and savings.

Uber and Lyft are replacing car services and cabs and are creating trust in unregulated strangers to take us to our destinations. Both Uber and Lyft have implemented a rating system of the drivers.

TaskRabbit lists more than 140,000 people you can hire to do household tasks. Once again, the credibility of service providers is based on customer quality ratings. The trust economy relies on the amassing of reputation data. Reputation capital becomes and forms the basis of credibility and worth.

On Airbnb, the reputation ratings given to both the hosts and the guests make the accommodations compelling or not so compelling, and the guests' behavior acceptable or not.

Credit history will no longer be the determining factor in how much something costs or whether you are approved. Reputation will be the determining factor of what we can access and, in many instances, will limit what we can do in the world. Reputation is the currency of trust in the twenty-first century. Résumés will become relics and tools of the past. Reputation scores will be the new modality.

Technology is the game changer in so many ways and is very much used to develop and build trust—but how much should we trust technology? How exposed are we? The Internet is currently a corporate monopoly, and monopolies are always a threat to democracy. Facebook, Google, and Amazon have built empires by using seas of data. These tech behemoths are managed from centrally controlled servers. To run efficiently, those programs and servers capture all the data that is created. When you enter data into your device, that data is being captured by their servers. After decades of unbridled enthusiasm bordering on addiction for all things digital, the public may be losing trust in technology and what it enables. First off, online information is not necessarily reliable, whether it appears in the form of news, search results, or user reviews. Hackers or foreign governments can manipulate social media in particular. Personal information isn't always private. Hackers keep getting more adept. There are so many examples of hackers' ability to either influence outcomes or invade and steal our personal information. When Trump first ran for US President, did the Russians influence voters by hacking technology communication? We have heard through the news that the Chinese have facilities and buildings manned by specialists whose mission is to spy and infect computers with malware. Can we trust the brilliance and the use of technology?

I serve on the board of Signature Bank in New York City, and I am a minority owner of a broker/dealer by the name of COVA Capital. The bank has employed technology and protocols to protect their clients from the technology used by hackers. As smart as those programmers are who create blocks and protections, there are those out there who are smarter and figure out ways to breach these preemptive protocols. It is a constant battle. The broker/dealer I am involved with is regulated by the Financial Industry Regulatory Authority (FINRA). FINRA requires that any personal information sent to clients must be encrypted, regardless of whatever other technologies the firms use to protect clients. Before the advances of digital technology, breaches were fairly uncommon. But today, I can't think of one person I know who hasn't experienced having his or her credit card number stolen and used for illicit purchases. Over the last five years, I have had to cancel my card and get a new one with a new number multiple times because someone has stolen my number and bought things that were charged to me.

How does this repeatedly happen? Clearly, every time you make a purchase through the Internet, your credit card number can potentially be stolen. In some restaurants, staff members can use a device that copies your credit card.

The damages incurred as a result of cybercrime are enormous. According to research from Cybersecurity Ventures's 2019 cybercrime report[22], the worldwide cost of online crime was estimated to exceed $6 trillion by 2021. In 2019 alone, online crime affected hundreds of millions of businesses and individuals. Some 52.5 million people were impacted by two breaches of a social media network that compromised user's names, job titles, email, employers, dates of birth, and relationship status. The personal information and possibly business card details of nearly 500 million customers were exposed in a data breach at a major hotel chain. In December 2019, the city of New Orleans declared a state of emergency and shut down its computers after a cybersecurity breach. A file-encrypting virus that demands money in exchange for the decryption key had infected a number of municipal and state governments. Governments and local authorities are very vulnerable as they are often underfunded and unable to protect their systems from some of the major threats.

In 2015, the Ashley Madison website was hacked. Touted as the premier site for married individuals seeking partners for affairs, Ashley Madison is the most famous name in infidelity and marriage dating. The hackers who breached the site appeared to make good on their threat to expose customer data, dumping the stolen information online. On the dark web, a 9.7 GB data dump was released. Account information and logins for thirty-two million people were contained in the files. Also released were explanations of what members were looking for. The leaked information spawned resignations, divorces, and suicides.

---

[22] Steve Morgan, "TaskRabbit lists more than 140,000 people you can hire to do household tasks." Herjavec Group. https://www.herjavecgroup.com/wp-content/uploads/2018/12/CV-HG-2019-Official-Annual-Cybercrime-Report.pdf.

What about online reviews? Are they legitimate?

Let's start with the experience of millennials (generally designated as those born between 1980 and 2000). Not long ago, if you brought up "millennial marketing," people would roll their eyes. That time has come and gone. Millennials are responsible for more than $1 trillion in consumer purchasing today. There are 91 million of them according to Goldman Sachs[23], compared to only 61 million Gen Xers (1965 and 1984) and 77 million baby boomers (1946 to 1964). And this savvy, youthful demographic has a significant impact on how your business is viewed. Why? First and foremost, this demographic is far more sociable than any other. According to social media software company, Sprout Social, in their findings from a report in 2017[24], 30 percent of millennials connect with a business on social media at least once a month, and millennials and Gen Xers are twice as likely as baby boomers to follow companies on social media. Plus, they're constantly sharing and resharing, tweeting and retweeting, Snapchatting, and Instagramming about their experiences with brands like yours. Thanks to that pleasure-inducing neurotransmitter dopamine, they check their phones an average of 150 times a day. Millennials don't trust advertising, celebrity endorsements, or any of the more traditional communication strategies. They're even growing skeptical of influencers, beginning to doubt their credibility. This skepticism is fueled by the obvious presence of fake reviews and testimonials. Nearly all millennials (97 percent) read online reviews. Millennials have changed how we do business altogether. They are the reason all things mobile matter so much and why doorstep delivery of everything is commonplace.

However, there is the questionable reality of ratings, the primary means of evaluating products and services in the age of millennial marketing. Holiday season rolls around, and we are all too eager all to buy presents

---

[23] Goldman Sachs, "Millennials Coming of Age," 2022. https://www.goldmansachs.com/insights/archive/millennials/.

[24] Sprout Social, "The Sprout Social Index: Edition XI: Social Personality." https://sproutsocial.com/insights/data/q2-2017/.

for our loved ones. If we go online, we are bombarded and practically brainwashed by ratings and reviews. They are a bid for instant credibility. Five-star ratings from anonymous reviewers give us such confidence that we often buy what's being sold. But again, what do we really know about the source or its reliability? Unfortunately, disingenuous product reviews are an epidemic according to Saudi Khalifah, founder and CEO of Fakespot, a site that ferrets out fake reviews. Khalifah says many product reviews are not real, and he has the data to prove it. Fakespot has created its own artificial Intelligence platform that enables consumers to examine and verify product evaluations. "Companies often manufacture good product ratings while sullying competitors' products with negative evaluations," Khalifah said. As a result, many of the ratings you read online aren't credible. For example, about 70 percent of the reviews on Amazon are not real, according to Khalifah.[25]

Bottom line: if something looks wrong, such as a product that seems too good to be true, it probably is. And if you buy it, you'll get what you paid for.

Fakespot combed through hundreds of thousands of product reviews for evidence of ratings given by people who were not actual purchasers. It graded each review from "A" to "F" based on purchase habits, language, and dates. On its website, you may see a complete list of winners. You can also download a browser extension that warns you when a review is fake. Fakespot analyzes ratings from Amazon, TripAdvisor, Yelp, and Walmart to determine which product reviews are not real. And while each site is trying to combat fake reviews, it's almost impossible to manage them in real time.

One of the big problems is that review sites like TripAdvisor and Amazon don't face any significant penalties for publishing fake reviews; neither do professional liars who seed these online sites. How many billions of

---

[25] Lauren Dragan, "Let's Talk About Amazon Reviews: How We Spot the Fakes," *The New York Times Wirecutter*, May 13, 2016. https://www.nytimes.com/wirecutter/blog/lets-talk-about-amazon-reviews/

dollars are being spent on shoddy products thanks to these fake reviews? This information is not available. So, if you are wondering if you should trust online reviews, the answer is no. You should not trust online reviews—at least not all of them. If you do not have the time to verify a review through a service like Fakespot, there are other ways to tell if the product review is legit. "If you see a product with nothing but five-star reviews, it's a major red flag that something is off," Khalifah said. "Because no product or shopping experience is perfect all of the time."[26]

Again, if it looks too good to be true, it probably isn't. As reported in *The Wall Street Journal* on October 22, 2019, Amazon might need to spend billions of dollars in the future to prevent the sale of counterfeit goods, expired food, or dangerous products on its platform to preserve customer trust. *The Wall Street Journal* detailed the availability of more than four thousand items that have been declared unsafe by federal agencies.[27]

Whom do you trust online? That question may be the number one litmus test for governments, companies, politicians, traditional news media, global websites, and anyone who uses digital technology over the next decade. In light of all this, I have become—and you should too—very skeptical of online interactions.

In the summer of 2019, I traveled to Europe with my kids, Benjamin, 22, and Talia, 19. We took a cruise from Rome to Sicily, Sicily to Malta, Malta to Dubrovnik, Dubrovnik to Slovenia, Slovenia to Mykonos, and finished in Venice. At each port, Benjamin Googled to find the best bakery in town, and we would visit whatever bakery the search and endorsement highlighted. Benjamin really believed that, in each case,

---

[26] Christopher Elliott, "This Is Why You Should Not Trust Online Reviews," *Forbes*, November 21, 2018. https://www.forbes.com/sites/christopherelliott/2018/11/21/why-you-should-not-trust-online-reviews/?sh=2c12eabd2218.

[27] Tripp Mickle, "Amazon Ready to Pour Billions Into Policing Products on Its Site," *The Wall Street Journal*, October 22, 2019. https://www.wsj.com/articles/amazon-ready-to-invest-billions-in-policing-products-on-its-site-11571787628.

we were at the best bakery. I guess he trusts Google's results. Objectively, I am sure that there were many bakeries equally as good as the ones we visited. The obvious point is just how much we trust a technology platform.

Google, among other search platforms, imply trust, but are the results reliable? According to the *New York Post*, two out of every five Americans have convinced themselves that they had a serious illness after consulting "Dr. Google." According to a poll of two thousand Americans, 43 percent of those who looked up their symptoms online thought they had a much more serious condition than they had.[28] The fact that more than half of all individuals in the United States use Google to learn more about their medical symptoms is concerning.

The Human Need to Trust

This reveals that we have an innate need to trust. That is our default mode. We are born believers. In no human realm is this more believable than in our trust of religious tales. We spontaneously accept what our holy books tell us. Each religious text is replete with extravagant and exorbitant stories we wholeheartedly embrace. Human gullibility is boundless. That is an inculcated aberration.

Brands violate your trust. The lust for profit propels CEOs to make unfounded promises. Historically, there are myriad cases in which companies have been sued for misrepresenting products. False advertising scandals cost some brands millions.

Many companies have been exposed for peddling ineffective products with exorbitant claims like "scientifically proven" or "guaranteed results."

---

[28] Marie Haaland, "Americans are quick to believe they have a serious disease after they Google their symptoms," *New York Post*, November 8, 2019. https://nypost.com/2019/11/08/americans-are-quick-to-believe-they-have-a-serious-disease-after-they-google-their-symptoms/.

In 2015, the Federal Trade Commission (FTC) filed a lawsuit against Volkswagen for deceiving customers with the advertising campaign that promoted its supposedly "clean diesel" vehicles, according to a press release. It came to light that VW had been cheating on emission tests on its diesel cars in the United States for the previous seven years. The FTC alleged that "Volkswagen deceived consumers by selling or leasing more than 550,000 diesel cars based on false claims that the cars were low emission, environmentally friendly."[29]

Volkswagen may face fines of up to $61 billion for breaching the Clean Air Act on top of potential fines for deceptive advertising.

According to ABC News, ads for Dannon's famous Activia brand yogurt resulted in a $45 million class action settlement in 2010.[30] The yogurt was marketed as "clinically" and "scientifically" proven to boost your immune system and help regulate digestion. The Activia ad campaign, fronted by actress Jamie Lee Curtis, claimed that the yogurt had special bacterial ingredients. As a result, the yogurt was sold at 30 percent higher prices than similar products.

False advertising is detrimental psychologically speaking. It foments hope and works on the principle of the placebo effect. Because false claims appear in boisterous TV commercials or persuasively written print ads, they convince an audience that wants to be hypnotized.

Red Bull, an energy drink manufacturer, was sued in 2014 for their tagline, "Red Bull gives you wings." The business agreed to pay a

---

[29] Federal Trade Commission, "FTC Charges Volkswagen Deceived Consumers with Its 'Clean Diesel' Campaign," March 29, 2016. https://www.ftc.gov/news-events/news/press-releases/2016/03/ftc-charges-volkswagen-deceived-consumers-its-clean-diesel-campaign.

[30] Troy McMullen, "Dannon to Pay $45M to Settle Yogurt Lawsuit," *ABC News*, February 25, 2010. https://abcnews.go.com/Business/dannon-settles-lawsuit/story?id=9950269#:~:text=Dannon%20to%20pay%20%2445%20million%20for%20false%20advertising%20of%20its%20yogurt%20products.&text=Feb.,digestion%20and%20boost%20immune%20systems.

maximum of $13 million to resolve the class action case, including $10 to every US customer who purchased the drink since 2002.[31] The tagline, which the company had used for nearly two decades, went alongside marketing claims that the caffeinated drink could improve consumers' concentration and reaction speed. The flamboyant drink became the favorite of an entire generation brought to rapture by the concept of an energy drink.

Some claims become ridiculous when they flaunt medical qualities for their plebeian products. With blatant audacity, they vouch their products as having healing qualities. Evil has never been so banal. According to CNN, Kellogg's iconic Rice Krispies cereal faced a dilemma in 2010 when the company was accused of deceiving customers about the product's immunity-boosting benefits. The FTC ordered Kellogg to stop their advertising claim that the cereal boosted a child's immunity by providing "25 percent daily value of antioxidants and nutrients—vitamins A, B, C, and E," claiming the claims were false. In 2011, the lawsuit was resolved.[32]

For deceptive advertising claiming that Frosted Mini-Wheats make you smarter, the corporation agreed to pay $4 million. According to the Associated Press, the cereal maker erroneously stated that Mini-Wheats enhanced "children's attentiveness, memory, and cognitive functioning." The ad campaign falsely claimed that the breakfast cereal could improve a child's focus by nearly 20 percent.[33]

In light of that, it is interesting to be reminded that cornflakes were invented by John Harvey Kellogg. While working as a superintendent

---

[31] Lara O'Reilly, "Red Bull Will Pay $10 To Customers Disappointed the Drink Didn't Actually Give Them 'Wings.'" *Business Insider*, October 8, 2014. https://www.businessinsider.com/red-bull-settles-false-advertising-lawsuit-for-13-million-2014-10.

[32] Saundra Young, "Kellogg settles Rice Krispies false ad case," *CNN*, June 4, 2010. https://thechart.blogs.cnn.com/2010/06/04/kellogg-settles-rice-krispies-false-ad-case/

[33] AP News, "Kellogg reaches settlement over Mini-Wheats claim," AP, May 28, 2013. https://apnews.com/article/dbf29739d9314ac886966919ca35d201.

of Michigan's Battle Creek Sanatorium, he hit upon the idea of making a natural breakfast for the inmates and the general public to prevent masturbation, which he considered responsible for many diseases. He invented cornflakes as the essential ingredient for a healthy diet, which, of course, had no impact on the masturbatory life of inmates or the general population.

New Balance once claimed that its shoes could help wearers burn calories. The toning sneaker claimed to use hidden-board technology, which was advertised as a calorie burner that activated the glutes, quads, hamstrings, and calves. Plaintiffs in the lawsuit claimed to have been harmed and misled by the athletic shoe company.

Lemos Labs falsely claimed its app Luminosity could help prevent dementia. In 2016, the FTC hit makers of the popular brain-training app with a $2 million fine.[34] The FTC argued that the company deceived customers with unfounded advertising claims. The app company boasted that their product could help prevent Alzheimer's disease as well as assist students to intellectually perform better at school.

The erectile dysfunction market has its share of fraudulent promises, and many men became prey to the product's promise of a more gratifying sexual life. For many, the expectations of an easy cure prove irresistible. Extenze asserted its pills were scientifically proven to increase the size of the penis. They were not. This company was forced to pay $6 million

---

[34] Federal Trade Commission, "Lumosity to Pay $2 Million to Settle FTC Deceptive Advertising Charges for Its "Brain Training" Program," Federal Trade Commission, January 5, 2016. https://www.ftc.gov/news-events/news/press-releases/2016/01/lumosity-pay-2-million-settle-ftc-deceptive-advertising-charges-its-brain-training-program.

to settle a class action lawsuit in 2010 initiated by many angry men who saw their hopes dashed, according to CBS.[35]

As bad as the marketing campaigns I've mentioned here are, even worse are some of the counterfeit products that are sold. Beware of fake eggs! This isn't a joke. Google fake eggs and watch the videos. In China, fake eggs are made with chemicals and sold to consumers. They are carcinogenic. The greater extreme of misrepresentations is outright fraud, including counterfeit goods. An estimated 10 percent of the goods in the global marketplace are counterfeit. This may seem like a high number, and it is, but it is also an accurate statistic. Counterfeiting is a huge business. It is run by super sophisticated cartels. If a consumer will pay $1 for something, it will be counterfeited.

I once heard a speaker who is in the business of catching these counterfeiting fraudsters. He has a massive warehouse filled with counterfeit versions of almost any product you can think of. One example he gave was a very large bucket of Tide detergent made in Turkey. It was a fake, probably costing $1 to make, but sold for $30. That is a $29 profit, and counterfeiters pay no taxes. Counterfeiting is huge and is tied to organized crime and criminal organizations. The sale of fake goods online has blossomed, as have the problems that accompany these illegal products. These include perfumes that contain urine, phone chargers that burst into flames in the middle of the night, and children's toys that contain dangerous levels of lead. Fake semiconductors in everything from toasters to military equipment threaten lives. With the growth of the internet has come a surge in sales of fake goods made by workers in dismal conditions—and an increasing number of people willing to buy them.

---

[35] Jim Edwards, "Extenze Settles a False Advertising Suit; Now the FTC Should Go After Jimmy Johnson," *CBS News*, December 1, 2010. https://www.cbsnews.com/news/extenze-settles-a-false-advertising-suit-now-the-ftc-should-go-after-jimmy-johnson/ https://www.cbsnews.com/news/extenze-settles-a-false-advertising-suit-now-the-ftc-should-go-after-jimmy-johnson/.

Prior to becoming more knowledgeable about counterfeit goods, I never thought about the extremity of this problem. I once thought it was limited, more or less, to Gucci and Prada bags being sold on the streets in Rome or Florence. You can buy one for $20 if you are a skilled negotiator.

My attitude was, why not buy one? You aren't hurting anyone, and you probably don't want to spend the money to buy a real one. No harm, no foul. This really was my conscious awareness of fake goods until I learned more. What an awakening I had. How extreme is the number of counterfeit products we ingest or topically put on our bodies? Again, if there is money to be made, someone will make a counterfeit.

Fake makeup is omnipresent. You must make sure that the cosmetics you are putting on your body are safe. Human feces, rat feces, and carcinogens have been found in counterfeit cosmetics.[36] I learned about a girl who used fake Kylie Jenner lip liner. It contained superglue, and her lips were glued together.

The World Health Organization (WHO) estimates that close to $83 billion worth of counterfeit drugs are sold annually, and one in 10 medical products circulating in developing countries are substandard or fake.[37] This includes high-demand, expensive medications such as various chemotherapeutic drugs, antibiotics, vaccines, erectile dysfunction drugs, weight loss aids, hormones, analgesics, steroids, antihistamines, antivirals, and antianxiety drugs.

Consumers who misuse pharmaceuticals or attempt to obtain meds at a bargain price are among those duped into purchasing counterfeit drugs.

---

[36] Amanda Jackson, "Police find animal waste in counterfeit makeup – so it's not such a bargain after all," *CNN*, April 15, 2018. https://www.cnn.com/2018/04/15/health/counterfeit-makeup-seizure-lapd-trnd/index.html.

[37] Fraud.org, "Counterfeit drugs are a global problem," https://fraud.org/fakerx/fake-drugs-and-their-risks/counterfeit-drugs-are-a-global-problem/#:~:text=The%20World%20Health%20Organization%20(WHO,countries%20are%20substandard%20or%20fake.

Counterfeit medications are sometimes made to seem almost identical to the genuine product, with almost identical labels and pills, duping unwary pharmacists and patients. Drug counterfeiters are known to use cheap and sometimes harmful materials such as brick dust, ground-up drywall, and flour.

Among the most egregious frauds are bogus cancer medications. It has been reported one out of five French citizens who die from cancer are sold cancer therapy medications that have no medicinal value. The person is reported to die of cancer, and hence, there is no crime. There is no autopsy. This is the perfect crime. Another sad story was about a kid who died after taking Xanax laced with fentanyl. It wasn't his Xanax. Make sure that you never take medication that belongs to someone else. You never know where they bought it.

A few years ago, 190,000 people died in China after taking fake medicines.[38] A few years later, they executed the top drug regulator. He was taking bribes. Sadly, some people don't care as long as they make money.

Each year, more than 11 million maritime containers arrive at our seaports. At land borders, another 11 million arrive by truck and 2.7 million by rail.[39] US customs simply isn't equipped to handle the volume, and this is how a plethora of counterfeit goods come into the country. It is truly important to realize that the purveyors of these bogus products do not care about consequences. It is strictly about making money.

In the United States, companies that launch and sell a product they know to be ineffective foresee their reckoning for false claims. At some

---

[38] Peter Goodman, "China's Killer Headache: Fake Pharmaceuticals," *The Washington Post*, August 30, 2002. https://www.washingtonpost.com/archive/politics/2002/08/30/chinas-killer-headache-fake-pharmaceuticals/00c10dff-0243-4ad8-a09f-c8fd42a46d01/.

[39] U.S. Customs and Border Security, "Cargo Security and Examinations," May 23, 2022. https://www.cbp.gov/border-security/ports-entry/cargo-security?language_content_entity=en.

point, they expect to pay fines for their transgressions. They calculate that, by then, they will have cashed in substantially on the sale of their product, and in their view, they can weather the punishment and still make a large profit even after paying their fines. It is a win-win outcome from their perspective. It's a sad statement, but in the consumer-products realm, lying succeeds.

Mass-Scale Violations of Consumer Trust

Vanity, arrogance, and feelings of invincibility have historically played a devastating part in the collapse of corporations, the violation of public trust, and the irreparable harm done to consumers, sometimes extending to mass catastrophe. In my view, one of the most dramatic and memorable parables of shattered trust is the story of RMS *Titanic*'s maiden voyage from Southampton, England, to New York.

In 1902, industrialist J. Pierpont Morgan bought the White Star Company. The sale meant an influx of American money to build larger luxury liners to attract wealthy passengers. Managing Director J. Bruce Ismay proposed that the company build the most luxurious ocean liners in the world. The three super ships would be called *Titanic, Olympic*, and *Gigantic*. The names alone suggest the overwhelming hubris that infused this project.

Considered an engineering marvel, *Titanic* was the biggest and fastest ship at the time and could comfortably house 2,200 passengers in her many decks. At 11:40 p.m. on April 12, 1912, an iceberg ripped her plates on the starboard side. She carried enough lifeboats for only 1,175 passengers, leaving the rest of the passengers and crew—around 1,500 people—stranded on the sinking ship. Captain Edward Smith of the *Titanic* was asleep when the iceberg scraped the longitudinal flank of the great ship. Despite Morse code messages warning of large icebergs floating in the North Atlantic, he had been encouraged by the White Star Line to sail at maximum speed using the full capacity of her four boilers to reach New York and break the transatlantic speed record. Even after being alerted of proximity of floating icebergs and navigating in the dark night, Captain Smith had ordered the slowing of the ship, which was perceived as indestructible—2,200 passengers and the world-trusted British seamanship and naval construction. It is interesting that, in all the press reports, years of historical writing, and documentaries, J. Piermont Morgan is never mentioned or blamed for the greatest naval disaster in commercial maritime history. Today, you can visit his home, which is preserved as a museum on the east side of Manhattan and find no mention of the tragedy. Morgan was a powerful CEO who was the ultimate principal in this tragedy—the hidden operative in this drama of pride and greed. His is a story not of trust regained but of blame avoided.

A different kind of tragedy, with a different kind of ending, played out in 1982 when seven people died after taking Tylenol capsules laced with potassium cyanide.[40] Johnson & Johnson wasn't responsible for that calamity, but they inherited this crisis and had to address it swiftly and vigorously. This disaster caused an unprecedented and still-unsolved public health scare that led to major industry changes and one of the first massive product recalls in the United States.

As a result of the event, over-the-counter drug packaging was reformed, and federal antitampering regulations were enacted. The company's and government's swift responses effectively dealt with the disaster. The brand was saved and faith in the product was restored.

What about Chipotle Mexican Grill? Beginning in 2015, the food chain was investigated for a nationwide spate of outbreaks of foodborne illnesses. According to the *Dayton Daily News*, more than seven hundred illnesses were traced to a possible outbreak at a single location in Ohio. According to the Delaware General Health District, 647

---

[40] Clyde Haberman, "How an Unsolved Mystery Changed the Way We Take Pills," September 16, 2018. https://www.nytimes.com/2018/09/16/us/tylenol-acetaminophen-deaths.html.

people experienced stomach problems after dining at Chipotle on Sawmill Parkway.[41] Executives of the restaurant chain announced the company would start retraining its entire staff on "food safety and wellness protocols." That's about 70,000 people across more than 2,400 locations. I for one am not running to Chipotle to have lunch.

The CEO of Boeing, Dennis Muilenburg, made many mistakes. Governmental agencies requested his resignation in the wake of two crashes in 2019 that claimed the lives of 346 people.[42] This is a case in which trust was sabotaged by the leadership of an organization. A mixture of greed, disregard, and moral lassitude worked in tandem to scuttle the most profitable product: the Boeing 737 Max. Use of the automated flight system that protected the pilots from stalling was not taught to the pilots; training had to be purchased à la carte by the airlines. Massive scrutiny of the aircraft is revealing more and more anomalies. It is becoming clear it was a shoddy product rushed in its fabrication to compete with the European Airbus company's new plane. Uncontrolled competitive fever played an essential role in the 2019 tragedy. The 737s remain grounded all over the world at this writing. The public's faith in Boeing has been eroded.

When will the Boeing 737 Max fly again? Boeing is facing massive scrutiny over its newest and most critical aircraft model. Boeing has thousands of orders on its books for the 737 Max, and over 330 of the planes have been delivered. In the future, how would you feel safe flying on this plane?

---

[41] Food Safety News, "CDC confirms bacteria in stool samples from Chipotle customers sickened in outbreak," *Food Safety News*, August 17, 2018. https://www.foodsafetynews.com/2018/08/cdc-confirms-bacteria-in-stool-samples-from-chipotle-customers-sickened-in-outbreak/#:~:text=Health%20district%20staff%20identified%20647,Parkway%20between%20July%2026%2D30.&text=Clostridium%20perfringens%20are%20bacteria%20that%20produce%20toxins%20harmful%20to%20humans.

[42] Leslie Josephs, "FAA chief Steve Dickson announces resignation midway through term," *CNBC*, February 16, 2022. https://www.cnbc.com/2022/02/17/faa-chief-steve-dickson-announces-resignation-midway-through-term.html.

History is full of stories in which making money was a priority regardless of the ramifications. During World War II, US companies were doing business with Nazi Germany. The collusion between corporations and Nazi Germany started with the pretext of helping to rebuild Germany, but it amounted to support for the Nazi regime. When the war began, these companies were desperate to keep everything going. General Motors pivoted and was able to keep its subsidiary Opel afloat, and Coca-Cola invented Fanta orange for the Germans with profits continuing to flow to Coca-Cola.

When Hitler came into power, his goal was to dismantle and destroy the Jewish community along with other groups such as gypsies, Jehovah's Witnesses, the disabled, and political opponents among others. This objective expanded to other groups so quickly that a computer was required to track it all, but there were no suitable computers with appropriate software in 1933. What was available was an IBM punch-card system that managed and stored data using holes punched in various rows and columns in cards just over three by seven inches in size. Engineers had to personally configure this data storage. Millions of people of all nationalities, religions, and backgrounds went through the concentration camp system, and that extraordinary traffic-management project required an IBM system in every railroad station and concentration camp. The system used numbers to identify concentration camps and the kinds of prisoners incarcerated. They were Jews, gypsies, Jehovah's Witnesses, communists, and others, and they were categorized by a number. Code 6 meant the gas chamber or a bullet execution. Code 5 indicated a Jew. Code 3 indicated a gypsy. And all this was enabled by punch cards driven exclusively by IBM technology. US IBM executives declared the company had no control over its German subsidiary, but in 1941, Thomas J. Watson, the CEO of IBM, met with Hitler, and the Nazi contracts were with IBM in New York.[43]

Corporate allegiance to profits trumps any allegiance to any flag. A recent treasury report revealed that, in one week alone, fifty-seven US corporations were fined for trading with official enemies of the United States, including terrorists and despotic regimes. Amazon, Caterpillar, Chevron/Texaco, Citibank, Exxon Mobil Corp., Walmart, and Wells Fargo Bank were among the culpable companies.[44] We live in a time of excessive violations of trust. It is difficult not to feel that many commercial institutions have deceived us and lack integrity.

We buy stocks, hoping the companies that we invest in will do well and our stock values will rise. But do we want their success and our returns to rest on a disregard for morality? Many investors do not care. I am in the minority that does.

Unfortunately, the stories we've considered here are examples of rampant and widespread corporate malfeasance. In this world, many corporations consider your health and safety cheap. In response, you should place a high price on your trust. Hold vendors to account. Make your consumer trust difficult to earn and easy to lose.

---

[43] Michael Dobbs, "IBM Technology Aided Holocaust, Author Alleges," The Washington Post, February 11, 2001. https://www.washingtonpost.com/archive/politics/2001/02/11/ibm-technology-aided-holocaust-author-alleges/6addc414-ecee-4058-bea6-7f4708912d6f/.

[44] Rex Nutting, "Trading with the enemy," CBS MarketWatch.com, April 15, 2003. https://www.marketwatch.com/story/us-companies-quietly-caught-trading-with-the-enemy.

CHAPTER 3

A Friend in Need Is a Friend Indeed

IT IS MY decision to trust you. Proving me right is your choice. The breach of a trusting and caring friendship is a horrible and upsetting experience. It makes you feel emotionally violated. Just as I wrote this, I thought about my crooked partner whom I implicitly trusted and shared so much with about my personal life. He was a confidant. I really believed naively he was my dear friend as well as my business partner. My poor judgment put me in a very precarious position. Since the beginning of 2019, I have been unwinding my business due to my poor judgment.

I am working with my other partner through the dismantling of our business. He lashed out at me. I called him out on something that I felt he had been remiss about. He sent me a text, and part of it said, "You were the one that trusted that piece of s——, and you gave him the latitude to f—— us all. I didn't like him from day one. He would have never been a partner that I would have chosen! But you not only trusted him; you let him in on all of the intimate things in your life. You empowered him. Do I really have to elaborate further? No one could have ever known what that piece of s—— was up to."

Most of the time, when something like this happens, we are not cognizant of what is happening while it is unfolding. We don't see it coming because we have our guard down and believe in someone. These type of breaches of trust have existed forever, and sometimes the outcome is worse than just getting hurt. Sometimes it is fatal.

The Roman leader Julius Caesar delivered a letter to the senate of Rome after a spectacular victory in the east against Pharnaces II of Pontus, demonstrating both hubris and immense military prowess: "I came, I saw, I conquered!" The future of the Roman Republic was likewise affected by this revelation. Despite being acclaimed at initially for both his military and leadership abilities, Caesar eventually instilled dread in the minds of many within and beyond the Senate. Finally, there was a storyline. Friends turned into foes, and the tyrant met a horrible end on 15 March 44 BC. As Caesar was stabbed to death, he saw his friend Brutus among the assassins, and uttered the famous phrase, "Et tu, Brute?"—"Even you, Brutus?" We believe in those we believe in and are deluded with a trust that is disingenuous. Sometimes, this mistake can be deadly.

This story reminds me of when I began to get suspicious, and my crooked ex-partner put his hand on my shoulder and said, "I always watch your back." But, in fact, he was holding a dagger in his other hand.

On August 16, 1972, four Northrop F-5 fighter jets shot at King Hassan II's Boeing 727 as it was returning to Morocco. The assassination attempt was ordered by his closest adviser and best friend, General Mohamed Oufkir. The king had already given his right-hand man immense power, wealth, and prestige. He trusted him completely and absolutely. This failure of trust was monumental. The king was devastated by the violation of his trust in his best friend. His faith was obliterated. King Hassan II retaliated, ordering his military to assassinate his dearest friend. The military that he commanded went to his home and machine-gunned Oufkir to his death.

Less than fatal but impactful to me was the occasion on which I met Heather in Rome six years before this writing. I was with my girlfriend on vacation, and she went over to an attractive woman standing near the Spanish Steps and asked her if she knew of a good hair salon in Rome. Jill was extremely outgoing and approached anyone, anytime.

Conversation ensued, and we all decided to go have the perfunctory glass of wine all tourists have when in Rome. We had a great time. I was very impressed with Heather. She was very bright and elegant. I instantly enjoyed our banter and was taken by her intelligence. She was from Toronto, and it turned out that she was living in Maui, and I was planning to go to Hawaii. We stayed in touch after our trip to Rome and started to speak regularly. We became long-distance friends. Over time, our friendship developed, and I felt that Heather was a good friend. I felt very comfortable sharing details of my life with her, including personal issues I was dealing with. She did the same with me.

Do you know that feeling that you have when you sense someone really cares about you, and they demonstrate implicit interest in your life and the outcomes of your troubling matters? Heather was that type of person with me. Our friendship grew even when we were not physically seeing each other. After meeting in Rome, we saw each other three, maybe four times. At one of those meetings, she met the girlfriend I was seeing then. My girlfriend really liked Heather and arranged to meet her one-on-one the following day.

Unfortunately, my girlfriend was over-the-top aggressive and made Heather feel uncomfortable. She was probing her for information about me. The following day, Heather warned me that my girlfriend wasn't right for me. She was right. We broke up a few months later. Heather shared things with me about her personal life, and I too was objective and had concern for what I perceived was a dysfunctional relationship and told her so. All of a sudden, Heather became ill and was hospitalized. She went radio silent, and I had no idea what was happening. I tracked down her son on Facebook to find out what was happening. Ultimately, she recovered, but she had a malady that wasn't going away. I was very concerned and checked in with her regularly. In 2018, she was in good spirits and had apparently met a new gentleman whom she was optimistic about. I was obviously happy for her.

One day, she called me in my office and asked if I could do her a favor. I was overwhelmed that day with business issues and very busy, but when my receptionist said Heather was on the phone and she said it was important, I stopped what I was doing to take the call. She was calling from Hawaii and told me her wallet had been stolen. She had made a reservation at a hotel on the Big Island, and they needed a credit card to keep the room. She asked me if I could give them my credit card number just to secure the room. She told me she should have a new credit card imminently. I was momentarily surprised, but I really didn't think much about her request. She was my dear friend. I said yes, of course, and the hotel emailed me a form to fill out to secure her room with my credit card.

Thereafter, I forgot about it until I received a bill for over $12,000 from the hotel charged on my credit card. I was stunned. Obviously, this had to be a mistake. I immediately called Heather and left a voice message. It was the Jewish holidays, and she was in synagogue. She called me back. I told her what happened, and she seemed embarrassed. She told me that they made a mistake, and she would call the hotel to fix it. She claimed she gave them a different credit card for the bill. Of course, I said okay and thanked her. The next month, I got my credit card bill, and the charge was still on the statement. When I saw it, I immediately called Heather and left a message. She didn't call me back. I called her several times before I got a return call. Then when I spoke to Heather, she vowed that she took care of this erroneous charge. The following month, the charge was still on my statement. Now I was getting really upset, and Heather wasn't returning my calls. I couldn't believe this was happening. I called the hotel and got the manager on the phone and told him the story. I said my card was to be used only to secure the reservation—period. After a couple of weeks of scrutiny, I got a refund. The manager shared with me that there was another $25,000 of charges that Heather didn't pay before she left the hotel.

I was in total disbelief. My misjudgment was so disappointing to me and made me realize even more that my strength is my weakness: I want to trust. But I promise I am getting smarter. I have never spoken to Heather again. I was sad, hurt, and felt truly violated. I trusted my friend and couldn't believe what she had done. I don't know if there is a moral that resonates here other than the question, Do you know who your friends are? I absolutely saw none of this coming. I was totally blindsided. I think this as a bizarre example, an outlier, but that doesn't make me feel any better.

You'll make a lot of different friends during your life, or at least you will spend time with people you think are your friends. But true friends are hard to come by. When choosing friends, there are so many parameters and variables to consider. Most people are attracted to others with whom they feel commonality. In the 1950s, sociologists coined the term homophily—love of the same. Homophily is the inclination for people to engage with people who are similar to them—or as the saying goes, "birds of a feather flock together." That theory highlights the influence of your social network. A study done by sociologist and physician Nicholas Christakis found that, if your friends are obese, your probability of being obese is 45 percent higher.[45] Gender homophily varies with age. During childhood and adolescence, same-sex friendships are more prevalent. Studies show that preferences change when people reach their twenties. Heterophily is the tendency to interact with others who are different. Heterophily is far less common than homophily. It is clear to me, for the most part, that my friends share commonality with me. They either are of the same faith or have similar interests, and I viscerally feel very comfortable being with them.

We all want people in our lives who care about us and bring value to us. The following are some attributes or signs of behavior you should note to distinguish sincere friendships from those that aren't.

Jealousy. This is a flashing red light and a flaw in character. Sometimes, friendships suffer from jealousy, especially if the two members are at

---

[45] Elizabeth Gudrais, "Costs and Benefits of Connection," *Harvard Magazine*, May-June 2010. https://www.harvardmagazine.com/2010/05/costs-benefits-connection.

different points in their lives, or something great happens for one, and the other resents it. This often results in one person ignoring or refusing to recognize the other's good fortune. It is not uncommon to dismiss this behavior even though you recognize that it bothers you. But good friends can learn to look past an initial jealousy and put the friendship at the forefront, provided the friendship is true and sincere. If the friendship is true and sincere, then in the end, there shouldn't be any jealousy.

Signs of jealousy include the following:

- Your friend tries to belittle your success.
- Your friend starts to avoid you suddenly.
- You friend constantly judges you.
- Your friend always talks about himself or herself and doesn't acknowledge what is happening in your life. Real friends truly care about you. Friends should be there for you. That means they are there both for the good times and the bad times (and particularly in bad times). Anyone who doesn't support you emotionally or who disappears in times of need isn't a true friend.

People are your friends if they do these things:

- They are proud of you and compliment you sincerely.
- They have your back, even when life gets tricky.
- They seem genuinely excited when you succeed.
- They empathize and support you when you're having a tough time.
- They call you out when you are wrong.
- They really go out of their way for you.

Keep friends who sincerely accept you for who you are. This also means friends who do not want you for what you have. Friendship shouldn't be based on superficial or external things. Fake friends are those people who just want things from you. Real friends support you for who you are as a person.

I have a friend in Miami who has a huge yacht. Everybody tries to be his friend. Fortunately, he gets it and has told me how wary he is about disingenuous friends who want to spend time with him so they will be invited to parties on his yacht. Friends call you out when you're wrong. When we're wrong and are not cognizant of a bad decision, a real friend will tell us regardless of the potential for contention. They really care, and it is obvious. We all have flaws and make mistakes. Real friends identify them and discuss them with us in a mindful manner. They do this not to be spiteful but for accountability's sake and to correct poor judgment. They're able to point out some of the negative things we do but in a constructive manner. This means that someone is really there for you. This is what really distinguishes genuine caring friendships from insincere ones. A new acquaintance or a superficial buddy won't say anything that could be misinterpreted or offensive. However, a true friend, someone you can trust, will tell you precisely what's on his or her mind. Some of the most crucial sorts of friends to have are those who are open and honest. Be aware of the distinctions between givers, matchers, and takers.

How many times have you tried to strike up a conversation with people just to have them return the discussion to themselves? The distinction between self-centered folks and those who are givers and truly care about others is that it is all about "me." Real friends don't have one-sided conversations.

The ability to have an open, two-way conversation with someone increases the likelihood of a healthier connection.

Organizational psychologist Adam Grant's book, *Give and Take: Why Helping Others Drives Our Success*, is superb. Givers, matchers, and takers are the three sorts of individuals he describes. The distinction between givers and takers is self-evident. Matchers are those who will contribute only if they get something in return. I strongly advise you to read this book. Keep friends who sincerely listen. If your friends always seem distracted when you're together and their interests are elsewhere, it is a sign it is all about themselves. Recently, I met someone I really liked, and we became instant friends. He is a very successful businessman, and we have commonality on many fronts. I found myself always listening to his personal issues and being very supportive. But I also noticed that our conversations were always about him. I accepted this foible because I rationalized our relationship, thinking it would evolve and he really cared about me. Recently, I called him out because the imbalance of our relationship had started to bother me based on a lot of things that had happened. He apologized and acknowledged my feelings and said he was sorry and extolled me. He agreed and recognized how I felt and apologized. My gut feeling is that nothing will change.

Watch out for two-facedness. Red lights should go off right away. Anyone who badmouths you to others isn't a friend. In fact, this is a relationship you should end promptly. If you're getting mixed messages from someone, don't ignore them. If you're picking up that someone is saying different things about you to your face than what he or she says to other people, you must know that person is not a friend. Talk to your other friends if you're curious about how you're spoken about in private. Good friends will let you know the truth.

- Anyone who bad-mouths you to your face is obviously not a friend. Joking around with someone is one thing, but if somebody puts you down and doesn't recognize that the words are hurting your feelings, you should not consider that he or she has your friendship in mind.
- Two-faced people are manipulative. When they see you are going through a rough time, they try to benefit from it by playing on your weaknesses.
- If people lie to you or make excuses for hurtful things they say, know that you need to exit the relationship

These points may seem like common sense, but human nature is sometimes remiss in what we really need—and need less of—in our lives. A friend indeed is a friend in need: always being there is probably one of the most important characteristics of a true friend. Sometimes, this way of being can be awkward and uncomfortable. Borrowing money or making a financial commitment for a friend often causes visceral discomfort. I for one have been in this position and have felt that way especially when I've not been paid back. In some cases, I didn't care because I didn't have the expectation that I would be paid back because that person had serious financial issues. However, I have had other experiences in which I have had to chase a friend to whom I loaned money. Then there have been bizarre episodes like the one with Heather. The rules are simple: if you borrow money, be mindful about paying back the money. Aside from being the respectful thing to do, paying back is expected.

Okay, now that you have read these criteria, how many real friends do you have? We now know who our real friends are. How many people do you know whom you believe are sincere? And how many of these people do you trust or have faith in? How many best friends do you have? What is a best friend? What is the difference between a best friend and other friends? Is a best friend someone you are emotionally committed to and that you feel safe with and with whom you share personal and private experiences about your life? Is that the difference? What does a friend mean to you? What are your expectations of friendship? Are these expectations realistic? How many friendships do you have that are disingenuous because the person's intent is to get something or to curry favor? These questions may sound somewhat redundant, but I am trying to make a point for all of us and make you think about this relative to your own life.

I have trusted stupidly. At times, I have been hurt, particularly by people I thought I could totally trust. I feel a sense of pain when I reflect on my naivete. Today, I see more clearly. So let me share my list of significant attributes that are important in friends: comfort, camaraderie, humor, respect, true care, being there when needed, and consistency. Those, for me, are the attributes that make someone a true friend.

But all this is individualized. We all, as individuals, must determine the characteristics of true friendship. We are all different. I had a relationship with someone whom I really cared about and always gave to. It was very one-sided in that I was such a giver, and she was a taker. Yet I overlooked the obvious imbalance and accepted abuse for a long time until I felt terribly violated, and I ended the relationship. I don't know why I allowed myself to be abused. The signs were there, and I ignored them. Maybe I place too much value on comfort. I was very comfortable with her, and we laughed all the time. She complimented and praised me, but she was disingenuous and said things behind my back. I guess that the good things outweighed the bad things until it didn't. Today, I am no longer emotionally attached, and I clearly see things and feel differently. I ran into her at Costco recently. She ran over to me and hugged me and called me by the endearing nickname she had given me. At that moment, I felt ill at ease. Sometimes, friendship and trust can develop in strange circumstances or under dire conditions. It isn't just that you met in school and grew up together or that you work in the same company. What type of person sacrifices himself or herself for another? And what does sacrifice mean? Going out of your way or taking a bullet for a mistake at work for a friend is an example of a "friend indeed for a friend in need." Most people are out for only themselves. But there really are an exceptional few who will do this.

I remember September 11, 2001, so vividly. All of us who are old enough do. I was in my office on Forty-Second Street and Madison Avenue that morning. I had a television in my office, and as the news was being reported, me and my coworkers were stunned, unable to turn away from what was being reported. Think about all those firefighters who ran up the stairs at the World Trade Center to save and protect people they didn't know. They put themselves in harm's way, and more than three hundred of them died.

Suddenly, an alert blasted through our office building. We were told to vacate the building by the stairs. The elevators were shut down. After exiting the building, I realized that I would be able to get home only by walking. There were no cabs, and mass transit wasn't operating. My residence was forty blocks north. I stood on the corner of Forty-Second Street and Madison Avenue. I was shocked by what I saw. People were walking from downtown north covered with white soot from the collapsing buildings. There were so many of them. I would metaphorically compare what I saw that day as a scene from the TV show *The Walking Dead*. Everybody was scared, shocked, and unaware of what had transpired.

I started to walk north toward my home, and I watched everybody I passed, feeling their duress. I wish the phones we had at the time had photo capabilities of those we use today. The only pictures I have are those in my memory. What was amazing and eye-opening was that, on that day, there was no prejudice—no black, no white, no Jews, no Catholics, no Asians, no discrimination, and no difference among us. That day, everybody was helping everybody. People were grabbing strangers and putting them in their vehicles to help them get home. That day, all of us were Americans—period. That day, we all cared about one another. Everybody was a friend to everybody else.

Another incredible sight I saw over the next several days were lines of people standing outside Lenox Hill Hospital. Hundreds of people showed up to donate blood for the survivors. They obviously didn't know who their blood would be transfused to. They were there to save strangers' lives. A friend told me that, the following day, he volunteered at a Red Cross table to accept donations. A boy who must have been no more than five years old walked up with an envelope full of change and handed it to him. The boy had obviously broken open his proverbial piggy bank and put his savings into an envelope. My friend thought, *No one could have taught him that—he's too young.* It was the very best of human nature, seen in the smallest among us.

Those memories are etched in my mind and in the minds of others. That day, every American was there to help every other American. What I saw was incredible and begs us to question how deeply we can befriend or care for another, and also to think about what circumstances bring out the best in all of us, which is the ability to put another before ourselves. This is a different definition of the depth of trust.

Airbnb: The House That Trust Built

Joe Gebbia decided to have a yard sale. He had just graduated from a design school in Rhode Island and wanted to make some money selling off some old stuff. After working the entire day, Joe noticed a guy pull up in a red Mazda. He got out of his car and then, after looking at a few items, bought a painting.

It turned out the guy was alone for the night and was driving around town because, the next day, he was going to enroll in the Peace Corps. Joe started speaking with him, liked him, and invited him out for a beer. Joe's new acquaintance told him how he wanted to make a difference in the world, and they were having an engaging conversation. Time started to go by, and Joe was getting tired. He was ready to leave when he made the mistake of asking this stranger where he was staying that night. Things potentially became risky for Joe in light of what he did and the way he reacted. His new acquaintance replied that he didn't have a place to stay. Joe felt badly and didn't know what to say. He felt comfortable about the fact that this guy was going into the Peace Corps, but he was still a stranger.

Regardless of his uncertainty, Joe said almost impulsively, "Hey, I have an air bed in my living room. You can stay with me." Joe invited a stranger to stay at his apartment. That night, Joe couldn't sleep. He lay in bed staring at the ceiling, asking himself what he had done. *There is a stranger living in my living room*, Joe thought. He began to panic. He became paranoid and thought to himself, *What if he is psychotic and dangerous?* Joe leaped out of the bed and tiptoed to his door, peeking into the living room.

Fortunately, everything turned out perfectly fine. The houseguest wasn't a psychotic, and Joe and his new acquaintance kept in touch. Fast-forward: The man is now a teacher, and the painting he bought at Joe's yard sale now hangs in his classroom.

Impulsively inviting a stranger to stay in his house was, in fact, Joe's first hosting experience. It began a series of events that altered commerce worldwide.

Joe thought to himself that we are culturally taught to fear strangers, but maybe some strangers are friends yet to be discovered. His first hosting experience completely changed his perspective and opened up the possibility for innovation. Joe soon moved to San Francisco and took his air bed with him. He was unemployed and almost broke when his roommate moved out. He acquired a new roommate, but they were hit with a rent increase. As this was happening, he learned that there was a design convention coming to town, and all the hotels were sold out.

Joe had an idea. He told his new roommate that he'd figured out a way to make a few bucks by turning their place into a designer bed and breakfast. They built a website, and Airbnb was born. Three guests stayed at Joe's place on air beds on the hardwood floor, and they loved it. Joe and his roommate took their guests around the city and had a great time. They realized that it was possible to make friends while also making their rent. They felt they had the greatest idea. And so, they did.

Imagine inviting total strangers to come stay in your home. Joe felt no discomfort knowing that strangers could see their bathrooms and possessions. He actually thought he could make new friends and also make money.

Shortly thereafter, Joe and his creative partners pitched their new idea to investors and did not get a positive response. No one in their right mind would invest in a business that allowed total strangers to stay in their homes because we have been taught since we were kids that strangers equal danger.

What Joe and his partner were trying to do was build Olympic trust between people who had never met one another before. Joe only knew design, and he was determined to design something that would create trust. A home is so personal, so it would be natural for a host to feel uncomfortable and untrusting. The business model was fraught with trust challenges. But in practice, guests generally turn out to be very responsible. A well-designed reputation system is the key to building trust. This system creates trustworthiness. The reviews by both the host and the guest became the solution to building trust. It created comfort and a sense of safety. The key seemed to be hitting more than ten reviews—and then everything changes, and trust kicks in. Also, disclosure is significant.

Being accepted and liked balances on what you say or don't say. Joe decided to use prompts to lead the guests about what to say. At the time, he and his partner were betting their entire company that the right design would overcome the stranger-danger bias. They felt trustworthiness would be verified by the review.

Then something incredible happened, and it was a testament to the all-around benefit of people doing the right thing. A guest at an Airbnb had a heart attack. The host rushed the guest to the hospital and donated blood. This is a true story. Joe's model was built and designed around testaments and reviews that are the foundations of trust both for guests and hosts. This story was an extreme example. It led to an epic and funny guest review: "Excellent house for sedentary travelers prone to myocardial infractions. The area is beautiful and has access to the best hospitals. Javier and Alejandra have become guardian angels who will save your life without even knowing you. They will rush you to the hospital in their own car while you are dying and stay in the waiting room while the doctors give you a bypass. They don't want you to feel lonely. They bring you books, and they let you stay at their house extra nights without charging you. Highly recommended!"

As it happened, the combination of luck, smart design, and a need-yet-to-be-filled was the genesis of Airbnb, and it was fueled by technology. The chief executive of Airbnb, Brian Chesky, has said, "We don't think you can be trusted in a place where you're anonymous."[46] In order to participate in services like his, Chesky argues, you must expose yourself. It is a model of consumerism that depends on customer transparency—on trust.

Technology advancements have changed so many aspects of our lives. The ability to connect through the Internet and the evolution of social media have enabled us to connect and develop relationships exponentially. This is great, but situations can turn very bad when trust is breached. Airbnb is a prime example of a trust system designed with reputation verification and checks and balances. It certainly isn't perfect, but it has won the trust of users worldwide and shows no sign of abating.

Can You Get a Sitter?

Speaking about a trust system, consider UrbanSitter. This service requires the ultimate trust because you'll be leaving your child with someone you don't know. UrbanSitter, like Airbnb, has designed a system of reviews and checks to establish trustworthiness. However, before social media technology, trust didn't work like this. Trust was more random.

---

[46] Kelly Faircloth, "Airbnb Is Gonna Need to See Some ID, Ma'am," *Observer*, April 30, 2013. https://observer.com/2013/04/airbnb-anonymity-brian-chesky-anonymity-government-id/.

I can personally speak to this. When I was five years old, my mother left me with a babysitter she didn't know. Now that was a long time ago, and the same kinds of trust systems didn't exist then. I don't know where my mother found this babysitter, but I was literally kidnapped and taken from New York City to a house somewhere in New Jersey and locked in a bedroom. I do remember that the room had a television, thank God. This woman and her dad (it was his house that I was abducted to) demanded ransom. All I remember was that, in the middle of the first night, I was awakened by police breaking down the door of the bedroom where I'd been kept captive.

Both my babysitter and her dad were taken away in handcuffs. I was fine and got to spend the rest of the evening in the police headquarters where I got to sleep in an empty prison cell until my parents came to get me. From what I am told, the FBI and the local authorities were all over this, and the story was aired on television. Anyway, it wasn't traumatic for me, but my parents probably felt differently. This is really a true story.

So how did UrbanSitter build a product that convinces parents that strangers can safely watch their children? Babysitters don't typically become your friends, but the trust component is essential. The secret sauce is a combination of product features, logistics, and customer service that have enabled them to become a reliable solution for hundreds of thousands of households nationwide.

First, there are several reasons customers visit UrbanSitter: they need a sitter right away, and time is of the essence; they want a lower-cost childcare solution; or they've just moved to a new area, and they don't know anyone to watch their child. To respond to all these questions, UrbanSitter immediately shows you available sitters, their average response times, their price range. Then, and using Facebook Connect, the site ranks the sitters based on your degree of connection so that your friend's sitters appear first.

When parents join UrbanSitter, the site gathers information, including which parenting groups such as a local mom's group they belong to, which specific PTA they belong to, and even which nearby museums might have significance to their family. When UrbanSitter launches in a new city, these groups are important because they already have established trust. In essence, UrbanSitter borrows brand credibility from other organizations so new users will trust them too.

The company provides a mix of quantitative and subjective data to help users determine if they can trust a given sitter. Two of the most important stats are how many ratings a sitter has, which gives a better sense of how accurate that score is; and the sitter's number of repeat families, which demonstrates satisfaction and relational consistency. The site has also built Facebook's like button into the sitter profile pages so that customers can post about individual sitters and the experiences they've had using the platform. And when these ratings are connected to people the user already knows on Facebook, the influence is that much stronger.

Do You Know Who Your Friends Are?

Most marketplace companies today rely solely on star ratings, but adding in more data specific to your service builds expertise. A big part of trust is believing that a company has your best interest at heart even though you are a paying customer.

Luckily, I have a lot of friends. Most people I ask usually tell me they have a few friends. Classic answer is, "I can count them on one hand." After thinking about the stories I've just shared, my takeaway may redefines and really clarify important things to consider. "Do you know who your friends are?"

CHAPTER 4

Do You Trust Yourself?

I KNOW I SHOULDN'T do it. I know it isn't good for me. But I am going to do it anyway. I know I am right, and I shouldn't be hesitant—but I am. I can't pull the trigger. I know I should, but I don't have the confidence. I don't like myself, and that is why I do what I do. I lie to myself and avoid the truth. I don't confront what I should because I am fearful of making a mistake.

Here's the simple question: "Do you trust yourself?" This touches on a wide range of intimate personal qualities. Some are more-or-less incidental while others have profound ramifications.

The issues involved include our ability to manage self-control, having confidence in what we do in our lives, and our ability to enter meaningful relationships. The person you must trust first in these matters is yourself. No one else can consistently impact your life.

If you're like most people, you will, at times, make terrible decisions based on emotions. Your rational objectivity will become clouded. Emotions affect not just the nature of the decision but also the speed at which you make it. Anger can lead to impatience and rash decision making. If you are excited, you might make quick decisions without considering the implications. Even relatively mild and short-lived emotions can have a long-term impact on your decision making and, therefore, your life. Your grounds for trusting yourself to do the right thing can suffer when emotions take over.

As a side note, it is well-known that human choices are affected by the way in which a question is phrased and how we perceive it. Your decision often comes down to how you react emotionally to a situation. For example, being told that an operation carries an 80 percent survival rate may trigger a different reaction from the one you might have if you are told that the same operation has a 20 percent mortality rate—even though both statements mean the same thing. Self-trust is at play when we eat things we know we shouldn't but we cannot maintain self-control. We're all guilty of this. I happen to love cookies. I know I am responsible about how often and how many I eat, particularly at one time. So, I still buy them and really don't eat more than one or two over a twenty-four-hour period. It seems minor, but it wouldn't be if I couldn't stop myself from consuming the entire box.

A good friend has a similar desire for apple crumb cake. When he is near a particular bakery not far from his home, he cannot control himself, and he always stops in and purchases the cakes. He recently told me that he is trying to lose weight, but he still had just bought an apple crumb cake. He was mad at himself. He couldn't trust himself, and he knew it. He told me that he decided to give the pastries to his doormen. By the way, he made that decision after he and I had a conversation about this chapter. (I wonder if he actually did give the cakes to the doorman. Maybe that was a white lie—another issue we'll consider.)

Are You Truthful about Trusting Yourself?

Recently, I was asked to deliver a talk about *Trust Is a Double-Edged Sword* while it was still in progress. There were about sixty attendees in the audience. I typically speak on an impromptu basis; I just go with the flow. After I was introduced, I spoke about my first two books and about my passion for networking and putting people together without a quid pro quo. I shared that I have been nicknamed the "master networker," and when you are this type of person, you must be a giver. Givers by nature have to be trusting—the two go hand in hand.

Well, I do trust, and I do so too much. This strength and weakness formed the genesis of the title *Trust Is a Doubled-Edge Sword: Trust Me*. Partway through my talk, I stopped and studied the audience. I spotted a gentleman two tables away from the front of the room where I was standing. I pointed at this fellow and said, "Sir, what is your name?"

He responded, "Alejandro."

I walked from the front of the room closer to him. When I was about eight feet from him, I asked, "Alejandro, may I ask you a question?"

"Yes, of course."

"Alejandro, the question I am going to ask you is an important question. Do I have your word that you will give me an honest answer?"

"Yes!"

Everybody in the room was leaning forward as I stepped closer. "Alejandro, there is one thing more I want you to know. I told you that this is an important question, and in fact, it is the title of one of the chapters in my new book." At this point, he was looking intently into my eyes as I was looking into his. "Alejandro, do you trust yourself?"

Clearly, I had caught him off guard. His left eyebrow arched up, and he immediately reacted, speaking very quickly with an obvious nervousness. "Of course, I do…one thousand percent… absolutely. Totally."

Everybody in the room saw Alejandro's reaction, and I noticed many were nodding their heads. I took a couple of steps back and said, "Alejandro, I know you totally trust yourself, just as I trust myself. Really I do. I totally trust myself—except when I don't. There are things that have happened to me both in business and in my personal life that I am now objective about. And I question my self-trust regarding these situations. Alejandro, I guarantee that, if you and I were to sit down for half an hour and have an open conversation, you would recognize decisions you have made that could make you question your trust in yourself."

Once again, I noticed people nodding. After the meeting, Alejandro handed me his business card and asked if we could get together.

Everybody suffers from some degree of diffidence. Learning by openly exchanging with others can make a major difference in our lives. In learning to trust yourself, you should stay away from naysayers. Avoid cynics or people who undermine your self-trust. Make every effort to keep promises to yourself. When you make those New Year's resolutions, follow through on them. Make a commitment and live up to it. When you get angry at yourself for making a mistake and blurt out "I'm so stupid!" just catch yourself and say, "That's okay. It was a slipup" or "Yes, that was a big mistake, but I'll learn from it."

Trusting yourself is, without a question, essential for a successful and happy life. It helps build confidence, inspires others to trust you, and makes the process of decision making much easier. Self-trust is the foundation of individual identity. Its consequences and benefits dramatically affect our lives. Our innate sense of self-trust either enables or impairs us.

Lack of faith in ourselves shows up in the way we force ourselves to do some things we might not want to do rather than doing the things we authentically want to do. It's the difference between being your own worst enemy versus your own best friend. If you spend a lot of time regretting things you've done or decisions you've made, you don't trust yourself.

People who don't trust themselves create self-perpetuating cycles of stress and anxiety to ensure that they never get to that place where they're happy or satisfied. This often leads to depression, and depression can be debilitating and, in some cases, fatal.

How often do people who fail to trust themselves ultimately commit suicide? This a rhetorical question because the answer is very complex; but I am astounded by the many cases of suicide that friends and family members never saw coming. Suicide is, in part, attributable to self-trust crises.

I recently visited Ernest Hemingway's house in Key West, Florida. His compound is a tourist attraction. I have always been mesmerized by his genius, his talents, and his life. I felt his presence as I walked through his house. Hemingway was a passionate man who was capable, as few are, of capturing his life experiences and sharing them with others.

Photos of him project strength and confidence. He was an icon. He loved to go fishing. There were so many pictures of him on a dock, proud of his catch. He would seclude himself in his home and share his experiences in his books. His death was a terrible loss.

There is one particular photo that shows Hemingway smiling, holding a shotgun under his arm. A plaque under the photo says it was taken just three weeks before he committed suicide. He killed himself with the shotgun shown in the photo. The museum guide told us the gun was cut up in pieces and buried in an undisclosed place.

After we left his home, my partner, Nicole, and I walked down Duval Street, which is the main drag of Key West. We went into an art store where a great many photographs were displayed. I noticed a large photo of Ernest Hemingway standing at a dock next to a marlin that he had apparently caught. I stood there for several moments, staring at the photograph, still taken by the experience of visiting his compound. I chatted with the owner of the store about the photograph. It turned out that he also was a big fan of Hemingway and seemed to be an authority about this life. He told me he had seen hundreds of photographs of Hemingway, but that one was one of only two photographs he had seen in which Hemingway was smiling. "He never smiled," he said. The only other one that I could identify was the photo taken shortly before the writer's suicide.

Asking whether you trust yourself may at first seem like a ridiculous question. Most people will say, "Of course I do." But I question that. Think about this once more, reflecting deeply about yourself. Do you trust yourself? Please really pause and think about this. Be objective.

You may start to focus on or recall something that you don't ordinarily think about or that you intentionally avoid. This isn't just about eating cookies when you know you shouldn't; neither is it necessarily about the extreme story of someone like Ernest Hemingway blowing his brains out. It is about you.

We all confront similar issues. Life is hard, and the obligations, decisions, and responsibilities we face cause stress. If you listen to your friends or people you know well and consider their lives, you should be able to put your own issues in perspective. Some issues are more extreme depending upon our own circumstances. Now, it is true that you can accomplish more in life if you have implicit faith in others; well-placed faith is empowering and adds to your resources. Alternatively, the risk of betrayal is the drawback of trust, and that unfortunate truth moves many people to prefer self-reliance. This way of thinking seems more secure because the only person you can truly count on is yourself.

In actuality, trusting yourself involves two people. They're both you. They are the present you and the future. I shouldn't eat so much even though I want to now. The future you may regret the craving that the present you gave in to. People want to think of themselves as trustworthy, so when their acts fall short of that ideal, they just forget about it. The future you forgets about the present you. These are the seeds of self-distrust.

What about times of duress? Everybody faces duress at one time or another. This goes hand in hand with having responsibility for others, financial obligations, health issues, and so on. Our decisions and judgments are sometimes clouded to protect our self-image or perceived interests. Fear can upend objectivity and good judgment. When desperation overcomes rationality, we can no longer trust ourselves.

We have all heard stories of self-sacrifice. Examples like a soldier jumping onto a grenade to protect other soldiers are not uncommon.

This example of bravery makes me think about priorities. Trusting myself to do first what is best for me doesn't always matter.

Again, let us face the question of what it really means to trust yourself.

- Do you trust yourself to do the right things for yourself?
- Do you trust yourself to protect yourself from harm?
- Do you trust yourself to take appropriate risks?
- Do you trust yourself to do the right things for yourself and for others?
- Do you trust yourself to handle adversity without being self-destructive?
- Do you trust yourself too much and hence act with no consideration or care for others?
- Do you compromise integrity to get what you want?

Self-trust implies that you can care for your own needs and safety. It indicates you have faith in yourself to get through difficult situations while still practicing compassion and decency. It implies that you will not give up on yourself. Being able to trust ourselves implies being able to try new things without condemning ourselves too severely. Probably like you, I immediately tell myself that, of course, I trust myself.

However, I also must pause and really consider the question. There are times when I am unsure about an important decision, and maybe that is because I don't trust myself. I honestly never really thought about that before now. Perhaps the genesis of this fear is the result of past experiences that didn't work out. Maybe my confidence isn't as great as it could be. That said, I really believe I am pretty confident, especially about things I know well.

However, I believe most people would say they trust themselves while dismissing or avoiding the revealing intention of this question; they will not be totally honest with themselves. Maybe there is a direct correlation between trusting ourselves and being truly truthful and realistic with ourselves. There is an absolute correlation between trust and truth on so many levels.

Again, do we trust ourselves to do the right thing, first for ourselves and then for others? I am sure you have seen some of the cartoons in which the good guy (angel) on a character's shoulder and the bad guy (devil) on the other shoulder each urge a certain behavior or action. We all want the best for ourselves in all regards. In most scenarios, we do sincerely try (or should try) to maximize positive outcomes. Yet in many situations, we know what to do but do not do it. Diffidence takes over, fear stops us in our tracks, and we avoid advancing. Worse than that is the fact that we can hurt ourselves or get in our own way and react by overcompensating for our actions.

Sometimes, people completely forsake trusting themselves and do things for immediate perceived need or want, disregarding morality, honesty, and healthy choices. These people can be dangerous to themselves and even to others.

Consider obese people, drug addicts, and alcoholics. These individuals have to know that they are hurting themselves and may be even slowly killing themselves. Obesity is a serious and pervasive problem. Nearly 40 percent of the United States population is obese. This means almost 40 percent of the population is overeating because they lack self-control. They know intellectually that they shouldn't eat so much, but they continue to regardless of the consequences. Many of those afflicted look in the mirror and are unhappy with what they see. Even worse, they know they are imperiling their health by risking diabetes, fatty liver disease, or heart attack—yet they don't stop eating. Recently, I had a discussion with a psychiatrist about obese people as an example of people who don't trust themselves. She disagreed with me. She said these people have an addiction. I countered by saying that, if they trusted themselves to do the right things for themselves, they would not have allowed themselves to become addicted to eating so much.

Do these people trust themselves? What do they tell themselves? How do they cope every day? What are they thinking? Do they simply not care? There is some of this in all of us. Be honest and look in the mirror. Can you think of some examples relative to yourself that show you cannot trust yourself to do the right things for yourself?

Until recently, my palliative was drinking wine at night. I could easily consume a bottle of wine, which reduced my stress and helped me to relax. Five thirty would roll around, and I would feel the urge to have a glass of wine. I knew intellectually that having wine every day isn't a good thing. But I rationalized that I didn't drink *so* much, and it made me feel good and relaxed. However, every so often, I had too much wine, and I would not feel well the next day. Yet I didn't stop. I wasn't an alcoholic, but maybe I was on some level.

The following June 2022 stats are from the Addiction Center[47]: In the United States, more than 15 million people suffer from an alcohol problem, yet only around 8 percent of them obtain treatment. More than 65 million Americans, or more than 40 percent of all alcohol consumers, report binge drinking. Low-risk drinking for women is defined as no more than three drinks per day and no more than seven drinks per week; for males, no more than four drinks per day and no more than fourteen drinks per week. Any higher than that, and you're in the danger zone. In 2017, 34.2 million drivers were caught driving under the influence (DUI): 21.4 million under the influence of alcohol and 12.8 million under the influence of drugs.

Unfortunately, so many people are on a path of damaging themselves.

These statistics aren't limited to any particular societal group. Affluence shields no one from becoming self-destructive. One might argue that, when you have too much, you no longer appreciate what you have. I now realize so much more about myself since I have curtailed my daily

---

[47] Nathan Yerby, Addiction Center, "Addiction Statistics," June 20, 2022. https://www.addictioncenter.com/addiction/addiction-statistics/.

wine drinking. I realized I was anesthetizing myself to the travails of my life. In fact, I was reacting to having a crooked and sociopathic partner, going through a terrible divorce, and living a life that is paved with bumps like the lives we all experience.

To some extent, I couldn't trust myself to do what was right and healthy for me because I also dismissed the ramifications of what I was doing. I stopped thinking about what was good or maybe even healthy for me. I just didn't think about it. Not trusting yourself is a hallmark of addiction; addiction saps self-trust.

Craig's Story

Craig Schmell co-authored with Ellis Henican, *The Uninvited: How I Crashed My Way into Finding Myself*, a must-read that is currently being made into a movie. A financier and entrepreneur, Craig is a good friend who was kind enough to share his story and epiphanies.

Craig was lost in the world and didn't know who he was; all his thinking and attitudes were upside down and backward. Craig shared his experience with me: "My life before I stopped drinking and before I met Dr. Knauer was about self, self-gratification, and doing whatever I wanted to do to please myself while living my way with no concern about others."

Craig had a big ego and felt as if he walked on water. His journey led him to crazy places, doing crazy things where there were no boundaries. One example he shared in the book was crashing the Grammy Awards. Somehow he got "on the stage and sang with Whitney Houston and Michael Jackson." Another time, while he was traveling in Russia, he got high in the Kremlin, and later that night, he climbed out of his hotel room window, walked the edge to the flagpole, shimmied out on the pole, and stole the Russian flag that was draped over the entrance of the hotel. On another occasion, back in the United States, he manipulated a federal security contingent to gain access to Ronald Reagan's presidential motorcade and drove in it.

His book regales the reader with outrageous stories and self-destructive behavior. Everything was about getting drunk or high and testing the limits. Craig Schmell had a world-class talent for talking his way into places where he did not belong and getting high from overcoming protocols. But when his self-absorbed life started to really crash down around him, he finally learned, with his parents' intervention, to eviscerate the demons that had him on a path of self-destruction.

I asked him if he trusted himself then and now. Here is how he replied:

> I thought I trusted myself then, but the truth was that I constantly made poor choices, which always led to bad consequences. How could I trust myself? I didn't even think about trust.
>
> I also was so arrogant. I was better than everybody else. I was infallible. I remember one time I was out to five in the morning drinking and picking up some one-night stand at a bar. I left her and had to drive to Long Island to go to classes at the law school I was attending. I was hungover, late, and was on the brink of dropping out. I was driving east on the Long Island Expressway, and there was no traffic heading east. However, the west side heading into the city was bumper to bumper. I said to myself, *Look at those losers sitting in traffic and going to work. What morons they are.* I really thought this and said this to myself. Truth was that I was the loser, and I was incapable of seeing that then. My views were upside down. I didn't see anything. I was just so self-absorbed in my own disturbed reality. My life changed radically when I met Dr. Knauer. My parents had had enough of my antics, and one day, my dad showed up

and made me wake up. He arranged me to see someone who was thoroughly apprised of my life. He knew my story and all the debauchery in my life. After some brief conversation during my first session, he asked me if I liked myself. I thought arrogantly at first that this was a stupid question, but I responded that I did. He asked me why. I told him that I have a pretty girlfriend, a nice apartment in New York City, great parents, and a great family, and I do what I like to do. He was pensive and told me, "Those are not reasons to like yourself."

I didn't get it, and I asked, "What do you mean?"

Dr. Knauer's office was on a low floor in a building in New York City overlooking the street. He swiveled his chair to the window and told me to come over to the window. Dr. Knauer pointed to a man standing on the corner across the street. He asked, "Craig, do you see that stranger on the corner? What if I told you that stranger is you? What if I told you that stranger underachieved in almost everything he did in life, including sports and school [which Craig did]. What if I told you that the stranger outside has a girlfriend and that he cheats on her with five girls on the side, which is similar to what you do. What if I told you that stranger outside, when he has a job, goes in late, leaves early, never puts in a full day, and never puts in a full effort to his career. What if I told you this stranger's life is about conning people, and he hasn't been a great son or brother, friend, and certainly isn't kind to others and is never charitable. Craig, would you like that person?"

Craig told me that he froze and started to cry like a baby. Dr. Knauer was describing Craig—and all of a sudden, he realized he really didn't like the epiphany. He saw who he was, and in fact, he didn't like himself. This reality was the starting point for Craig to change his life.

Craig asked Dr. Knauer what he should do. His response was, "Every day, show up and do estimable acts, and you will begin to feel self-esteem."

"What do you mean?" Craig asked.

"Every day, you are a man of honor, integrity, and commitment. Every day, you go to work early, and you stay late. Every day when you make a commitment to a woman, you keep that commitment. You try to be the best at whatever you do. You get involved in charity and be a good son, and friend. Things will change."

Craig shared that this realization happened twenty-nine years ago, and he has been performing estimable acts ever since. Craig's life changed on that day when he became dedicated to Dr. Knauer's principle.

Trusting Ourselves

Craig's story returns me to the question, "Do I trust myself?"

I do today because, most of the time, I make good choices. I try to live by an attitude of sober discipline.

Here are my favorite mantras:

- Easy does it.
- First things first.
- Less is more.
- You never make anything better by making it worse.
- Pause, quiet, and respond with intellect.

I have discarded drunk behavior and attitudes. I stopped thinking of me first. I gave up the attitude of "I want what I want when I want it." I gave up thinking that I can screw it up now and worry about the consequences later. I stopped reacting with emotion, and I began to pause and get quiet. I committed to stop talking while never listening.

I can listen today. If you scramble the letters of the word *listen*, you get the word *silent*. Funny, isn't it? Another thing I learned is that true humility is not thinking less of yourself but thinking of yourself less. When you're thinking of others, you do not have the chance to wallow in your own self-pity and your own resentments. Today, I don't live in fear and resentment. Another of my favorite quotes is, "Knowledge speaks, and wisdom listens." American rock guitarist Jimi Hendrix said that!

A Friend's Bad Decision

I want to share another example of a non-sober attitude that produced an atrocious decision. A rather successful friend of mine worked in New York City and lived in Old Brookville on Long Island. He was married and had five kids. But he always avoided going home and would go to a local bar after work. One time, he met a woman at the bar who gave him her telephone number, which he put in his jacket pocket. He didn't pursue anything, but his wife, before taking the jacket to the dry cleaner, found the piece of paper with the girl's name and number when she checked the pockets. She became furious and confronted her husband. Instead of apologizing and being contrite, he launched into a non-sober rant. He said to her, "Do you know who I am? How dare you?" Things escalated, and his wife left him.

After a few weeks, he went back to the bar by his office and met another woman. He got drunk and took this woman in his car and got into a bad accident. The woman was killed, and my friend was charged with vehicular manslaughter. He was sentenced to six and a half years in prison. This happened all due to arrogance and emotion irrationality exacerbated by alcohol. He too made very poor choices.

Do You *Like* Yourself?

I think we first must like ourselves in order to trust ourselves. Are you constantly performing makeovers of your appearance, personality, and image? When you look in the mirror, what do you see? Do you see imperfections and wish you could make them go away? Do you feel the same way with your personality? Before you are due to interact with people at a social or business event, do you worry or feel discomfort instead of relaxing? Do you want to kick yourself for being so anxious? Do you overcompensate? Do you go home questioning yourself afterwards, and are you upset about that day?

Think about your relationship with your significant other. How often, when you go out with your other friends, do you spend the entire time discussing the issues with your relationship? Obviously, this isn't applicable to every relationship, but I bet it is for the 50 percent of those who get divorced.

The nadir of disliking yourself is when you do things to hurt yourself to a point of degradation. The most extreme example is suicide. Approximately 700,000 people worldwide die by suicide every year[48], which is roughly one death every forty seconds. Suicide is the leading cause of death in the world for those aged fifteen to twenty-four. Think about this for a moment. At this age, people are at the genesis of responsibility and achievement. How hard is it for them to take on life? Do you think those who kill themselves have no trust in themselves or others?

Depression is the leading cause of disability worldwide. It's estimated that 19.4 million adults in the United States—7.8 percent of American adults—have had at least one major depressive episode in a given year.[49]

---

[48] World Health Organization, "Suicide," June 17, 2021. https://www.who.int/news-room/fact-sheets/detail/suicide.

[49] Healthline, "Depression Facts and Statistics." https://www.healthline.com/health/depression/self-care-for-depression#4.-I-am-changing-how-I-look-at-myself-in-the-mirror.

Self-awareness is your best ally; it's opposite your worst enemy. Craig had to hit a terrible low point where self-destruction was imminent, and then he was guided to become self-aware and thus to change.

So, what happens when you don't have self-awareness?

- You don't see yourself objectively (and maybe you don't know how to).
- You don't understand your own strengths and, much more importantly, your own weaknesses.
- You are unaware of your cognitive biases.
- You are unaware of thought patterns and mental addictions that prevent you from achieving what you want.
- You delude yourself.
- You reject criticism and feedback.
- You reject ideas simply because you don't like them.
- You make lame excuses for your failures instead of taking responsibility for them.
- You don't know your self-limiting beliefs.
- You don't recognize repeat patterns of self-sabotage.

Self-awareness underpins nearly every other skill. If you're self-aware, you can grow, improve, learn, and get better. If you are not self-aware, you usually plateau and end up stuck. You stay exactly where you are.

What about the more extreme situations? Did Jeffrey Epstein trust himself? Here was a guy worth $500 million dollars who lived a life of extreme affluence—and he did what he did. Do you think there was a good side to him that knew the distinction between right and wrong? Did the bad side, driven by a sick desire, overwhelm him? In the model that we've been exploring, during his life, did the present Jeffrey Epstein disregard the future Jeffrey Epstein? He was able to achieve success to such a great level by trusting his business judgment and decisions. Yet, on a personal side, his decisions ultimately led him to end his own life.

Think about some of the stories in books or films in which a killer leaves clues intentionally. He taunts his pursuers and dares them to find him. In real life, maybe one side of this ill person is trying to repent. Maybe he is emotionally guilty. Am I reaching here? So, what is a psychopath? A psychopath is a person who suffers from a chronic mental disorder and displays abnormal or violent social behavior. Most psychopaths are untroubled with the need to trust anyone—including themselves—because they are, by design, not "vulnerable."

I don't say this to be self-serving, but as a normal person, I always intend to do the right thing. If I ever feel that I did the wrong thing or handled something poorly, I feel guilty and say to myself, *I can't permit the same mistake again.* I trust myself to correct my error. Aside from the correlation between trust and truth, there is another correlation relative to trusting yourself, which is self-confidence and execution.

Fear of Failure

"I've missed more than nine thousand shots in my career. I've lost almost three hundred games. Twenty-six times I've been trusted to take the game-winning shot and missed. I've failed over and over again in my life. And that is why I succeed." That's Michael Jordan talking.[50]

Fear of failure is one of the most powerful deterrents to self-confidence. When you put your confidence in yourself, you run the danger of making a mistake and failing. More precisely, when you trust yourself, you're compelled to take responsibility for the consequences of your choices; you can't blame others for your mistakes.

Is it, however, truly a bad thing to fail? No, I don't believe so. It's something I'd recommend evaluating. Everyone you look up to has made more blunders than you have. They've also failed more than you. Failure has an eerie quality that makes it seem permanent. It isn't. When

---

[50] Forbes, "Forbes Quotes." https://www.forbes.com/quotes/11194/.

you experience results that you don't like, it's your job to try something new. New actions produce new results. This is the only way we get new results. Without failures, there would certainly be no successes.

Going a bit deeper, failure tends to exist more in our heads than in real experiences. When you reflect on your life, you'll often notice that, when you took a chance, everything worked out fine. During the rare instances when it didn't, you were able to bounce back. One of life's most enduring lessons is that things have a way of working out. While we're suffering through the disheartening and gut-wrenching pain of failure, we're often focused on surviving, not thriving. When we fail, it makes us question everything, right down to the heart of who we are and why we have been put here on Earth. But failure, as much as it hurts, is also a necessary steppingstone. In fact, the most successful and famous people in history endured the most failures in life. They failed repeatedly but also got back up and kept going. And that is just what it takes to succeed.

Do You Trust Yourself Too Much?

I want to close this chapter by considering what happens when self-trust becomes too much of a good thing. Some of us have a high degree of confidence. When confidence is taken too far, the negative side emerges as arrogance and a total disregard for other people's opinions, perceptions, needs, or suggestions. The extreme example is a control freak—possibly a despot with a very specific agenda. I can think of several figures who could be viewed this way. Adolf Hitler comes to mind. He was an insane megalomaniac who listened to no one and who was obsessively driven toward what he conceived to be perfect solutions. It is a historical fact that Hitler distrusted his own generals and made some disastrous military decisions. His maniacal confidence was unstoppable until the very end.

More relevant to all of us as of this writing is Donald Trump. He is never wrong. Anyone who goes against him either gets debased or fired. He clearly trusts himself too much to the point he can never be wrong and refuses to recognize when he is. Every day, he makes a fool out of himself, and he cannot see what is obvious to everybody else. This goes back to my definition of "perception of self." It isn't how you see yourself. It is being aware of how others see you.

What about Bernie Madoff? He didn't start off being a crook. He was a money manager who built his credibility by achieving above-market returns. When the pressure developed to maintain those returns, he created a Ponzi scheme and believed that he wouldn't get caught; he probably thought he would make back the money. Did he trust himself too much? Did that form the root of his self-delusion and epic fraud? How do you interact with people who think they are always right? They trust themselves too much or delude themselves by trying to control or overwhelm those they are speaking to.

Your relationship with people who always insist on being right can prove challenging, especially when you've got no escape dealing with them. Perhaps you have friends or family members who always asserts their points of view even when you know they are wrong. They may either try to wear you down with their opinions or tell you and everyone else what you should think or how you should live. Recent findings on emotional intelligence and personality disorders reveal that people with certain types of behaviors are likely to lack the interpersonal awareness necessary for controlling their overcontrolling impulses. This is another way of labeling the absence of emotional intelligence.

Emotional intelligence is the ability to understand how your behavior impacts others. People high in emotional intelligence can adjust their behavior to that of the people they are with rather than insisting on having their own way. These opinionated people are, in this framework, people who are low in emotional intelligence because they cannot recognize and respect your point of view.

Entering endless arguments with these types of people is likely to prove frustrating, if not counterproductive. Here is a tip to help you regulate your emotions when this off-putting behavior is making your life miserable: walk away. You simply cannot overcome a personality disorder.

Practiced healthfully, trust is an Aristotelian virtue, which means that it lies at the midpoint between two extremes of excess and deficiency. Having too much trust makes you gullible. Gullible people believe almost anything just because another person says it. They trust far beyond what is justified and prudent. At the other polarity, people who are deficient in trust are paranoid in the sense of accepting virtually nothing that anyone else claims unless it matches what they already believe. For these people, there are never any good enough reasons to trust; all the evidence in the world would still be insufficient to win their trust.

Trust of self and others requires reason: it is a recognition of your foibles and strengths.

CHAPTER 5

Whom Are You Fooling?

> Magic is the only honest profession. A magician promises to deceive you and he does.
> —Karl Germain
> American magician and lawyer

IF YOU LIE to me, can I ever trust you again?

I think the response to that question depends on the severity of the lie. It is a fact that everybody lies and probably does so every day. That being said, the majority of these lies are "white lies." These are harmless or trivial lies told, in many cases, to avoid hurting someone's feelings or to avoid something you'd rather not deal with. Can you relate to this?

I decided I would track how many lies I told in one week. Here are the examples:

- My lawyer called me in the morning. I didn't take the call. I texted that I was in a meeting. But I really wasn't.
- My son wanted to use my car, and I told him no because I was going to use it—but I really was not going to.
- I made a dermatologist appointment for 11:00 a.m. The office called and said that I had to come at 9:00 a.m., and I agreed. Turns out, I couldn't make it at 9:00 a.m. and showed up at 11:00 a.m. anyway. When they said they called me to change the appointment to 9:00 a.m., I pretended to know nothing about the change. They honored my original 11:00 a.m. appointment.

- I ran into someone I really don't like and ended my conversation by saying, "Nice to see you again." It really wasn't.
- My girlfriend's friend bought new shoes and asked me if I liked them. I said, "Yes, they are elegant." I really thought they were ugly.
- My dear friend Dennis told me about a promise he made to his dad. When his dad turned ninety, Dennis promised him that, every year for the rest of his father's life, Dennis would put a tattoo on his arm. His dad is now ninety-seven, and Dennis has seven circles on his arm. Dennis told his dad that, when his dad reached one hundred, he would put a tattoo on his rear end. Dennis told me this story a year ago. I had a conversation with him about this, and I told Dennis that he'd said I could pick out the tattoo. He replied, "I never said that. I am getting the smallest possible tattoo on my ass." I replied, "You don't remember! You promised me that I could pick out the tattoo. I have good taste." He said he never would have agreed to that. He was right.
- My girlfriend asked me to have dinner with her parents, and I said I couldn't because I had to have dinner with one of my investors. In reality, I was only meeting my investor for cocktails.

So, in one week, I was guilty of seven white lies. I think you should test yourself and see if your count is greater than mine.

If you are saying to yourself that this isn't applicable to you, then you are lying about not lying. Maybe you've seen the movie *Liar Liar* starring Jim Carrey. Can you imagine if that film depicted reality, and you couldn't lie? Aside from always being truthful, you would face a plethora of embarrassing and revealing moments.

Do you palter?

I am a word guy and actually send out a "Word of the Day" email Monday through Friday to more than a thousand people. The email includes the word, its definition, a sentence for context, and its etymology. *Paltering* is a new word for me, and it is a great one. Everyone I ask says they've never heard it before.

There is a methodology of lying that deceives others through truthful statements. It is a manipulative form of deception called paltering. Paltering means speaking in a way to bamboozle others. Politicians are paltering experts; they palter when they omit important information. People palter when they have something to hide or just don't want to discuss. Paltering can pervade all kinds of personal interactions, from romantic relationships to international politics. In business, such behavior is rampant. Deception in business can take many forms, ranging from outright lies to half-truths.

Consider the following example. A human resources (HR) manager has determined that only one candidate is worthy for an in-house promotion to a particular position in the organization. Sharing this information with the candidate could inspire the candidate to use the information to gain an edge in the negotiations about the terms of the job (e.g., salary, bonuses, benefits). Thus, the HR manager has a motivation to mislead the person about the competition for the position and could do so in different ways.

An outright lie would involve stating something like, "We have many other qualified candidates who are interested in the position and could fill it perfectly." Another possibility would be to omit information about this very issue from the conversation. For example, the HR manager might remain silent about whether there are alternative candidates, which might lead the person being considered to form a mistaken impression.

Research suggests that, in a negotiation like this one, paltering is the most likely strategy used. It might involve telling the candidate something like, "After announcing the open position, we received more than a hundred résumés. My secretary shortened these down to ten applicants, each of whom has great skills, credentials, and experience." These statements may be true, but they express the false impression that other qualified applicants could fill the position when, in fact, that is not so.

Another example was Trump's response in the September 26, 2016, presidential debate to a question about a federal lawsuit that charged his family's company with housing discrimination. His answer was, "When I was really young, I went into my father's company. We, along with many, many, many other companies throughout the country—it was a federal lawsuit—were sued. We settled the suit with zero—no admission of guilt. It was very easy to do. But they sued many people."[51]

A 2017 research paper entitled "Artful Paltering: The Risks and Rewards of Using Truthful Statements to Mislead Others" starts with a portion of a PBS News interview on January 21, 1998, in which Jim Lehrer asked President Bill Clinton about the accusations that he had had an affair with former White House intern Monica Lewinsky.[52] In his answers, President Clinton spoke in present tense as a way of evading Lehrer's questions.

> Jim Lehrer: "No improper relationship. Define what you mean by that."
>
> President Clinton: "Well, I think you know what it means. It means that there is not a sexual relationship or any other kind of improper relationship."

---

[51] The Commission on Presidential Debates, "September 26, 2016, Debate Transcript." https://www.debates.org/voter-education/debate-transcripts/september-26-2016-debate-transcript/.

[52] Todd Rogers, Richard Zeckhauser, Francesca Gino, Michael I Norton, Maurice E Schweitzer, Artful paltering: The risks and rewards of using truthful statements to mislead others," PubMed by National Library of Medicine, December 12, 2016. https://pubmed.ncbi.nlm.nih.gov/27936834/.

> Jim Lehrer: "You had no sexual relationship with this young woman?"
>
> President Clinton: "There is not a sexual relationship—that is accurate."

Politicians usually palter by changing the theme or by giving an answer that doesn't directly address the question. They may be asked difficult questions they don't want to answer, so they focus on making true off-topic statements. Technically, they are telling the truth even though they are actually evading it.

In business, the dangers of paltering are significant. If the dishonesty is revealed, negotiations often reach an impasse. Even worse, negotiators who palter can do serious damage to their reputations and can permanently break relationships. This is because targets of paltering feel deceived and consider the practice to be just as unethical as lying by omission.

Some may think that "lies of omission" are similar to paltering. In both cases, the deceiver isn't saying the truth. But the two are different: Lying by omission is a passive failure to reveal something a negotiation counterpart doesn't know. Paltering, on the other hand, is the active use of true statements to mislead.

Say you are negotiating with a buyer over a used car you are attempting to sell. If the buyer says, "I assume the car is in great shape and the engine runs reliably." If you simply fail to correct the buyer if the engine has problems, you are lying by omission. But if you say, "I drove it the other day, and it drove well." Even though the car has been in shop two times in the past months, this is paltering.

Paltering runs rife in the legal profession, particularly in litigation. Do litigators ever tell the truth? This is rhetorical question, but clearly, cases are fought with a range of distortions and outright lies. Consider matrimonial law. It is all about money and disparaging litigation to create impressions that will maximize monetary allocations. As I have discussed before, even the children are fair game. If you want the whole truth and nothing but the whole truth, get a subpoena.

People are concerned about paltering in the news. Fake news is not a recent phenomenon. It has been part of news culture as far back as the birth of free press. Sensationalism sells, and media moguls are all about getting our attention and building an audience, and therefore increased advertising revenue. Too often, they use false or misleading news to achieve this goal.

Fake news has expanded because the business model of media companies shifted from paper to digital, making the distribution of fake news easy and low cost. News websites that currently publish fake news have names and branding that make them appear to be actual newspapers. An example of such a website was the now defunct Denver Guardian, which even included fake local weather forecasts. Since the fake news attracts many visits, website operators can easily acquire advertisers. It is said that talented writers who find it tough to make a living in traditional media are willing to accept high payouts to "report" fake stories, regardless of their personal ideology.

Orson Welles proved that Americans are very susceptible to believing anything, even a story as outrageous as armed aliens from another planet invading New Jersey. His brilliant radio broadcast in 1938 of an adaptation of his novel, *The War of the Worlds*, created such fear that it even surprised Welles. The broadcast created chaos because people believed the invasion was really happening. The morning after, Welles owned up to his unintentional "fake news" and apologized for the havoc it caused.

Today, the most despicable spinners of horrific, hateful, and fake stories show absolutely no indication of remorse or regret for the damage they cause. On the contrary, an unwillingness to display civil decorum or own up to their lies even when confronted with the truth often strengthens their reputations. Fake stories that manipulate the beliefs of viewers aren't likely to disappear, as they have become a resource for some writers to make money and potentially impact public opinion. Pew Research Center suggests that 23 percent of US adults have shared fake news knowingly or unknowingly with friends and others.[53]

In April 2018, Malaysia, citing national security concerns, enacted the Anti-Fake News Act, which stipulates that anyone convicted of creating or circulating fake news online could face imprisonment for up to six years or fines in excess of $120,000.[54]

What are the consequences of fake news? Inaccurate reportage poses a threat to democracy and creates bias. It is a particularly egregious and direct avenue through which inaccurate notions are propagated.

Misinformation can lead to poor decisions about consequential matters. The untrue beliefs that are promoted this way are persistent and difficult to correct. As a result, false information may continue to influence beliefs and attitudes even after they are widely debunked.

In 2016, it was falsely reported that the pope had endorsed Donald Trump. This "news" was shared more than 960,000 times and reported by BuzzFeed, a news and entertainment website. In reality, the pope rarely speaks on politics. Following the story, the Catholic leader told

---

[53] Michael Barthel, Amy Mitchell, and Jesse Holcomb, "Many Americans Believe Fake News Is Sowing Confusion." Pew Research Center, December 15, 2016. https://www.pewresearch.org/journalism/2016/12/15/many-americans-believe-fake-news-is-sowing-confusion/.

[54] Gulizar Haciyakupoglu, "Malaysia's Elections and the Anti-Fake News Act," April 26, 2018. https://thediplomat.com/2018/04/malaysias-elections-and-the-anti-fake-news-act/.

reporters, "I never say a word about the electoral campaigns," adding the voters should "study the proposals well, pray, and choose in conscience."[55]

Here's another case in point: In 2019, a video appeared allegedly showing a Tesla "self-driving vehicle" crashing into a robot prototype at the Consumer Electronics Show (CES), an annual trade show organized by the Consumer Technology Association that is attended by many tech reporters across the globe. It was not long before the video went viral and a number of media outlets running headlines claiming "Self-Driving Tesla Car Kills Robot."

The problem was that the video was fake. Tesla, during that time, didn't have a self-driving model, and the robot that was "killed" was actually part of an elaborate publicity stunt made up by the Russian firm that developed it.

When We Deceive Ourselves

To deceive ourselves about ourselves is metaphorically like burying our heads in the sand. Sometimes we do this out of ignorance. But I think most of us know, on some deeper level, when we are fooling ourselves. Every one of us, regardless of how evolved and self-aware we are, harbors pockets of denial, misconception, defensiveness, and ignorance. By accepting that as a given, we initiate the process of waking up. There is a direct correlation between deceiving ourselves and cognitive dissonance.

Cognitive dissonance is the state of having inconsistent thoughts, beliefs, or attitudes, especially relating to behavioral decisions and attitude change. So, for example, you might be going out with someone, and you see a blatant red flag in his or her behavior. The part of you that is not denying reality is saying that something is mentally off key about

---

[55] Hannah Richie, "Read all about it: The biggest fake news stories of 2016," MSNBC, December 30, 2016. https://www.cnbc.com/2016/12/30/read-all-about-it-the-biggest-fake-news-stories-of-2016.html.

this person, but you deny that and come to an illusory belief in his or her sanity. Cognitive dissonance can apply to many different situations, but it is, in essence, a finely crafted form of self-deception, a kind of illusory state created by your fear of reality.

What are the ramifications of lying to ourselves and then to others? In our daily lives, we engage in many acts of self-deception, large and small, but we rarely notice them because we so strongly believe that we are right or justified. We often fool ourselves—but not others. This predicament can cause relationship difficulties and undermine your credibility and the respect of those you love and care about.

False beliefs can also magnify a sense of self-achievement and satisfy important needs of the individual. People most of the time twist bad behavior to reflect positively on themselves, for instance, by cheating on an exam and believing that their inflated performance echoes their true ability.

This way of thinking is an element of what is called confirmation bias— the tendency to analyze new proof as confirmation of one's existing beliefs or theories. Confirmation bias enables people to hold all kinds of illogical beliefs. For example, someone who believes in tarot card readings or astrology will notice all the times a reader or a horoscope is correct, and they will blatantly ignore all the times the predictions and findings are inconsistent with reality. There are numerous examples in which people deceive themselves about the "peaceful" nature of their religious beliefs or traditions.

But what happens to the self-deception when self-deceivers must face reality? What happens when the next test comes, and the self-deceiver cannot cheat?

Visualize a stock trader who has access to inside information on a particular company and, as a result of using this information, is rewarded with remarkably high profits. If he assesses his stock-trading skill by this performance, he may deceive himself into expecting higher profits when he invests in other companies; he may deny that his cheating was the cause of his performance in favor of fooling himself that it was all due to his skill. Will the trader eventually readapt his beliefs and reach a more realistic understanding of his true skill? Probably not. The Bernie Madoff story is an on-point example.

Self-deception is a skill that humans have mastered. We deceive ourselves into believing erroneous information and refuse to believe truthful information. In fact, we tell ourselves lies about everything from why we choose designer clothing instead of nonbrand clothing to how our upbringing influences our love partners. Most of the time, we are entirely oblivious of our own mind's wild fabrications. Given the nature of self-deception, seeking to become honest presents us with a serious dilemma: how do we know when we are lying to ourselves?

Self-deception usually happens on the unconscious level to help us fulfill certain goals and maintain psychological balance. People are usually unaware that they are deceiving themselves, and as soon as someone tries to expose them to the truth, they often become defensive and even aggressive.

Self-magnification is one of the most prevalent forms of self-deception. We evolved to overestimate our positive characteristics, according to psychologists, because it makes us feel good and impresses people who listen to us. Some think that self-magnification increases motivation, which leads to better achievement. However, if motivation were the only aim, humans would simply have evolved to be more driven without the costs of reality distortion.

I have a friend who is guilty of deceiving himself regularly and says things that the listener who knows him recognizes as untrue. A recent example involved an email disagreement with me in which he started off by saying, "My time and life experiences are priceless." He was bragging. The fact is that he is twice divorced, he has kids who have not seen him in years, he has never achieved any real business success, and he is broke. His self-delusion continued throughout his defensive retorts.

He has a tendency to always say things about himself that are braggadocio—and are absolutely untrue. I always thought his assertions were bizarre or just efforts to overcompensate. The amazing thing is that he knows that I know who he is and isn't. Yet he says unrealistic things anyway. Many people deceive themselves just to prevent themselves from feeling inadequate.

People might deceive themselves to protect their egos. One of the most common examples of self-deception is believing in luck. After all, if people believe that they have failed because of bad luck and not because of a mistake, then they can maintain their sense of self-worth. The consequence is that no lesson is learned.

Procrastinators are among the worst self-deceivers. Procrastinators might claim that they are awaiting the "right mood" or the "right time," while actually they are just afraid to fail or to even test her abilities. Were they brave enough, they would face the truth about their self-doubts instead of hiding behind lies.

Life is unfair! This statement is familiar, huh? In most cases, it is nothing more than another attempt at self-deception. After all, it will hurt less to say that life is unfair than to say, "I didn't manage to reach my goals," right?

If you want to avoid self-deception, then don't escape; be brave enough to face the truth and decide you will change what you don't like about your life instead of living a lie.

How Do You Spot a Liar?

Spotting a liar sometimes is very easy, and we can tell right away that we are being told a fabrication. Other times, it is not so easy to tell, and we are deceived.

Author Maria Meyer did popular a TED Talk on spotting a liar.[56] She described how you can become a lie spotter and why you may want to go the extra mile from going from lie spotting to truth seeking and ultimately to trust building. The following were some of her observations from Meyer's TEDx:

> Lie spotters are armed with scientific knowledge of how to spot deception. They use it to get to the truth. They do it with a core proposition, and that proposition is lying is a cooperative act. It begins when someone believes the lie. You got lied to because you agreed to be lied to.
>
> However, there are times we are unwilling participants in the deception, which can have dramatic cost to us. Leading up to the 2008 Wall Street–induced collapse, a multitude of financial products were falsely marketed. Buyers were deceived. Lies can betray our country, they can compromise our security, and they can undermine democracy; deception is a serious business.
>
> Lying is an attempt to bridge that gap to connect our reality with our fantasies about who we wish we were. Studies show on a given day you could be lied to as many as ten to two hundred times. Some social scientists have found that strangers lie three times within ten minutes

---

[56] TEDX Talks, "How to spot a liar - Pamela Mayer." https://ne-np.facebook.com/tedtalksgroup/videos/how-to-spot-a-liar-pamela-mayer-ted-talks/3211011625784054/.

of meeting. Extroverts lie more than introverts. Men lie eight times more about themselves than they do about other people. Women lie to protect other people. If you are a couple, you will lie in one out of ten interactions. If you are unmarried, that number drops to one in three. By the time we enter the work world, we are breadwinners, and we are accosted by spam, fake digital friends, partisan media, ingenious identity thieves, world-class Ponzi schemes—and all this adds up to a deception epidemic.

Lying starts very early. Babies will actually fake a cry, pause-wait to see who is coming, and go right back to crying. One-year-olds learn concealment. Two-year-olds bluff. Five-year-olds lie outright and manipulate through flattery. Nine-year-olds are masters of the cover-up. By the time you enter college, you are going to lie to your mom in one out of every five interactions.

Lying is complex and deeply woven into our business and personal lives. Society has sanctioned it. It is part of our history. It is about how we live and interact. We live in a post-truth society.

So, what are the signs that indicate someone is lying?

- Freud said there is more than speech. If the lips are silent, you chatter with your fingertips—something we all do.
- The next pattern is body language. Liars are known to freeze their upper bodies when they are lying.
- We think that liars don't look you in your eyes. In fact, they look in your eyes a little too much.
- Smiles are supposed to evoke sincerity, but a lie spotter can detect a fake smile. Your eyes tell the truth, and they can't be consciously contracted.

- Attitude is probably the most overlooked most telling trait: truthful people are generally cooperative and helpful.
- A deceiver is withdrawn, looks down, and lowers his voice. He often pauses, and his movements are herky-jerky.
- Remember: we rehearse our words, but we don't rehearse our gestures.
- Liars behave in a discursive manner. O. J. Simpson is a great example. During his trial for killing his wife, he smiled and exuded a sense of comfort, which was completely disingenuous and out of keeping with the situation.
- These behaviors are red flags; they are not proof of deception, but when you see clusters of them, that is your signal that something is amiss. Another element to watch for are off-key patterns of speech. Studies show people who are overdetermined in their denial often resort to formal rather than informal language. You will also hear distancing language. Liars intentionally distance themselves from their subject using stock phrases, superfluous expressions, or overstatements. Richard Nixon used the statement "in all candor" when speaking of Watergate. Bill Clinton called Monica Lewinsky "that woman."

When I replay the tape, I realize my ex-partner was even more extreme. He was a pathological liar and had no boundaries to the extremity of his lies. Consider the lie that he put his kids on the company's payroll because they were taking classes that required them to be on a company's payroll. He is an example of a pathological liar.

Can You Trust Your Eyes?

Law professor Danielle Citron told a chilling story in her TED Talk "How Deep Fakes Undermine Truth and Threaten Democracy." Rana Ayyub is an Indian journalist who has revealed government corruption and human rights crimes via her reporting. She's become accustomed to controversy surrounding her work over the years. None of it, however, could have prepared her for the events of April 2018. When she first viewed a two-minute, twenty-second film of herself performing a sex act, she was with a friend. She was stunned because she had never filmed a sex video before. Unfortunately, thousands of people believed it was her.[57]

Sadly, the law did very little to help. Sex is frequently used to humiliate and discredit women, particularly minority women who dare to stand up to strong men, as she did at work. In just forty-eight hours, the fake sex video became viral. Screen images of the video with graphic rape, death threats, and remarks about her Muslim beliefs filled her social media accounts. She was seen to have advertised herself on the Internet as being available for sex. Her home address and mobile phone number were doxed, which means they were posted on the Internet. The video has been seen over forty thousand times. The consequences of this sort of cyber-mob attack are severe. She was heartbroken and terrified of the threats. She was unable to continue writing because she was emotionally paralyzed. She was concerned about her own safety. What she faced was a deep fake. Deep fakes are audio and video recordings that have been manipulated or fabricated to depict individuals doing and saying things they never did or said. Deep fakes have the appearance of being genuine and lifelike, yet they are not. They are complete fabrications despite the fact that the technology is still evolving and readily available.

Deep fakes first arose in connection with pornography. In 2018, someone posted a tool on Reddit, a social media site that connects people who have similar interests. Reddit enables users to insert faces into porn videos. What followed was a cascade of fake porn videos that featured people's favorite celebrities. Today on YouTube you can find countless videos that provide step-by-step instructions for making deep fakes on your desktop application.

---

[57] TED, "How deepfakes undermine truth and threaten democracy," TEDSummit 2019." https://www.ted.com/talks/danielle_citron_how_deepfakes_undermine_truth_and_threaten_democracy?language=en.

Researchers have found that hoaxes spread ten times faster than most accurate stories online. Deep fakes have the potential to cause grave individual and societal harm. Imagine a deep fake that shows American soldiers in Afghanistan burning a Koran. That deep fake would provoke violence against US soldiers. Imagine that the next day, we see another deep fake of a well-known political figure praising those soldiers. We might see violence and civil unrest not only in Afghanistan but across the globe. This isn't far-fetched. We have seen falsehoods spread on WhatsApp and other online message services that have led to violence against ethnic minorities. Deep fakes have the potential to corrode the trust we have in all media.

Imagine that just before an election, a deep fake video shows one of the candidates gravely sick. The deep fake could influence the outcome of the election and our sense that elections are legitimate. Imagine a deep fake video that disparages a company going public and disrupts the public markets. Our investments could be manipulated and our confidence in the stability of financial markets could be shaken.

Deep fakes can exploit and magnify the distrust in which we already hold most politicians and business leaders.

Technologists predict that, with advances in AI, it may soon be difficult if not impossible to tell the difference between an untouched video and a manipulated one. Politicians might insist that real damning audios are fakes. We won't be able to believe what our eyes and ears are telling us. Danielle Citron and Robert Chesney study deep fake technologies. They have coined the term *liar's dividend*: liars labeling something a deep fake (when it is not) to escape accountability for their wrongdoing.[58]

---

[58] Danielle K. Citron & Robert Chesney, *Deep Fakes: A Looming Challenge for Privacy, Democracy, and National Security*, in 107 California Law Review 1753 (2019). Available at: https://scholarship.law.bu.edu/faculty_scholarship/640.

Social media and technology companies must monitor and ban deep fakes—and that is expensive. Current law isn't up to the challenge to counter deep fakes. Laws need to be tailored to address deep fakes and mitigate their damage.

Rana Ayyub reported the deep fake to law enforcement in New Delhi, and they told her nothing could be done. The sad truth is that the same is true in the United States. We need new legislation to address this. We also need new forms of media training and education so that journalists and other gatekeepers can more readily identify deep fakes. We need better radar for fakery.

The moral of the story is that, in many cases, not only can we not trust what we are told, we also cannot trust what we see. Maybe the question shouldn't be, "Who are you fooling?" but rather, "Who is fooling you?"

CHAPTER 6

Maybe My Brain Needs to Be Smarter

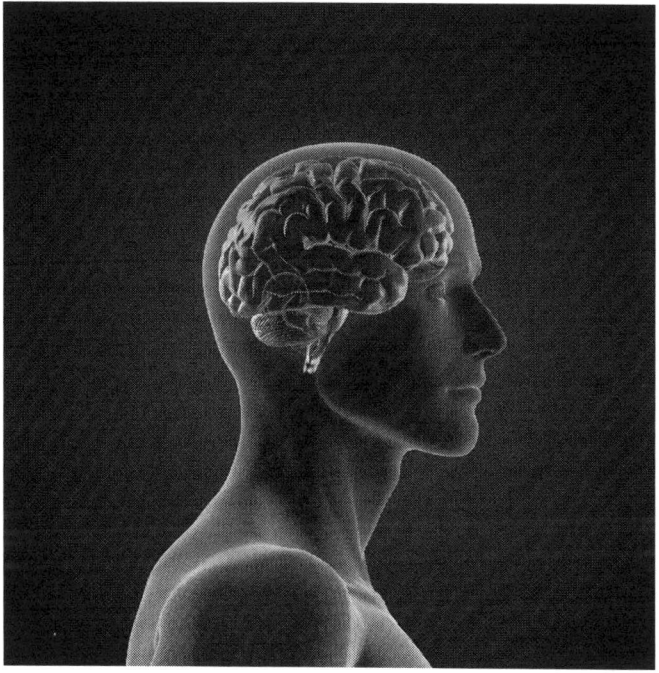

NOT A SECOND goes by when millions of people around the world are not constantly making decisions. Their brains are telling them what to do or not to do.

From mundane decisions to significant decisions, your brain dictates how to dress for the day, whether to return a phone call, what to eat for your next meal, what to purchase, and whom to trust and believe in. Your brain also twists and distorts incoming information so that it aligns with your attitudes, beliefs, and assumptions.

How much do we really think about what we do? That is mostly a figurative question except when it isn't, and the decision is important. It also must be noted that overthinking a situation often leads to a statistically evident deterioration of decision quality.

Perhaps the most damaging flaw is the brain's tendency to think that it is right. In fact, the brain often insists it is right even in the face of contradictory evidence.

Our brains, metaphorically, are supercomputers that direct us. Ideally, the output is objective, logical, and serves to produce the best possible outcome. This is too often not the case. I think it would be great if we had two brains that could confer and evaluate what we should do before we do it. Maybe then, our decisions would be better. If our brains had self-checking mechanisms, we would make better and more objective decisions. But the brilliance of our brains is limited by our perception.

Analyzing just how we decide is actually very difficult. We could talk about neurons and other physiological analytics, but that takes us only so far. Philosophers and scientists have spent decades trying to figure out why we pick one option over another and why some individuals act quickly while others take their time. Despite the fact that such problems are perennial, we have just scratched the surface of the intricacy of our human decision-making mechanism. Objectively, most of us do things we believe in and have faith in.

However, we are deeply influenced by people in our lives, our culture, the mores of our society, and our natural inclinations. There is a branch of philosophy called epistemology that probes how we know what we believe we know. Epistemology raises questions like these: What is truth? Do we really know what we think we know? How can knowledge be made more reliable? It is one of the oldest branches of philosophy, reaching back in time before Socrates. Today, epistemology is connected with many areas of philosophy and science.

Epistemology considers three main conditions: truth, belief, and justification. First of all, truth to ourselves occurs when we cannot recognize false propositions. Consequently, for something to be considered knowledge, it must be true in nature. Epistemology analyzes the nature and origin of what we think knowledge is and how it relates to our thoughts, such as the beliefs and justifications that underscore our actions or positions. Epistemology also deals with the origins and production of our supposed knowledge and our skepticism about what is presented to us. Epistemology is the investigation of what distinguishes verified fact from belief or opinion.

In short, it asks why we believe something is true. Some people are brought up thinking that people from different origins and beliefs are different from them or in some way alien; they are sometimes taught by influencers (such as religious or ethnic leaders) to stay away from other groups because they are inferior or threatening. This is an example of a belief that becomes a "truth" that manifests as unjustified prejudice. People are taught to be biased because the ideas are proselytized without justification.

How do we know what we know? What is the source of our knowledge? How do we know when something is true? We must assess the veracity of what we know and believe. For example, a lie cannot be truth because it is not factual and is false. Do we do what we do because we are deluded, fearful, or deceived or maybe irresponsible? Our minds are powerful tools. Our minds' convictions are overwhelming persuasive even when they are false. There are sometimes serious ramifications of belief that we are manipulated to accept as truth. This manipulation can affect our brains to the point where we lose all objectivity and forsake morality and do things to others that are heinous and even criminal. Have you ever thought about what it takes to kill someone? I just don't understand this ability or, better said, mental disability. Yes, I understand extreme circumstances, such as self-preservation when there is a need to kill someone to protect ourselves. But for a normal, healthy mind, there must be hesitation. What happens when a normal, healthy mind is influenced by other factors and loses all objectivity or capacity for clear thinking?

Drugs and Decisions

During the Blitzkrieg in 1939, German soldiers were ordered and expected to go to battle in a Panzer tank and to continually attack for three days straight without being allowed to sleep. How is this humanly possible? It really isn't under normal circumstances. These soldiers, or maybe better said human robots, were proselytized by their commanders to commit themselves totally to the Nazi cause regardless of what is normally plausible. Regardless of the personal cost and the health consequences for their soldiers, the high command's sole intention was to literally blitz the enemy and conquer Poland rapidly. They didn't care or think about their soldier's welfare, much less that of their victims. The people were used like tools to create the outcome the Reich wanted to achieve. In September of 1939, the weather was extremely hot, and it would have tested anyone's resilience to attempt the demands dictated by the hierarchy. Without artificial inducement, no one could endure the severity of the demands. The only solution was drugs. Life in Germany after the First World War had been extraordinary difficult: massive unemployment, civil unrest, and hyperinflation. But during the 1920s, Germany got itself back on track again. Suddenly, there was a sense that anything was possible. Berlin became a party city; it was a very open society. People took advantage of free time, spending it in cabarets and nightclubs, and free love and drugs were everywhere. Basically, people could do anything they wanted.

From a business perspective, drug manufacturing was an important part of the German economy. The pharmaceutical industry became a pillar and resource for the fulfillment of business aspirations—and eventually those of the Third Reich as well. Germany became the world supplier of cocaine, heroin, and morphine. The Germans invented methadone in order to help deal with pain. This led them to develop new drugs that could be used to inspire and manipulate the military. New substantive linkages were developed between the needs of a militarily expanding nation and the pharmaceutical industry that supplemented the goals of the leadership. Drugs, therefore, were legitimized by the Nazi regime; they became a good source of energy and stimulus in the military.

Hitler's soldiers were mandated to drive for days without stopping or sleeping. They literally were ordered to overwhelm anyone in their path. The high command wanted an advantage, and the German pharmaceutical industry became the manufacturer of a resource that could make that happen. The soldiers didn't have to rest because they had been inoculated with stimulants that enabled them to keep going, which was a major advantage because their enemies had not been similarly inoculated, and they had to sleep. The fact is, Nazi soldiers were taking Pervitin pills by the millions. Today, we know this drug as methamphetamine or crystal meth! Panzer drivers were taking two to five tablets a day. They didn't sleep, and they didn't stop.

During protracted periods without sleep, the human mind is affected, and the dreaming world starts to bleed into the waking world. People experience deterioration of their mental health because they increasingly lose the ability to distinguish between what is real and moral from what is illusion. Reality becomes a blur. As a result, behavior is affected, and people lose their moral compasses. They became paranoid and start thinking differently and lose control of their normal faculties.

There is a new finding by scientists that there is a mechanism in our brains that inhibits us from killing, and there are ways to circumvent that mechanism. The Nazi hierarchy used Pervitin as a tool to manipulate their soldiers so that their brains were influenced to follow orders without rest, self-thought, or moral consideration. We have certainly heard many stories about people who kill out of rage, often when they are drunk or affected by drugs. In Nazi Germany, synthetic stimulants, including Pervitin, proved to be effective ways of bypassing that inhibition to kill.

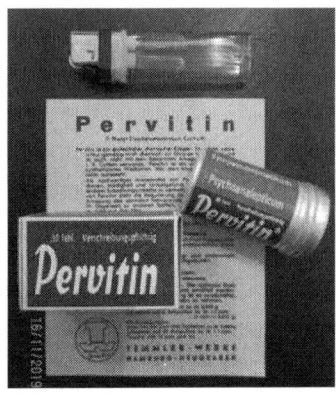

In today's parlance, their brains were hacked. The Nazis' slaughter and genocide of innocents was exacerbated by the excessive use of Pervitin. Many armies in history have taken drugs to improve their fighting capabilities. In Germany, however, the practice was brought to new levels. When Temmler Werke, a Berlin-based pharma company, released its methamphetamine compound in 1938, high-ranking army physiologist Otto Ranke viewed it as a real "wonder drug" capable of keeping fatigued pilots awake and an entire army happy. It was the perfect anti-war medicine. Ranke tested the medication on university students in September 1939 and found that they were suddenly capable of outstanding productivity despite a lack of sleep. The Wehrmacht, Germany's World War II army, began distributing millions of the tablets to soldiers on the front lines, and the stimulant was soon called *Panzerschokolade* ("tank chocolate"). German soldiers were allegedly taking a "wonder drug," according to British media.

For many troops, though, the miracle turned into a nightmare. The drug's short-term effects on the human body were equally as severe as its long-term consequences. Short rest intervals were insufficient to compensate for lengthy periods of vigilance, and the troops got hooked on the stimulant. Sweating, dizziness, sadness, and hallucinations were all symptoms of addiction. Some soldiers died of heart failure while others committed suicide during psychotic episodes. In light of these adverse effects, several doctors were dubious about the medication. Even the Third Reich's senior health official, Leonardo Conti, tried unsuccessfully to restrict the drug's use. Methamphetamine is a very potent substance, so it certainly has a very strong effect on the soldiers. Hundreds of thousands of soldiers on methamphetamine had a definite effect on the outcome of battles and entire campaigns. The drug temporarily mitigates fatigue and fear and enhances aggression and confidence. It produces a sense of euphoria. Soldiers didn't need to be brainwashed. For days at a time, they felt good and didn't realize that addiction to the drug builds up, and severe side effects follow.

Hitler, too, was influenced and affected by drugs. His personal physician was always by his side prescribing drugs and injecting him with substances. The drugs Hitler took actually made him look older. His brain was severely impacted. His decision making was deluded. Hitler's drug consumption exacerbated his ultraparanoid tendencies. He became a serious addict, and as Germany was going down, Hitler became completely maniacal and ordered the complete destruction of Germany, essentially a scorched-earth policy. The last drug he took was cyanide, with which he committed suicide. The irony is the salute "Heil, Hitler." Heil in German means "health."

Suicide Missions

Consider another Axis power, Imperial Japan during World War II. The Japanese military drafted pilots and asked them to volunteer for suicide missions. These pilots were called *kamikazes*. The military designed planes for the purpose of crashing into targets, and during these attacks, the pilots sacrificed their lives. Imagine that your son enrolls in the Air Force, and he comes to say good-bye to you because he is going to kill himself in his next mission. What would you tell him? What in his brain would allow him to end his life this way? Can you fathom the absurdity of fulfilling this order? But that was the reality then, and it remains today, just with different acolytes and delusions.

Why would someone choose to accept death? Well, at that time, the sense of duty was manifested by the culture of Japan. In Japan, shame is an important aspect of society. It is a tool of influence. Pilots were asked by their superiors to volunteer for the suicide missions. If a pilot refused, his response wouldn't bring shame to just him; it would bring shame to his entire family. Also, if he volunteered and died, he would be posthumously promoted by two ranks. So, from the pilots' perspective, they really didn't have much of choice. They could stay alive and shame themselves and their entire family or die and be hailed as a hero.

Hara-kiri is a ritualized method of suicide that originated in Japanese samurai society in the twelfth century. Rather than being captured, a vanquished swordsman would stab himself in the stomach, drag the blade to the right, and pull it upward. It was meant as atonement for defeat. This act was thought to win back some measure of honor in defeat. I don't know. Self-disembowelment seems a bit harsh to me.

The Islamic terrorist group al-Qaddafi carried out a series of four coordinated terrorist strikes on September 11, 2001. The assaults claimed the lives of 2,977 people, injured more than 25,000 people, and caused at least $10 billion in infrastructure and property damage.[59] In the months and years following the strikes, more individuals died of cancer and respiratory illnesses that were linked to the attacks. There were nineteen terrorists on four separate planes that day. It is clear that, regardless of generation, zealots can be proselytized to sacrifice themselves and others for a cause. Unfortunately, this mind manipulation and warped decision

---

[59] Students of History, "The September 11 Terrorist Attacks." https://www.studentsofhistory.com/9-11-attacks.

making isn't going to go away. From 2001 to 2014, 3,802 terrorist attacks resulted in 37,562 deaths and 96,644 injuries.[60]

Humiliation, revenge, and altruism appear to play key roles in shaping subcultures that promote suicide missions or the killing of noncombatants. Humiliation is an emotional process that seeks to discipline people's behavior by attacking and lowering their own and others' perceptions of whether they deserve respect. People have a strong antipathy to what they perceive to be injustice, with retribution as the dark side. One result of the drive for revenge is a person's readiness to suffer self-sacrifice in order to carry out a deed. Men place a higher priority on revenge than women, and young people are more willing to behave vengefully than older ones. It's no surprise, therefore, that the majority of suicide volunteers are young men. Suicidal behavior is viewing one's life as less valuable than the honor, religion, or some other shared interest of the community. Political organizations can use suicide missions as an outlet for their people's feelings of desperation, deprivation, hostility, and injustice because of religiously and nationalistically coded attitudes toward death, which stem from long periods of collective suffering, humiliation, and powerlessness. So, what were the 9/11 hijackers thinking about as the planes were approaching the World Trade Center? It is scary that someone's brain can justify that kind of act. Our brains are the computers. Our minds execute. We rely on our minds for everything—every thought, decision, opinion, and idea is believed to come from the mind. But our minds can't always be trusted. Living inside our heads can be dangerous. This is where our fears are triggered, where our internal enemies dwell, where patterns creep in, and negative self-talk takes over.

---

[60] Harmon, Vanessa, Edin Mujkic, Catherine Kaukinen, and Henriikka Weir. "Causes and Explanations of Suicide Terrorism: A Systematic Review." Homeland Security Affairs 14, Article 9 (December 2018). https://www.hsaj.org/articles/14749.

Deprograming Yourself

Constant thoughts weigh you down and have a negative impact on your decisions. They can, however, be managed, and once they are under control, you may start making judgments based on facts and conscience. The human brain is a marvelous tool. But its most damaging flaw is the tendency to think it's right all the time. The brain sees what it wants to see. The brain acts as a filter, constantly screening incoming and outgoing information. Unfortunately, it tends to screen out information that contradicts our prevailing view of the world and lets in that which supports it. We avoid what we don't want to see and refuse to even acknowledge it. Does this sound a little strange? Actually, this happens in every realm of our lives. Ever been jilted by a romantic partner and wondered why you were the last to know? The signs were usually there all along. Your brain just didn't want to see them. And how about when you are in a negative relationship but refuse to confront the facts until you are terribly hurt or taken advantage of? Incoming information is also twisted and distorted by the brain to match our prior attitudes, beliefs, and assumptions. Because we are already committed to a cause or a conviction, we mislead ourselves. If you have any doubts, turn on Fox News or MSNBC. There, broadcasters make their careers by distorting and manipulating facts to fit their own objectives in order to affect our opinions. Perceived credibility can influence our thoughts, perceptions, and decisions. Our brains by themselves do the same thing when we accept what we are told by people we believe are credible. We all know that drunk driving is dangerous, and texting behind the wheel is even worse. Yet we do both anyway. Be honest: do you do either? Why? Because your brain says you won't get caught and you won't get into an accident.

Even when it is clear that the old approach is no longer functioning, the brain seeks solace in what is known when it is anxious. That is why individuals remain in unsatisfactory professions or relationships. Our minds choose what is known rather than what is unknown but potentially excellent. The brain also has too much confidence in its own abilities. Research shows that experts are only slightly more accurate than nonexperts when making predictions in their fields. Moreover, when confronted with errors, experts almost never blame their thinking or change their beliefs. Instead, most attribute their mistakes to factors beyond their control.

Albert Einstein once said, "Two things are infinite, the universe and human stupidity, and I'm not sure about the universe." I don't think we are stupid. But I do believe we can be hoodwinked by our own brains.

The brain loves to solve problems. But as soon as *a* solution presents itself, the brain wants to accept it as *the* solution. There is no seeking of alternative answers, no exploring other possibilities. This is a terrible business strategy since there are numerous viable solutions for most issues in commerce, and the process of pursuing multiple viable options typically leads to a variety of successes. The ancient adage "trust your intuition" is backed up by plenty of scientific data. Intuition-related systems in our brains react considerably faster than systems responsible for deeper cognition and conscious analytical judgments. Not only are they quicker, but they are also more accurate. Instinct is a valuable evolutionary trait that keeps us safe during battle. Things that humans have understood for a long time are now supported by neurological data. Often, your initial idea is the best thought. Are "gut instincts" the brilliant distillation of all our wisdom and experience or just an expression of our brains' impulses? Do they lead us to oversimplify or stereotype? Or do they help us avoid danger before we can even fully process the threat? These questions are the stuff of heated academic debate. As I mentioned, my gut feeling usually seems to prove correct. Sometimes it is obvious, and other times it is not, but your visceral sense is great to bet on.

We can argue that intuition is the key aspect of knowledge relative to a reliable gut feeling. Intuition comes from experience, and those experiences can spot trends and patterns that are either positive or negative indicators. How many times have you gone against your gut feeling and wound up being disappointed or hurt? My gut feeling about my crooked ex-partner started five years before he was exposed. I ignored the uncomfortable feeling and moved on. I confess that I was stupid, lazy, and avoidant. That understates the severity of how bad my decisions were about the situation.

Brain Massage

Our brains are sometimes in a state of discomfort, and meditation has been used to resituate the mind in times of turbulence for millennia. Meditation, like many other beneficial endeavors, requires practice and a time commitment. Many people feel that the best approach to begin meditating is to set out time every day for it, but you may start small. I occasionally sit quietly in a comfortable position for a few minutes at a time, emptying my mind of any lingering ideas and concentrating on simply being there. I have a tremendous feeling of inner calm when I let my mind wander instead of striving to be something or someone. That is the most beneficial aspect of meditation. The chemistry of trust is a hormone known as oxytocin—it is the brain chemical of trust. It is an elixir and intoxicant. It is called the love hormone. It removes suspicion and distrust. A burst of that chemical in the brain makes us bond with another. Once released, it increases our capacity to affirm and embrace others. It has properties that create attachment, closeness, comfort, and empathic engagement.

That chemical is both a curse and a blessing. When oxytocin is injected into test subjects, xenophobia and discomfort toward others dramatically decreases, and strangers appear less threatening. Subjects become more accessible and receptive. Trust expands significantly. Oxytocin promotes social bonding because it reduces social anxiety. Is that a good thing? Those who can manipulate the levels of oxytocin in our brains can gain power and dominion over us; they can alter our trust. Can you imagine such a radical ideology?

In his book *Negotiating the Nonnegotiable: How to Resolve Your Most Emotionally Charged Conflicts*, Harvard professor and conflict resolution expert Daniel Shapiro discusses the power of affiliation, which is the emotional connection one person feels toward another. That connection engenders connective emotions and a desire to cooperate. The feeling of affiliation releases oxytocin, which further enhances the feeling of trust. This is a fundamental ingredient in networking.

But affiliation is a two-edged sword. Affiliation can be a factor in allegiance to a political party, a leader, a spiritual sect, or any ideology. What is your affiliation? Can it have a negative side? The answer is yes, especially when affiliations create bias and prejudice. In the mass psychology of ideological, political, or spiritual movements, individuals who enter a community no longer feel alone; harried by doubts; or persecuted by feelings of inferiority, insecurity, and death anxiety. The new member has entered a larger self, a vast group of souls, a mass matrix. New members entering the jihad movement are consumed and controlled by their reason for being. As a member of this radical entity, they may not fear death.

Every party has its spokesman, and every affiliation has its "prophet" who summons new recruits to buy into group ideology and bypass the boundaries of their own selves. What these affiliations offer their acolytes is the release of personal identity and acquisition of a vast self. Chemically, these affiliations flood the brains of their believers with an abundance of oxytocin.

Most historians have no knowledge of brain chemistry. They catalog events, report on significant happenings, analyze data, and structure theories according to certain historical developments. Brain psychology rarely enters their understanding of history. But before the United States entered World War II, President Roosevelt ordered Walter Langer, a psychoanalyst and chief of research and analysis head of the Office of

Strategic Services (OSS), to issue a report on the mind of Hitler.[61] Langer dispatched a team of researchers to Germany to speak to witnesses and gather all kinds of biographical information about the führer. Langer analyzed all the data and produced a psychological dossier for the president. Langer predicted many events, decisions, and actions Hitler would take. The president trusted this document and was guided by it in his war against the führer. This was the first time modern psychology was used to predict an uncertain future. But when it comes to the knowledge of brain chemistry, there has been no commensurate effort.

How much do we rely on our feelings to direct our behavior? And should we trust our feelings? Over the last few decades, it's been common knowledge that we should trust our gut instincts. That is, if we have strong feelings about something, those feelings deserve to be recognized as real or true. The phrase "trust your feelings" has nearly become commonplace in recent years. But in the end, how logical—and safe—is it to trust that, if we have strong feelings about something, we should trust them and allow them to dictate our actions?

The wonderful sensation of falling in love is one example of needing to be cautious about "running" with our emotions. Falling "madly" in love with someone doesn't always mean that the person we're smitten with is the ideal one for us, even though it nearly always feels that way in the moment. However, because falling in love is more of a chemical process than a cognitive one, we must exercise extra caution while making a commitment due to the intensity of our sensations. Falling "head over heels" might indicate exactly that: our desire has put us off balance, and we must continue with extreme caution. In some respects, falling in love with the wrong person is just as simple as falling in love with the right one, especially if we're just so eager for the experience or if the other person is highly appealing. In a similar spirit, the word *infatuation*

---

[61] Jewish Virtual Library, "Adolf Hitler: Psychological Analysis of Hitler's Life & Legend." https://www.jewishvirtuallibrary.org/psychological-analysis-of-hitler-s-life-and-legend-2.

literally means "to make fatuous or stupid." Alternatively, when things don't work out and we get hurt, we may emotionally overreact.

At some time in our lives, most of us have been disappointed or betrayed in love. And we've all experienced how difficult it is to regain trust when someone has betrayed us. Trusting is difficult in and of itself, but if you have pistanthrophobia, it may be nearly impossible.

What is pistanthrophobia? It is an unjustified fear of developing a close and personal contact with people. Fear overrides the urge to trust people because of past trauma or negative experiences. People who suffer with this condition feel as if everyone sooner or later will disappoint or betray them. They become extremely distrustful. They're afraid that past harms may be repeated, and they don't want to let that happen.

Your emotions are busy sending you messages all day. Those messages often provide vital information. Events and insights can deepen or weaken some of these feelings. And some feelings can attach themselves where they do not belong.

A Unique Method for Determining Whether or Not You Can Trust Your Feelings

- First, sit with the emotion and consider it. Try to name the emotion or emotions, bearing in mind that many strong emotional reactions are the consequence of a combination of emotions. What is going on in your life right now that makes you feel this way? It might be something that looms huge or something that appears little at first. Make the best decision you can.
- Second, imagine a friend tells you about a problem: "This happened, and I feel this way." What would you say to your pal? Do you think your friend's sentiments are well-founded or exaggerated?

- Third, consider the past. Have you ever had this sensation, or a combination of feelings, before? If you have, what caused it? Could any of those past feelings be resurfacing again and attaching themselves to your current situation?
- Fourth, close your eyes and focus once more in on your feelings. Visualize a meter that measures the old feelings from the past. How high does the needle register? Now do the same but register the feelings from the current situation. How high does that needle go?
- This method of sorting out your emotions is a powerful tool for self-awareness. You'll get better at it the more you do it. As powerful as your sentiments are, and as perplexing as they may appear at times, you can learn to connect with them and use them in the way they were intended. Being clever is all about being aware of what you're doing and why you're doing it. Take a few deep breaths and consider the benefits and drawbacks of your next step in a realistic and conscious manner the next time you have to make a decision. Then, for your own sake and that of others who are impacted by your life, do the right thing. Your brain is far more intelligent than you believe.

CHAPTER 7

Until Death Do Us Part

(Though Probably Not)

HAVE YOU EVER heard the expression, "Beware of the lady in red"? Generally, when I am at an event or a social gathering and I see a lady wearing a red dress, I ask her that question. Most women have heard the expression but have no idea what it means, and they don't know its origin. I so enjoy telling the following story.

In the 1930s, the FBI's public enemy number one, at the top of the FBI most-wanted list, was John Dillinger.[62] He was a gangster and bank robber, and possibly a killer.

John Dillinger was the master of disguise and always outmaneuvered the authorities. The FBI assigned an agent by the name of Melvin Purvis to track him down. One of Dillinger's weaknesses was his desire to be with beautiful women. After a lengthy pursuit, Purvis was able to get to Dillinger by setting him up with a beautiful woman. Dillinger met this woman and was enamored. She was actually a brothel madam. And she was Dillinger's friend. She agreed to cooperate with the FBI in exchange for leniency in an upcoming deportation hearing. One night, they went to the movies, and his date was wearing a red dress. It was a setup. The red dress was the signal that she was with Dillinger. The FBI and Purvis were waiting outside the theater for Dillinger and his date wearing the red dress to exit. When Dillinger walked out, FBI agents approached him. He tried to flee, but he was machine-gunned to death. Hence the saying, "Beware of the lady in red."

Being with the wrong person in the ordinary world generally doesn't have such serious consequences. But marriage breakups often can be severe on so many levels. Divorce is the legal remedy. The process and the ramifications are destructive and life changing. When you walk down the aisle at your wedding, you assume and hope that the commitment of a sustaining marriage ensures love, friendship, and trust. The couple vows to sustain its bond "until death do us part." But for many marriages, it becomes one more broken promise.

Consider the realities:

- 41 percent of first marriages end in divorce
- 60 percent of second marriages end in divorce
- 73 percent of third marriages end in divorce

---

[62] FBI, "Public Enemy #1." https://www.fbi.gov/audio-repository/news-podcasts-inside-public-enemy-1.mp3/view.

- 90% of marriages with children who have special needs end in divorce[63]

For couples in their twenties, the risk of divorce is very high. According to George Blair-West, a prominent psychiatrist who has done a multiple TED Talks, the older you are when you get married, the lower your chance of divorce. Why? There are several reasons that younger spouses are more prone to divorce. First, trends in modern relationships discourage marrying young, and this may place peer pressure on the couple. Second, the human brain is still growing at least until age twenty-five, which means that the people think and what they think keeps changing until the brain matures. Third and most important, people's twenty-year-old personalities don't correlate with their fifty-year-old personalities, but their thirty-year-old personalities do. So, when people who divorce in their twenties say they grew apart, that is often very an accurate statement.

A person's twenties can be seen as a decade of rapid change and maturation. We could argue that people might want to be older before they get married. Of course, these factors aren't always predictive. In fact, there are some very successful marriages based on true love, best friendship, and most importantly, implicit trust. This chapter address both realities.

What works, and what doesn't? How do long-lasting marriages work? I will share with you the insights offered by those so fortunate. I think that being with someone who watches your back, cares for you so much that you feel truly safe, and empowers you to tackle life every day defines marital trust.

I wasn't so lucky. I got married when I was thirty-four. I was ambivalent, and my visceral sense told me that I was making a wrong decision,

---

[63] Wilkinson and Finkbeiner, "Divorce Statistics: Over 115 Studies, Facts and Rates for 2022." https://www.wf-lawyers.com/divorce-statistics-and-facts/#:~:text=Almost%20 50%20percent%20of%20all,first%20marriages%20end%20in%20divorce.

but I fell into the peer pressure thing, and I rationalized away my uncertainties. I didn't even factor in or consider trust. My marriage lasted twelve years, and my divorce never seems to end. My ex-wife literally is on her nineteenth attorney. This is not a hyperbole.

In the hierarchy of terrible things that happen in life, divorce is right there at the top of the list. When divorce commences, trust shifts. We each hire a matrimonial attorney to represent us, and we implicitly trust that our attorney has our best interests at heart. Unfortunately, it doesn't always work that way. In fact, the very nature of the system is broken. Matrimonial representation is muddied by a built-in conflict. People who are getting divorced want to get it over with as quickly as possible, and matrimonial attorneys make their money by prolonging the process.

I will tell you unequivocally that going through a divorce is one of the most invasive, violating, and deprecating experiences. You have no control and no privacy. The system is geared by extortion, and life-affecting decisions are made by a judicial system that is overburdened, bankrupt, and financially uninformed. In addition, personal biases also take a toll. Judges are human beings. They can disregard objectivity and make decisions based on how they feel.

My experience is a heinous example that is all about fees and egregious unfairness. When my divorce was commencing, I was certain that the jurisdiction would be Florida. My ex-wife and children lived there, but we also had an apartment in New York City. I started making appointments to meet attorneys in Miami, and then I got served in New York by a New York–based law firm. I was truly surprised but reacted by finding a local lawyer. Getting divorced is like jumping into a pool of quicksand. Once you are in it, you start to sink, and you can't get out. I began to realize that I knew nothing about divorce law and nuances of the process. I liked my lawyer, but I felt insecure. He wasn't a businessman, and he was very process oriented. I decided that I wanted to connect with guys like me—New York dads with young children who were successful in business and going through a divorce.

My friends started to introduce me to some of the peers I was seeking. I was amazed that, at every meeting, I made new friends and learned so much based on their experiences. It wasn't only about venting; the knowledge shared proved invaluable. In fact, I learned one thing that was deeply meaningful and relevant to my situation and that significantly impacted the financial resolution to my divorce—but that my lawyer never even told me. It wasn't that he was intentionally withholding information; it just didn't come up.

Are you ready? If you recall, I was surprised when I was served in New York. What I learned in conversation was that Florida is a permanent alimony state, and New York isn't. In Florida, at that time, if you had been married for more than eleven years, the income-generating spouse could be subject to paying the other spouse alimony forever unless that ex-spouse remarried.

New York has no regulations or laws in that regard. My ex hired one of the most prominent matrimonial firms in New York City, and they took the case knowing that my ex and children were domiciled in Miami Beach. As time went by and I was becoming more knowledgeable about this terrible process, I started to realize a lot of things. One critical item I learned was that it is incumbent and expected that the representing attorney must advise his or her client as to the best course of action to maximize the outcome of the case. It is their fiduciary responsibility. This did not occur.

In June 2014, I was having cocktails with one of my investors at Cipriani's in Grand Central Station in New York City. As we spoke, I glanced to my left at the two gentlemen who were seated next to us. Lo and behold, one of them was my ex's first lawyer, Steve. He was only one foot away from me. I mentioned earlier that my ex is on her nineteenth attorney now, and, for me, this man is now a faded bad memory. However, sometimes, I see Steve on the street and acknowledge him with a mere nod. Coincidence would have it that he is good friends with a dear friend of mine, so he knows me from several different perspectives.

When I realized that Steve was sitting next to me, my blood started to boil. I told my client who he was, and I said to him, "Watch this." Calmly, I turned toward Steve and said, "Steve, how are you? It is so nice to see you." He smiled. I then said, "Steve, would you believe Joyce [my ex] is now on her fifteenth attorney, and I am in court again with her in three weeks?"

"Oh, I am so sorry to hear that," he replied.

I said sarcastically, "I am sure that you are."

I looked at my investor, smiled at him, and then returned my attention to Steve. "Steve, I just want you to know something. I have no ill will toward you. I know you are a good guy, and our mutual friends say nice things about you. I also realize that, back then, you were just doing your job as you should have, and I have no personal angst for you. I don't like a lot of things that your firm did, but I don't have bad feelings for you."

He responded, "Thank you."

I turned away again for a minute, percolating, and then I interrupted his conversation again. "Steve, excuse me. As I said a moment ago, I have no issue with you. However, your partner, Bill, who ran day-to-day litigation in my case and reported to you, is a lowlife. It became crystal clear quickly that there would be no possibility to negotiate anything. Bill did everything he could to create contention regarding all the matters. He methodically poured gasoline on a fire and created unrealistic expectations just to run up the meter. I am curious, is your work all about driving up fees? You don't have to answer. Bill, in my opinion, is a predator and represents what is truly bad with the divorce process."

I then looked at Steve's client and said, "You should pay attention to this." All of a sudden, Steve stiffened up; his complexion, which is normally pale, turned to rigor-mortis white. I noticed that his client was staring at me while I spoke, appearing shocked. I let a minute go by to let both of them absorb what I had said. Then I started again. "Excuse me, I am sorry to interrupt again, but one last question. Steve, when Joyce came to interview you prior to retaining you and you learned she and my children lived in South Florida, I am curious as to why you didn't tell her that she would be better off adjudicating our divorce in Florida." Before he could answer, I added, "Oh, by the way, I owe you a giant thanks because I had to pay alimony for only three years, so I really thank you so much, but let me get back to my question. Because, as you know, or should know, Florida is a permanent alimony state, and New York is not."

It is clearly common knowledge among matrimonial attorneys that every state has different laws. I have spoken to several retired matrimonial judges. If a prospective client has residences in more than one state, their unanimous opinion is that, prior to being retained, the matrimonial attorney must research which state better serves a prospective client from a legal perspective. In fact, the first question I ask someone seeking my advice about the divorce process is, do you have residences in more than one state? Matrimonial attorneys must tell prospective clients what state is best for them regardless of the state they practice in. If an attorney doesn't know the answer and doesn't research the answer, what are the implications? After speaking to several retired judges, I learned that the consensus answer is that such malfeasance is both immoral and an act of malpractice.

Steve looked as if he were going to have a heart attack. He paused for what seemed like an eternity; his client was still staring at me. Steve, pale and shell-shocked, replied, "I am not at liberty to discuss client matters. They are privileged."

I smiled and responded, "That's it? That's your response. You have to be kidding me! You don't have to discuss it or answer me. I already think I know the answer. I am sure you made a lot of money, and by the way, I am going to tell this story in my new book, and I'll be sure to mention you and Bill." I then got up, smiled, and said, "Have a nice day."

Sadly, my ex-wife shouldn't have trusted her matrimonial attorneys. They were more interested in their fees than in giving her the right advice.

How many times have you been in love? Seriously, how many times? What did that mean at the time, and what does that mean now? I think I have been truly in love twice—once when I was in college, and the second time after a bad breakup as an adult. I wasn't in love when I walked down the aisle. You may ask yourself why I got married. The answer is for the wrong reasons. Hence, I found myself early on in a really bad place.

I hired a very good attorney. (He came recommended by one of my investors for whom I have a high regard.) Even that being the case, I felt very insecure because I knew nothing about the divorce process. The expression "live and learn" couldn't have been more appropriate. I didn't understand a lot of things. My ex had two attorneys at the firm she hired to represent her. I had a sole practitioner representing me. Her bills were two and half times what mine were. When I asked my attorney about this, he just said, "You don't know about the firm that represents her, what they are about." I immediately felt more insecure. I am known as the networking guy, and in fact, I have written two books on the subject. You'll recall from the previous story what I learned from my peers about each state having its own laws and how material that was in my divorce. Every new revelation was scary and sometimes very costly. It also became clear to me how valuable it would be to learn from other people's experiences. I decided to send an email out to my database, which read:

> Subject: Divorced or Divorcing Dads with Young Children Luncheon

> If you are going through what I am going through—a process in which your children are being used as pawns—you are subject to a broken system, you are being financially extorted by the legal and judicial process, you are petrified and unsure as to the outcome, and you are fearful as to the emotional effects and ramifications the divorce is going to have on the children.
>
> I am putting together similarly situated dads to vent, strategize, create a community, and most importantly, confer about the well-being of our children. If this is you, please respond, or if you know someone like this, I would greatly appreciate your forwarding my invitation to that dad.

I clicked "send," and over time, I received almost two thousand responses. What is perhaps eye-opening and interesting is that I sent that invitation to over 8,500 people. So many of them forwarded it to divorcing dads. With great effort, I responded to all those who wrote back and ultimately selected seventy-five guys whom I thought had some relevance to one another. Then I held the event. I didn't have any idea what would happen. I also invited my attorney, Mark, to attend for legal guidance.

There we were in a large conference room. I approached the lectern with all piercing eyes staring at me; they were like deer in headlights. I started to tell my story. I shared what had happened to me, and I became emotional. My raw emotional state was most transparent when I started to speak about my kids. My pain was oozing out, and the audience felt it. Many of them could relate. At that time, my ex-wife had already worked with fifteen attorneys. Some she had fired, and some had fired her. I had appeared in front of four judges and one referee. I spoke for twenty minutes, sharing crazy, outrageous stories. Mark, my attorney, who has practiced matrimonial law for thirty years, told me that my divorce ranked in the top five worst divorces he had ever had to litigate. When I finished, I stared at the men in the room; all the eyes were glued on me. I stopped speaking and asked if anyone would like to say something or share his experiences. I was shocked. No one stepped forward. There was just dead silence. I knew some of the men in the room, and those I didn't know were referrals. I immediately called on a friend, Eric, whom I had spent some time with a few days prior to the event. (Eric committed suicide a year later. The combination of the divorce and his financial collapse overwhelmed him.) I asked him to please stand up and share the horrible story he had told me. Eric got up and spoke. Then another guy got up. Soon the participation became volcanic. Aside from emotional release, the stories, insights, and bantering were very meaningful. No one wanted to leave. The event went on for almost three hours.

After the event, I received incessant calls; the overall gist: "Waywill, this is incredible. You can scale this all over the country and create a platform. Waywill, I have a name—DAD: Dads after Divorce. Waywill, this is brilliant. Waywill, you have to do this." Since I speak often on networking and I share the things that I do, every time I tell this story about this luncheon, I get the same response.

In October 2015, I had lunch with an old friend whom I had not seen in twenty years. It was one of those wow-twenty-years-have-gone-by-and-we-just-caught-up-on-everything experiences. I started sharing my networking activities. When I told him about the Divorcing Dads forum, he looked at me intently and said, "Waywill, this is the most incredible idea. You have to do this." And he is happily married.

Well, my friend's comments were a tipping point. My initial reason for starting Divorcing Dads events was to help those going through divorce. In addition, I thought that, by doing these events, I would meet interesting people and create new relationships. These new relationships could generate a multitude of possibilities.

The theme of my last book, *The Opportunity Magnet*, was what we must do to make ourselves stand out. I contend that, if we make ourselves stand out, we will create possibilities. If we create possibilities, some of them will turn into opportunities.

There I was, doing these unique events that involved panels. I was on the dais running the room in front of fifty people, many of whom I didn't know. What a great networking opportunity. In addition, I thought these events gave me more brand dimension of being a great connector. Two weeks later, I sent out the following email to my database of ten thousand.

Divorcing Dads Council

Are you currently getting divorced and experiencing what I went through and am going through?

- Your children are being used as pawns, and you are scared of the damage that will ensue.
- You are subject to dealing with a broken system.
- You are distressed by the uncertainty of the judicial and legal system.
- You feel financially extorted.
- You are concerned about the impact the divorce will have on your business.
- You are thoroughly disgusted and emotionally enervated.

  OR

  Are you contemplating getting divorced? You don't know the ramifications and are uneducated about the laws and the litigation methodology.

> I am putting together similarly situated dads to strategize, learn by the experiences of others, and create a relevant community to help one another in all aspects of the divorce process.
>
> If this is you, or if someone you know could clearly benefit, I would greatly appreciate an introduction. Or you can simply forward my invitation. Please respond if you are interested so I can explain the details.

In a month, I had received almost one thousand responses. Shortly thereafter, we launched the Divorcing Dads Council, which became DivorceForce. My terrible divorce experience created something very meaningful. I became a cynosure. I often receive calls for help or advice. I became a source—a person who is objective and sensitive to this horrible experience. There are so many bad things about divorce, but the way children are used and how deeply negatively they are affected ranks the worst. One of the most heinous aspects of divorce is the total disregard of children or, even worse, their use ss pawns. Unfortunately, this isn't uncommon.

When my divorce was in the early stages, my children were affected horribly. My ex-wife tried to alienate me from them, and for weeks I was unable to speak to them, much less see them. Regardless of my efforts, the system was ineffective, and I couldn't do anything about it.

One time, after not seeing my kids for a couple of weeks, I bumped into them at a hair salon where my ex-wife was getting a pedicure. Coincidently, I had walked in to get a haircut. My son and daughter were sitting on a couch at the entrance of the salon, waiting for their mother. As I walked in, my ex-wife saw me and started yelling. Having no regard for anyone else, she started cursing at the top of her lungs. I ignored her and walked over to my son first, leaned over, and kissed him on his forehead. He was eight, and my daughter was four. When I leaned over, he backed away. I asked him what was wrong, and Benjamin said, "Mommy said we are not allowed to kiss you anymore." I did not react well to this. Anger and hate are very toxic and destructive. I began to shake and felt emotionally overwhelmed and started to lash back. Quickly, I gathered my composure because it dawned on me that this display would be very hurtful to them. I stopped speaking and turned around and left the salon.

One of the psychiatrists I spoke to shared a story about the wife of a gentleman who was in therapy with her. Apparently, he was having an affair and was having lunch in a restaurant with his girlfriend. His wife had their twelve-year-old son put on a disguise and go into the restaurant with a camera. She instructed him to take pictures of them at the table. This mother clearly had no regard for her child and the potential emotional damage she was inflicting. Several therapists told me stories about children being used as messengers, "Tell your father …" or "Tell your mother …" It seems strikingly apparent that this can't be good or healthy for the children. Yet divorcing parents commonly do this. The prevailing view is that children who live through a divorce have a high probability of getting divorced themselves. Depending on extremes, kids may withdraw, become obese, and as they grow older, succumb to drugs or alcohol more readily than children who come from parents who maintain a healthy marriage.

Our kids are in this world because of us—their parents.

Maybe we made a bad decisions with regard to choosing our significant other, but that is our concern and our shortcoming. Regardless of what we and our family think about our partners, our kids are one-half of each of us. Take note of that because, each time you mention to your kids what an idiot their dad is or what a "fool" their mom is or how awful the absent parent is or what awful things a parent has done, you are telling these kids that a portion of them is terrible. That is something reprehensible to do to kids. That isn't love. That is ownership and control. If you do that to your kids, you will estrange them. Your actions will be like cutting them into pieces because you are impacting their feelings. I genuinely hope that you don't do that to your kids. Think more of your kids and less about you, and love selflessly. Don't be stupid or narrow-minded; only then will your kids endure.

I am closing this chapter with a wonderful piece of writing by Dr. Michelle R. Kohn, a clinical psychologist, which is used with her permission:

> Everything in life has a beginning, a middle, and an end ... even life itself. We can debate when those exact moments occur for many events, and most of the time we don't realize what's happening until after the fact, when it's too late, and it feels like you have been hit by a truck, like, for example, the minute when it dawns on you that your marriage is really over. However, sometimes, we can pinpoint those pivotal times as they are taking place, like a first kiss, a graduation, or the birth of a baby. In these situations, we can anticipate and plan on how to cope or deal with any upcoming changes. Divorce, the ugly, all too common D word—but is it really ugly? Is it even really an ending, and can one plan to survive it?
>
> No one enters a marriage thinking one day this will end with the sharp sound of a judge's gavel in court after there's been so much anger, hatred, and a path of destruction that makes a tornado look like a passing summer drizzle. We fall in love, and we make promises to care for each other till death do us part.
>
> Well, the definition of death is up for discussion. Death doesn't only have to be a physical demise. Maybe it refers to when this relationship no longer works or meets the needs of both involved. After all, don't most people change over time? All people learn new things about

themselves as they mature and are exposed to different life experiences. People grow up, are inclined to want to try new things, and challenge themselves, which may influence who they are as a person and change what they want out of life and from their relationships. Couples ideally grow and change together and use the art of compromise to stay bonded and committed to each other. Sometimes, though, people just grow apart, see the world differently, and it becomes too hard to continue to be life partners. This isn't failure; it is just honesty about what can happen between two people over time.

So how can one end a marriage without all the bruises, debilitating injuries, and permanent war scars? What happens when your partner has cheated or behaved so badly that your heart has been ripped out of your chest and left bleeding? How can you be able to move forward in any kind of amicable way if you have been traumatized or abused by your partner, and you feel like you have been gutted like a fish? The truth is, if you want to walk away strong and whole, then you don't have a choice but to proceed with dignity, respect, and a calm confidence. It is the only way to preserve your own sense of self and prevent horrific damage to those who are the innocent bystanders, your children.

Before I tell you how we are going to get you through this, I need to make sure you are clear about the following: if your situation truly involves a parent that is physically, sexually, or emotionally abusive to you or your children, then your first priority is to ensure their safety with the help of family, friends, the authorities, and the court system. That being said, all children love their parents differently. They even love an abusive or negligent parent and crave their attention. All relationships are unique, so how we feel about someone and how we love them and act toward them are unique as well. It is not comparable, nor should it be. So don't ever ask, "Who do you love more, me or Mom/Dad?" It's not a fair question and has no real answer. Children gain different things from both parents, which are equally important for their growth, development, and overall well-being. Therefore, here are rules you need to follow.

Rule number 1: You should not deprive your children of time with your ex. They need to know that it is okay for them to spend quality time with their other parent and that it's okay to smile and laugh and have fun with them. In fact, you should encourage it since it only helps them feel calmer and more secure about themselves and the world, which will help them succeed in every aspect of their lives.

Rule number 2: This is related but very different. No matter what you feel about your ex, no matter how disgusting and despicable he or she is, do not under any circumstances bad-mouth your ex to your children or to others in front of your children. When a child hears terrible things about a parent, it is very hurtful. It makes them feel badly about having any love or positive feelings toward that parent since they will feel disloyal to you. Also, this is their parent, so if they are called horrific names, it will have a negative influence on their own self-esteem since all children identify with some aspects of each parent. So by all means, let it rip…curse, scream, use every nasty word or phrase in the book, just not in the vicinity of your children.

I get asked all the time how parents should tell their children about the final decision to proceed with divorce. Ideally, it should be done with both parents together in a private and safe setting when there is ample time for your kids to ask questions and have their reactions. The message needs to be unified and consistent and include the fact that the kids had nothing to do with this and that your love and commitment to them is unwavering. Reassure them that they will always be provided for, and their physical and emotional needs will always be met. It is okay not to be sure about custody or visitation arrangements, but just say that additional time is needed to figure it all out, but they have access to both parents whenever needed.

Rule number 3: When the children are with you, they should be allowed to communicate with your ex. This is important for the closeness and consistency needed from parental relationships. They should be able to touch base daily with both parents whether it's to share something important about their day, talk about a concern or problem they are facing, or simply to say good night. Divorce is the end of a marriage, but it is much more than that. It is the conclusion of something that has likely been idealized in your head since you were a child, something you promised yourself you would be great at, and a broken promise to someone whom you chose to be your lifetime best friend, your co-parent, the person who was going to be there through the good, the bad, and the ugly and never let go of your hand. You need to properly mourn the loss of this relationship. People go through all kinds of negative feelings—sadness, frustration, anger, rage, and anxiety. They have fear of loneliness, fear of social judgment, fear of independence, and all that goes with standing on your own two feet for a change. Your children will be going through the same kind of feelings, but kids express them differently than adults. They may not have any initial negative reaction; in fact, some might seem to be totally fine, even happier than usual. Children process information slowly, in phases, and their emotional reaction comes in waves.

Rule number 4: It is okay for them to see you have a genuine emotional reaction, to cry, to scream out, to be fearful. But then it's critical for you to also demonstrate how to cope successfully with those strong feelings, thereby modeling that expressing those emotions will not be overly consuming. It will help your children be able to identify and better understand their own feelings and then learn how to cope with those intense reactions so they can continue to function well in their daily lives. So, can divorce also be cause for celebration? Umm, of course! It is the excitement of the unknown and thinking about what possibilities lie ahead that allows us to recuperate, get strong, and realize that the sun will come out tomorrow and might just seem a bit brighter this time!

Rule number 5: It's okay to smile. Yup, and you should, even in front of you kids. Kids need to see that life will go on and might even be better than before since there will be less tension, less fighting, and less chaos in the home. Your kids will get hopeful watching you be okay. They need to be reassured that whatever will happen next, they are a permanent part of it and are your priority always. You can't divorce your kids. Which brings us to the next rule.

Rule number 6: Your kids are brilliant and very intuitive. They know when you are honest, and they know when you're hiding something, so you must always communicate truthfully about any changes that are taking place while taking into consideration your child's age, developmental level, and maturity. If not, their minds wander, and they will unnecessarily assume things that are far-fetched and frightening. But this doesn't mean that you should give them too many details either as this can also be overwhelming. Going through the process of a divorce is usually a horrific nightmare, nothing like you could have ever imagined. But why does it need to be so torturous and dragged out for so long that it leaves you depleted of your time and energy with a red mark in your bank account? This situation often leaves a person feeling so desperate that they resort to doing the unthinkable—they use their children as bargaining chips, investigators, and master negotiators.

Rule number 7: Leave your kids out of this no matter what. Your children cannot be the middleman to your chaos. Even if you think it's no big deal to send a simple message through them to your ex, like a reminder for a pickup time, don't do it! All communication between the two of you must only ever be directly between the two of you and with so many instant ways to accomplish that these days, there is really no excuse to involve your kids at all. When even an innocuous request or question is sent through children, it puts them in the uncomfortable position of causing upset to one or both parents when it is relayed. This burden weighs heavily on them, is completely unnecessary, and places them at risk for additional harm. It can cause them to withdraw and experience increased anxiety, sadness, frustration, and anger, which really takes away from the positive time they desperately need to spend with both parents.

Rule number 8: It's okay to get divorced; don't wait. If you have gone through the process and tried everything you could to repair the relationship and fix the marriage, then you can know that there is no other option. Although most of the time watching the initial reactions of your children is heartbreaking, they will adjust in time, so do not second-guess your decision. In addition, if the marriage is broken and cannot be fixed, then you would actually be doing your children more harm than good by trying to stick it out for their sake. Parental fighting and constant tension in the home are horrific for children and place them at risk for many psychological disorders. In fact, research shows that those parents who wait to divorce until the kids are grown and leave the home cause significantly higher risk to their adult children. These children tend to question the foundation of their lives, replaying past events and not knowing what was real and what was a charade put on for their benefit. They start to have trust issues and begin to feel insecure in their own relationships, leading to depression, anxiety, and anger. Although we enter a marriage with the intention of it lasting a lifetime, we have a way out if need be. Divorce actually shows your children that we can't always anticipate what will happen in the future. Most importantly, you are demonstrating to them that if you are in a bad situation, you are not stuck. There are always solutions, and it is critical to make healthy choices to protect yourself from prolonged harm. The next rule is a tricky one as some kids will appear as if they are totally fine. Don't be fooled. Children, especially the oldest, can get easily parentified. They will do whatever they can to ease any burden for their parent, so they will go through their day without a hitch and then come home and take on additional parental tasks, such as caring for younger kids or cooking for example.

Rule number 9: They all need a therapist or at least someone neutral and safe to be able to talk to on a regular basis about all their private thoughts and feelings without judgment or consequences. This will allow them to be guilt-free when showing negative feelings or complaining and will help them process all the inevitable changes that lie ahead. They all need it to some degree, so it should be a choice.

Rule number 10: You can't go through this alone, so don't even try to. It would be like standing in the middle of a mountain during an avalanche, totally vulnerable and easily knocked down. I know most people are devastated and embarrassed to tell even close friends or family about the divorce, but that makes little sense since they will find out eventually, and you need all the support that you can get right now. The most important thing that others can do first is to help you let go of the anger and rage. Anger is very toxic, and not only is it emotionally debilitating, it can cause real physical symptoms and illness. Do everything you can to release it; don't hold a grudge as this will only keep you trapped. You will need someone to cry with, someone to make sure your refrigerator is stocked with fresh food, someone to check that you have actually gotten out of bed and are dressed for the day. You need people to keep things in perspective, to take you out to a restaurant or comedy club and show you that even though your world seems to be caving in, life is still going on out there, and it's okay to still participate in it and laugh a bit. The bottom line is if you are going to get through this and be able to walk away with enough energy to move forward, you must follow.

Rule number 11: Take care of yourself! It is so easy to want to shut the shades, pull the covers over your head, and hide in the darkness. Forget about that. Life is too short, and if you are getting divorced, then you have already spent too much time alone and sulking; it's enough. Get up, really do it, put this book down, and get up. Look in the mirror and see what you want to change about the person looking back at you. Easier said than done, I know. There will be dark days, but then there are days that are easy, and you tend to forget what you are in the middle of. It's really one step forward and then two steps back. But eventually, you will be able to walk far enough ahead that you will be so light on your feet and will be able to skip, dance, and leap forward. Be good to yourself. You can't properly take care of your children if you are a mess. Oh, wait…you think I forgot? The answer is that divorce is not just an ending. It is the chance at a new beginning. It is a new start, a refresh button, a do-over for you and your children. So get up already, challenge yourself, reevaluate your bucket list, step outside and breathe fresh air, smell flowers, eat a cake, be thankful that you are alive to enjoy another day, and get hopeful that your life will once again be filled with joy, love, and the hope of seeing another rainbow.

Last one…rule number 12: Go celebrate! Congratulations!

CHAPTER 8

Thirty Plus: Happily Ever After

A SK YOURSELF THIS question: What is the difference between loving someone and being in love?

Loving someone is about how the person makes you feel; being in love is about how you make the person feel. When you love someone, all you care about is how much he or she makes you feel cherished, unique, or valued. When you're in love, you're also concerned about how to make him or her feel cherished because it's just as essential to you. Loving someone can feel just as fierce, passionate, and consuming as being in love, but it's ultimately different.

Stop reading and consider your own response. I have thought about this question a lot over the years, and I have replayed the tape of my life in my head. Prior to writing this book and really taking the time to consider this introspectively, I really didn't get it. I came to realize that trust is a fundamental pillar of both loving and being in love. The two or three times that I thought I was in love, I really didn't consider all the attributes that I now believe are the true fundamentals of loving someone, which also sustain the longevity of the relationship. I further believe that the qualities of love change as we mature. When I was a twentysomething, it was about passion and comfort. When I was in my early forties, it was about beauty and feeling easy about being with someone. The last time, when I was in my fifties (which is recently), it was about laughing, comfort, and great compatibility.

When I was in my twenties, I knew nothing. When I was in my forties, I was exiting a bad marriage, and I felt resurrected. When I was in my fifties, I'd benefitted from a lot of experiences and thought I learned what I truly needed and wanted.

Today, I learn every day that I really want a best friend and partner whom I implicitly trust, who makes me better than I would be without her, whom I am proud of, who stands next to me through thick and thin, and whom I love to hold in my arms when I fall asleep. And of course, I want to have passion for her. The last chapter dealt with a lot of pain (and also second chances).

This chapter is about the kind of love that lasts. Unsurprisingly, the factor of trust is omnipresent in sustained love. For this purpose, I interviewed people who have been happily married for more than thirty years to learn the truth about their trust and love for each other and how they grew and maintained a sustaining, sacrosanct partnership. My criteria for the interviewees were as follows: You love or are in love with your spouse. You are fulfilled or content with your spouse. You have implicit trust in your relationship. Your spouse is your partner, soul mate, and best friend.

I sent the following questionnaire to those I interviewed beforehand. I think that the responses are mandatory reading for anyone who is getting married for the first time. It is a lot easier to learn from others who have been there before you.

1. What advice would you give to someone getting married for the first time?
2. What makes your marriage so special to you? (Share meaningful stories or experiences.)
3. Over the years, when something bad happened that caused major friction in your relationship, how did you overcome this fractious issue?
4. What would you consider unforgivable in your marriage, and why?
5. What are three things you and your spouse have in common?
6. What is the difference, in your opinion, between being in love with someone and loving someone?
7. Today, in your relationship, how important is intimacy, and how would you define intimacy?
8. How much of a role does patience and forgiveness play in your marriage?
9. What is the role of selflessness in your marriage?
10. How important are or were your in-laws relative to your relationship with your spouse?
11. How do you handle fights or disagreements?
12. It is clear that couples who experience marital longevity share common traits and points of view. More than thirty years is a long time. Many things occur over the years. Some things are great, and some are very upsetting.

So, what is the secret sauce?

Responses to the first question—What advice would give someone getting married for the first time?—were resoundingly consistent:

- Never be with someone because someone else pressures you to.
- Never succumb to self-inflicted pressure to get married because you are getting older, and your friends are getting married. Marry only for the right reasons.
- Intimacy and passion change. Realize that. Romantic love changes.
- Make sure you really like each other.
- Be objective about expectations.
- Your partner's family relationships are key.
- Discuss and define what a breach of trust would mean to you and be clear about it with yourself and your partner.

Dennis and Laurie have been married for more than forty years. They love each other so much, and it was apparent when I spent time with them. Their story stands out because of an event that took place that changed both of their lives in an instant. Dennis was a very successful and prominent investment banker. He engineered the sale of some very prominent companies, most of which were public. Dennis's reputation as a financier put him in the company of the so-called masters of the universe. In the movie *Wall Street*, starring Michael Douglas, the character known as Gordon Gekko is said to be a composite of several people, including Dennis.

Unfortunately, Dennis was arrested, prosecuted, and imprisoned for insider trading. Prior to his arrest, he was living the big life. He had a fancy apartment on Park Avenue, drove a Ferrari, and enjoyed significant personal wealth.

One day, the FBI showed up at their residence, and Laurie answered the door. The agents said they were looking for Mr. Dennis. She responded, "Oh, you must have the wrong Mr. Dennis. There are others living in the building." She was completely caught off guard and had no idea what had happened and what was about to happen. Unfortunately for Dennis, he was the Mr. Dennis they were looking for, and he was arrested. Laurie was stunned and blindsided. She was also pregnant with their daughter at that time. In a flash, both of their lives changed.

Laurie was devastated when this occurred. She was confused, scared, angry, and couldn't understand why he had done what he did. She had no knowledge about his illicit activity.

Despite this life-changing, terrible event, their relationship got even better for some very important reasons. Laurie explained to me why she loves Dennis so much even in the wake of his trauma. She told me that Dennis is her best friend and always put the family first ahead of everything. In fact, Dennis didn't tell her about his insider trading to protect her. He was always respectful and totally compassionate. She said they always laughed, which is so important. Even after his arrest, their relationship even got better. Adversity really can be a huge difference. Either you grow, or you come apart. Laurie said that they grew. The only deal breaker would have been if Dennis had cheated. She said if he did that, she would have been out of there. When I spoke to Dennis, he extolled Laurie and more or less described the same attributes about their relationship. I asked him how he had handled his situation with Laurie. His response was, "I lied! I said everything will be okay, and I was scared to death. It took time to regain her trust. She is my better half, and we even got closer."

In total, I interviewed twenty people who had been married over thirty years. There was some consistent commonality regarding points of view. Make sure you get married for the right reasons. One respondent, David, said, "If you are getting married for money, you will earn every dollar." Sue said, "Don't get married for the first time. Get married for the second." She is married twice, now forty years, to Ted. Review the character, the patterns, their behavior and how they tick. Learn from your blind spots or failures.

Here are some common themes I heard:

- Being a best friend. This attribute was expressed by almost everybody. Respect the person. Be proud of the person. You believe in the same things.
- Understanding each other. Gloria said, "I understand him. I know what ticks him off. I know how to approach him. I want to explain my side." Life is a compromise. You have to give of yourself.
- Counting on each other. This quality is essential and was expressed by the majority of those interviewed. Lisa said, "I always have Cliff's back, and I know he has mine. He will do anything for me."
- Having intimacy. The definition of intimacy changes and takes on different meanings as years pass. Being considerate and doing sweet things sustain intimacy. How you make your spouse feel is everything. David told me that, after fifty years of marriage, he decided he wouldn't buy cards for his wife anymore. Instead, he writes and designs his own cards—and that is an example of intimacy. Intimacy is more than sex. It's holding hands; it's kissing each other good morning and good-bye. It's spending time together without outside distractions like cell phones and television.
- Not going to sleep angry. It sounds like an old saw, but this came up many times. A rule shared multiple times is don't go to sleep until you resolve the issue. Lynda told me that she and her husband have stayed up until three in the morning more than once until they settled an issue.
- Being really comfortable with your partner. Jill said that no matter what, she always feels relaxed around Phil. "He knows who I am and accepts and embraces me. Ultimately, it comes down to respect and knowing whatever opinions I express, whatever I find funny or engaging or insulting, Phil listens whether he agrees or not."
- Trusting decisions made together and supporting them. Once you've given your word or agreed with your partner, do not reverse yourself.

- Communicating always. Never retreat into silent resentment.
- Having empathy. "Being in love," Jay said, "means having deep empathy for your partner."
- Saying reminders of love. Let your partner know you're thinking about him or her throughout the day. Kathy, married thirty-eight years, shared this point. Bill calls her when they are apart and regularly lets her know that he is thinking about her. She said that makes her feel safe and creates a greater sense of trust.
- Knowing that compromise is key. Know what fights are worth it and when you should meet your spouse halfway.
- Having money values. Make sure you have the same financial priorities.
- Having patience is a must. Do all you can to cultivate it.
- Being a TEAM: *t*ogether, *e*veryone *a*chieves *m*ore. Karen said that, after forty-four years of marriage, she and her spouse still approach all significant decisions as a team. That has nourished their relationship.
- Avoiding codependence. Ryan said he maintains his personal interests, and Linda encourages him to do so. She too has her own interests outside the marriage. Space is healthy.
- Listening to yourself. Don't be overinfluenced by friends or parents. Don't allow another's opinions and advice to infiltrate your marriage. Only you and your spouse must be in sync. "You need to totally rely on each other," Henry said.

A few statements really blew me away, including one from Gloria, married fifty-two years, who shared the ups and downs of her marriage. All her experiences were very moving to me, but one really pushed me back in my chair. She said that her husband "anticipates her needs." My dear friend Peter told me something that was very sagacious: "The best relationships are the ones in which both parties think they got the better part of the deal." He's been married for thirty-four years.

I don't want to sound too overly philosophical, but life goes by quickly, and for most people, having a loving, trusting partner is much more fulfilling than being alone. To accomplish that goal, we must be open-minded, considerate, and want to share our lives.

CHAPTER 9

Should I, or Shouldn't I?

DO YOU VACILLATE? If you say no, I will call you out. You aren't telling the truth. Having doubts about meaningful decisions can be mentally exhausting. Being afraid of making the wrong choice is understandable but being indecisive can chip away at your confidence. Second-guessing is often a paralyzing form of self-sabotage, which can disrupt our sense of inner peace and drive us to overanalyze and stagnate. Decisions that have major consequences obviously do need mulling over—but not obsessing over.

Actions always have unforeseen or unintended repercussions, according to the law of unintended consequences, which is frequently mentioned but seldom defined. There is never a problem when a decision's unexpected outcome is positive. The positive outcome is seen as a bonus. When the unanticipated outcome has a negative impact, the decision-making process, as well as the leader who made the choice, is questioned. The decision by NASA to launch the space shuttle *Challenger* on January 28, 1986, despite warnings about inadequacies in rubber components by engineers at the Morton Thiokol company[64], shows a choice driven by immediate interest. NASA had promised Congress a launch frequency that was far too aggressive and unachievable. Due to the pressure to achieve this deadline, the *Challenger* was launched in poor weather circumstances, considerably below the ambient temperature at which the solid rocket booster O-rings were intended to function correctly.

The engineers' recommendation was to delay the launch due to risks to the astronauts and the shuttle. One NASA official replied, "I am appalled by your recommendation." Another stated, "My god, when do you want me to launch—next April?"[65] NASA went ahead and launched *Challenger*, and shortly after the launch, the O-rings failed, resulting in an explosion and the deaths of seven astronauts and loss of the shuttle.

In January 2020, President Trump downplayed the severity of the COVID-19 virus. He either didn't listen to what he was being told or decided there were other priorities, so he diminished the dimensions of the pandemic. The unintended consequences caused six-figure casualties in the United States.

---

[64] Joe Atkinson, "Engineer Who Opposed Challenger Launch Offers Personal Look at Tragedy," *The Researcher News by NASA*, October 5, 2012. https://www.nasa.gov/centers/langley/news/researchernews/rn_Colloquium1012.html.

[65] Stan Silverman, "One former CEO's 8 principles for success in your business and career," *The Business Journals*, June 6, 2017. https://www.bizjournals.com/bizjournals/how-to/growth-strategies/2017/06/one-former-ceos-8-principles-for-success-in-your.html.

The wildcard is not anticipating or giving merit to the possibility of unexpected events. Unfortunately, bad things happen fairly often. People become ill, get divorced, and suffer accidents. Markets crash, house prices drop, and friends prove unreliable. It is discouraging to over consider the possibility of negative events in our lives, but in reality, life is filled with good and bad outcomes.

You must have a decision-making methodology. Most decisions are reflective or intuitive. In a reflective decision, you consider the known variables. Some people believe that an intuitive decision is the same as a gut decision, but there is a difference. Intuition is based on experience. With intuition, you just know. Fear is absent, and you feel absolutely clear in your direction. On the other hand, the gut tells you a lot, but it's not your intuition. Either way, we have to live with the results of our decisions.

So here is the big question: Do you trust your decisions? Absolutely yes is, for many of us, a knee-jerk reaction given with little thought. Replay the tape of your life and ask yourself the question again. I think about so many mistakes that I have made in my life. Some were bad decisions I went ahead with even though I viscerally felt I was making an error. I don't know why I proceeded. My gut told me something was wrong. I think I went forward either out of laziness or what I thought would be an easier road to travel. I am honestly getting mad at myself now thinking about this. My most relevant lax decisions involved my crooked partner. I instinctively knew something was wrong, and I didn't probe or dig deeper for way too long. I now know that I was avoiding or hiding from Armageddon. I am honestly embarrassed by my stupidity. I guess I had a fear or lack of trust in myself to better examine what he did on an operating level, or maybe I was avoiding confrontation. I now realize my horrific mistake for which I paid a tremendous price.

Many people don't trust themselves and chronically seek advice or review details. This lack of confidence probably emanates from the way these people were brought up. If you think you aren't qualified to make a good choice, then you're going to be afraid to make any choice. Ask for advice if you feel you need it, but in the end, you are the one who must live with your decision. The guru won't shoulder the consequences of your choice.

These icons of history didn't vacillate. They were confident, made decisions, and were prepared to live with the consequences. It is also important not to slip into the bravado of overconfidence or arrogance. General Patton was unquestionably overconfident at times. Being aware of this way of thinking may be the first step to battling it. Recognizing what we might not know can help us gain an objective perspective. Balance is key where confidence is concerned: Too much of it, and you risk making poor, cocky decisions. Too little and you live with inertia and never risk anything at all because you are afraid to make a decision.

Success can bring fame and recognition. As a businessman, I realize that my positive recognition is based only upon positive accomplishments. Alternatively, failure is the catalyst for being looked poorly upon or being disparaged. The mistakes I made trusting my partner caused me great harm in all regards. In the future, I want to be more deliberate and analytical. I want to employ a more evolved method of introspection. For example:

> A *heuristic methodology*, often known as a heuristic, is any approach to problem solving, learning, or discovery that uses a practical method that is not guaranteed to be optimum or flawless, but is enough for the immediate aims. Heuristic techniques can be used to speed up the process of finding a suitable solution when finding an ideal solution is unattainable or impracticable. Heuristics are mental shortcuts that reduce the cognitive strain of decision-making. A rule of thumb, an informed guess, an intuitive judgment, a guesstimate, stereotyping,

profiling, or common sense are all examples of this approach.[66]

You must listen to the TED Talk given by Ray Dalio, a preeminent hedge fund money manager and the founder of Bridgewater Associates. As of this writing, for twenty-three of the last twenty-six years, he has made more money for his investors than any other hedge fund investor.[67] Eight years after founding Bridgewater, Dalio experienced his greatest failure. It was the late 1970s, and Dalio had calculated that the American banks had lent more money to emerging countries than that the countries could pay back. As a result, he believed we would experience the worst debt crisis since the Great Depression and, with it, an economic crisis and bear market in stocks. It was a controversial bet. Mexico defaulted in August 1982, and a number of other countries followed suit. We faced the worst debt catastrophe since the Great Depression as he had warned. Dalio was asked by regulators to testify. After the fact, he recognized that his manner had been arrogant. He was right and yet so wrong. Yes, the debt crisis had happened, but the economy and the stock market had gone up. His fund lost so much money that he had to shut down his operations and let all his employees go. Dalio said it was one of the most painful experiences in his life. He had to borrow $4,000 from his father to pay his personal expenses. It then turned out to be the greatest experience in his life because it changed his attitude about decision making. Rather than thinking he was right, he started asking himself how he believed he was right. He gained the humility he needed in order to balance his audacity. He searched out the smartest people who had disagreed with him to try to

---

[66] Kleining, Gerhard & Witt, Harald (2000). The Qualitative Heuristic Approach: A Methodology for Discovery in Psychology and the Social Sciences. Rediscovering the Method of Introspection as an Example [19 paragraphs]. Forum Qualitative Sozialforschung / Forum: Qualitative Social Research, 1(1), Art. 13, http://nbn-resolving.de/urn:nbn:de:0114-fqs0001136.

[67] Megan Sauer, "Billionaire Ray Dalio credits his market savvy to a conversation he had as a 12-year-old golf caddie," *CNBC Make It*, June 8, 2022. https://www.cnbc.com/2022/06/08/billionaire-ray-dalio-credits-market-savvy-to-conversation-at-age-12.html.

understand their perspective or to have them stress-test his perspective. Hence, he would reach future decisions by meritocracy. Radical truth and radical transparency drive the way he has operated his hedge fund for the last twenty-five years. This methodology eliminates people who naively or arrogantly hold promulgating wrong opinions. Collective decision making fueled by algorithms is superior to individual decision making. It is the secret sauce behind Dalio's success. As I will note several times, good judgment comes from experience, and experience comes from bad judgment.

Decision Guidelines: Go with Your Gut Most of the Time

Making decisions based on your visceral sense may make you feel more certain that you have made the right decision. Gut instinct should increase your confidence. There may be no need to think it over or to get another opinion—you just really believe. Even taking this into consideration, you may still vacillate. The process of trusting your gut is not as simple as the phrase implies.

Because we are frightened of what may happen, we typically wait too long to make decisions. As a consequence, we go through meticulous preparation, in-depth analysis, and thorough consideration of the advantages and disadvantages. It takes a long time to complete this analysis. Instead, develop the ability to trust your instincts. In most cases, your original inclination is right or the path you actually desired to take.

Even if you end up making a mistake, going with your gut still makes you a more confident decision maker compared to someone who takes all day to decide. But anyone who thinks intuition is a substitute for reason is indulging in a risky delusion.

Intuition is a fickle and an unreliable guide. It is just as likely to lead to tragedy as it is to success. Intuition, according to most people, refers to the brain's process of understanding and drawing judgments about events without the use of conscious cognition.

Decisions—or, more accurately, indecisions—can cause a drag on your time for days, weeks, months, or even years. Choosing well doesn't always have to mean choosing slowly. Making the incorrect decision is frequently worse than being indecisive. The people who are most immobilized by dread are those who feel that one mistake would lead to their demise. When you make a choice, follow through on it. What does it mean to make a genuine choice? A genuine choice is taking action on what you have decided. Making a decision and then doing nothing about it is useless. That's the same as not deciding at all. When you make a choice, follow through on it.

When our inherent desire to be productive is challenged or inhibited, we become lethargic. Our inner anxieties lead us to seek ineffective kinds of comfort; this is a reflection of our fears of failure, imperfection, and holding unrealistic expectations. I love the statement, "I knew I should have sold." This is a comment very relevant to investments in the stock market. One of my investors said this to me when the coronavirus pandemic struck. He said he knew he should have sold out in the very beginning of the crisis, but he didn't, and now he was very annoyed with himself. Indulging in hindsight is always easier than acting. The irony is that since he didn't sell, he probably not only recovered but may have prospered since the market shortly thereafter excelled.

Learn from Your Bad Decisions

Reed Hastings, cofounder of Netflix, experienced a sad twist of destiny in the year 2000. Officials at the video rental service company Blockbuster were requested by Netflix to promote their service in its stores. Netflix recommended assisting Blockbuster in selling their brand online as well. This agreement effectively amounted to Blockbuster having the opportunity to acquire Netflix for $50 million.[68] Blockbuster was quick to reject Hastings's request and slammed the door in his face. That was a bad decision! Who'd have guessed that moviegoers would forego video rental outlets in favor of the ease of Internet streaming? Maybe because it's logical? Blockbuster filed for chapter 11 bankruptcy protection less than a decade later in 2010. Netflix has over 200 million members globally (as of December 2020) and $20 billion in income, which is a horrible twist of destiny.[68]

When it comes to making decisions, the fact is that you will make mistakes at times. Rather than blaming yourself, use your bad decisions to your advantage. Consider what was beneficial about the decision you made. What exactly was the issue? What can you take away from this experience to help you make better decisions in the future? Don't just dismiss bad decisions and forget about them. Learn, edify yourself, and don't be afraid to take risks in making another decision. I'm sure most of us would like to pretend like we've never made any errors. It's easy to talk about successes or just about mundane topics.

But of course, things go wrong. We need self-confidence to face the challenges of the day, and errors can erode our feelings of purpose and drive. But you must use them as tools to strengthen your future judgment.

Maintain a Flexible Approach

I know this might sound counterintuitive, but making a decision doesn't mean that you can't be open to other options. Responding to change often requires adjusting your approach to meet the unexpected. Keeping an open mind is important when you are considering the

---

[68] Minda Zetlin, "Blockbuster Could Have Bought Netflix for $50 Million, but the CEO Thought It Was a Joke," Inc. September 20, 2019. https://www.inc.com/minda-zetlin/netflix-blockbuster-meeting-marc-randolph-reed-hastings-john-antioco.html.

overall situation. The objective is to take the current circumstances and move them toward a future goal. Don't be stubborn and try to seek out only one way of making a decision.

You must be open to change in order to develop flexibility in decision making. Even the best-laid plans run across unexpected roadblocks. Embrace any new knowledge that brings you closer to accomplishing your initial goal. Ask confidants their opinions. You will become more confident with peer affirmation and maybe wiser with views that are different from yours. And always remember, any decision is better than no decision at all.

CHAPTER 10

Trusting Too Much Can Put You in Harm's Way

MOST OF US, by our very nature, believe that people are sincere and well intentioned except when the opposite is obvious. The reality is that many of us trust too easily and too much—and that puts us in harm's way. Too much trust might stem from a good heart, faulty judgment, or simply human nature. It might also be a result of emotional difficulties that you need to address. You may have an insatiable want for approval, a desire to be liked and accepted, or a lack of self-control. Moreover, we sometimes have difficulty distinguishing trustworthy people from untrustworthy ones. This can be a real problem. Do you know the difference between trust and faith?

I was sitting with Stephen, a trust adviser and sounding board, and he asked me that question. I sat there and pondered for a moment. I was taken off guard. I certainly know what trust means, and I think I know what faith is, but what is the difference?

Faith is the "the substance of hope." Faith does not require proof. The sheer essence of faith presupposes the absence of visible evidence. Trust, on the other hand, is primarily based on evidence that is true to the senses and human reason. Trust is the basic conviction of judgment based on information, instinct, and experience. Faith is complete trust or confidence in someone or something without any proof or evidence. The key word is *complete*.

Faith is a higher degree or level of trust. Trust is a conscious trait. Faith is an unconscious one. I've heard from many from people who were in bad relationships and who suffered deep challenges and even trauma in the aftermath of trusting the wrong person. I know I am one of them. If you misjudged someone and had faith in a faker, cheater, or emotionally unstable individual, learn from that mistake. You don't want history to repeat itself.

In all cases, the reasons are similar. I've learned that there are five underlying reasons that we get duped by people we shouldn't trust and why we're susceptible to chronically trusting untrustworthy people.

Five Reasons We Trust the Wrong People

1. **We rely too much on what people say instead of what they do.** Even if we know what they're providing is too good to be true, we want to trust people because we believe we need them. We often overlook all visible and internal signals that suggest if someone should be trusted when we're in a scenario in which we badly need or want to change. The biggest problem with trust comes when we rely too much on what people say instead of what they do. If they keep saying they are going to do something, but never actually do it, why should we believe that they will ever actually follow through? We go with what sounds impressive and what we think will get us what we expect. We jump at something even though we know it's too good to be true because we want to believe. The first golden rule of *trust* is judge someone not by what they say but by what they do.
2. **People validate what we need and want to believe about ourselves**. They are excessively charming and complimentary. Notice if they constantly seek to know more about you yet never reveal much about themselves. Untrustworthy people with an agenda often know exactly what to say to us to get us hooked and manipulate us. They obviously don't have our best interests

at heart. They deceive us into believing we are safe. They are acutely aware of (and scan for) our power imbalances, as well as our lack of confidence and self-esteem, what we wish to think about ourselves and our life. And they tell us what we wish to hear. That makes us feel good, so we follow them.

3. **People give the impression of being "winners."** They're enticing, compelling, and impressive. Narcissists can view the world only through their own eyes. Nothing matters more to them than themselves, and everyone else's job is secondary. They are masters at assigning blame and ensuring that others bear the brunt of their faults, which they would never admit to. From their egotistical viewpoint, the blame is always placed on someone else. Narcissists are people who suffer from a personality disorder. They are emotional manipulators, and we frequently put our confidence in them when we shouldn't. Why? Because they aim to be powerful, confident, in command, and extremely successful. We want part of their success to rub off on us since they appear to be "winners" in their own lives and jobs. They make a positive impression on us. And we're honored that these "winners" have chosen us to be a part of their team. It boosts our self-confidence. However, when we get to know them and dispute what they say, think, or believe, we quickly realize that they are not trustworthy and are not who they claim to be.

4. **They make us feel as if somebody finally recognizes our talents.** We need to watch out if someone excessively praises us for us talents and abilities and talks about how we stand out from the competition as if they seem able to understand what we are all about and who you we at our core. They make us feel understood, valued, and protected. They puff us up so we feel terrific in their presence. But this type of flattery and praise is short lived. Many people do not consider or evaluate enough before they allow themselves to trust, even when they are going to participate in something significant with them.

5. **We hand over our power and skip due diligence.** Even though they're about to engage in something very important with an

individual, many people don't conduct the necessary evaluation of the person before they just plunk down their trust in them. This may be due to wishful thinking, laziness, or the result of overwork and stress.

6. In milliseconds, your brain decides whether or not to trust someone. Imagine you're in the supermarket parking lot, struggling to open your car door while carrying your child and your grocery bags. "Here, let me hold your baby," a stranger offers as he approaches. Should you give him permission? According to research conducted by New York University, understanding whether or not to trust someone is so crucial that we can detect whether or not a face is trustworthy even before we are aware of its presence.[69] Previous study has shown that when it comes to judging the trustworthiness of a face, people are quite similar. They sought to see if this was true if individuals viewed a face for only a brief moment—a period of time so brief that it would normally prohibit people from making a conscious judgment. "Higher inner eyebrows and prominent cheekbones are viewed as trustworthy, while lower inner eyebrows and shallower cheekbones are considered as untrustworthy," the NYU researchers stated. So, do you have faith in the person in the parking lot? Your brain is already aware of this.

7. Relationally, there are certainly telltale signs that untrustworthy people always exhibit. The danger zone is entering into relationships with people who see trust as something they can use to manipulate the truth to serve their own purposes without regard for the impact on others. Their vision of reality has been formed in such a way, and at such a young age, that nothing short of a direct emotional nuclear strike will remove the survival and coping strategies they've developed. What's more, these folks

---

[69] NYU, Why Do We Trust, or Not Trust, Strangers? The Answer is Pavlovian, New Psychology Research Finds," January 29, 2018. https://www.nyu.edu/about/news-publications/news/2018/january/why-do-we-trust--or-not-trust--strangers--the-answer-is-pavlovia.html.

don't only dislike others, they also make grand statements like, "Trust me." They don't even have faith in themselves. In other words, while their acts may disappoint, injure, or harm others, they are largely self-defeating in the end.

Signs of Untrustworthy People

- **They believe their own lies.** One of the most remarkable characteristics of untrustworthy people is that they perceive themselves in ways that are just not true. When you come across people who appear detached and don't recognize the true consequence of their acts and behaviors, it's a definite indicator that they're attempting to construct a false world that corresponds to their wants rather than the reality of their actions.
- **They project behavior onto you that you are plainly not displaying.** People who are untrustworthy have an incredible knack of accusing others of activities that they themselves are engaging in or considering.
- **They breach confidentiality.** When agreed upon, confidentiality is a sacred bond. Once breached, there is no second chance. There is zero hope for trust when there is no respect for confidentiality. This is a red flare over the bow. People who breach confidences are emotionally unpredictable. Untrustworthy people often experience mood swings, impulsivity issues, volatile emotional polarizations, and other issues of mental health.
- **They have zero empathy.** Failing to exude compassion and empathy when something horrible happens is a quality that murderers hold. However, this character flaw can also be found in untrustworthy people. They are able to rationalize being untrustworthy by diminishing the impact, pain, damage, or inconvenience they cause others. This is their most dangerous behavior. Worse, those who really lack empathy are either

unaware of their lack of empathy or are selectively compassionate when it suits their goal. It's all about them, really.
- **They are unfavorable.** They are perpetually pessimistic about other people's achievements. If someone talks badly about everyone around them, chances are they'll do the same to you when your back is turned. Their enmity will begin to grow. They are two-faced. The moment you leave the room, they start spreading rumors about you or harshly criticize you in front of others, despite the fact they had just told you how amazing you are.
- **They live in denial.** Untrustworthy people live in their own worlds and justify their behavior and actions. My ex-partner had no sense of wrongdoing about putting his kids on our company's payroll and was totally stoic when I confronted him. What's more, he unabashedly lied when I confronted him.

Do You Trust God?

For many of us, God is sacrosanct and the source of faith and security. God is the entity believers fall back on especially in times of duress. Nonbelievers can become zealots. Religious faith is the foundation for unity and alternatively the basis for division and apathy. When you are aligned and you believe, faith manifests unity. When you are different and of another religion, your devotion can create division and apathy. I am not a very religious person, but some of the biblical stories resonate. One of the classic stories is that of Job. This biblical story encompasses the significance and importance of trust in the relationship between man and God. It illustrates the value of endurance and persistence regarding unwavering faith fundamentally based on trust between believer and his deity. The book of Job tells the story of an affluent farmer whose life is blessed with good health, a loving family, and a prosperous agricultural business. His whole life is based on a spiritual foundation, the foundation of success: his belief in God. Because he has complete allegiance and trust in his God and he knows God has trust in him, Job asserts that the Almighty favors him for the benevolence of his thoughts and actions. His ethics and morality are exemplary as his charity is generous, impacting many indigent people in his world.

All is well until Satan (the adversary) enters the stage and presents God with the challenge that Job's fidelity to God is possible only because of the farmer's life success and his wealth. Satan tells God that Job loves and trusts him only so long as he reaps the benefits the divinity grants him and that, if God withdrew his beneficence and caused him distress, Job would reject him and abandon his faith in divine supremacy. In other words, Job's worship and trust are conditional on God continuing to assist and protect his devotee. Satan proposes that if God withdrew his support, Job would likewise break his alliance.

God accepts the challenge and proceeds to test Job's devotion. God deprives Job of his health, wealth, and family. A loathsome disease disfigures Job's skin, his children die, and the lands become arid. The agony is indescribable. Even his wife entreats him to curse his cruel and heartless God. His wife hopes to foment a rebellion, a mutiny against the divine. Friends, who are alarmed by Job's condition, visit him and propose that this punishment could be the consequence of some unethical crimes or religious heresies that offended God. But Job rejects such explanation, convinced of his purity and innocence of heart.

Job feels blameless. His love and trust in God are a constant in his life. He has never strayed from his absolute belief in God's majesty. He wishes he could speak to God and clarify the matter, which is, in all probability, an oversight on God's part, he reasons. An extraordinary dialogue takes place between God as a voice in a whirlwind and Job. God establishes his supremacy, and Job acknowledges the divine omnipotence. Satisfied, God reestablishes the health and wealth of Job, who is blessed for his steadfastness and unwavering trust in the divine.

What we find interesting in this tale is the concept of an unshakable trust—the immovability and unbending status of that emotion. Job's trust resists doubt, uncertainty, and the lack of absolutes. It's a victory of conviction, the confidence of faith, and the empowering nature of that belief. The moral of the story is the endurance of faith-trust can overcome of excruciating ordeals. In this biblical narrative, trust is given a spiritual value of essential and fundamental significance. Trust gives power and force to individuals. It emboldens and expands our humanity.

Job in Our Time

In the real world, we can face similar challenges to Job's. My friend Stephen had a client, Gemma, who came to him for help. Her emotional state was impacted because of a breach of trust. Gemma is an emergency room nurse. She practiced at some of best hospitals in the New York tristate area. She is excellent at what she does. She has fought a war against death for more than twenty years. At the end of her shifts, she is covered with blood, bone fragments, and urine. She has saved hundreds of patients who were wheeled in damaged and broken. She's so good at what she does that, on many occasions, ER physicians let her completely handle seriously injured patients. She's a diagnostic wizard, describing the internal damage before sonogram, X-rays, and MRI results.

She's loved and admired by her husband and three children. Hiram, her husband, owned and managed a plumbing store. About ten years ago, he increased his drinking and his use of cannabis. He attributed his dependency to work stress due to a weak economy, which was affecting his industry. Renovations to old homes and new constructions had diminished, and his business floundered. He freelanced as a plumber. He didn't advertise or use social networks to get business. He relied totally on word of mouth. His wife felt he was losing his competitive drive. It seemed he had lost that fire in his belly. Without trying to investigate this anomaly, she accepted her husband's inertia, which had become the new normal. That was a serious mistake. She was in denial. Her need to trust was an imperative urge. She was the woman who trusted too much. She trusted unquestionably. Hiram had a lot of time on his hands. And everybody knows, and his wife certainly should, that idleness is the devil's playground.

To help with the finances, Gemma started to work double shifts. She gave her husband a substantial weekly allowance. Unbeknownst to her, she was subsidizing his purchases of alcohol and drugs. The strain of her arduous schedule was wearing her down. She wasn't getting enough sleep. She was exhausted all the time and complained of body aches. One afternoon in a mall parking lot, Allie, their twenty-two-year-old daughter, spotted her father in his car drinking and smoking with Maria, the twenty-eight-year-old nanny. Visibly shaken, she drove home and waited for her mother to return from her shift. She informed Gemma, who was devastated and experienced wave after wave of blinding rage. Her trust and faith in her life companion were shattered.

Hiram had not seen his daughter witness the presence of Maria in his car. Gemma didn't want to disturb her husband with the raw truth yet. She wasn't ready to expose his perfidy. She wanted more evidence. Hiram, in his arrogant blindness, didn't have a clue he was being investigated by his wife. She accessed his cell phone. He felt invincible and therefore never changed his password, which she knew. He was so sure of himself, of his invulnerability. After all, Gemma was the workhorse in the family, the dedicated wife, not the jealous, hysterical, paranoid type.

His telephone contained a trove of compromising material. The affair had been going on for many years while Maria babysat his young daughter in the family home. A myriad of texts revealed he was paying for her wine and cannabis with the allowance given to him by his wife. He paid for her lawyer as well when she was arrested for speeding while using an illegal substance.

Gemma woke up from her unconsciousness. For many decades, she had devoted her life to a man she cherished and trusted. She had been very kind and supportive to the nanny, helping her with tuition when she was taking culinary classes. Gemma suffered a rude awakening. She realized the magnitude of her naivete and the immensity of her gullibility. She sought psychotherapeutic help to understand her psychological blindness. She blamed herself for this catastrophe. She became depressed at the thought that she was lacking emotional intelligence. Indeed, she lacked any trace of suspicion. The absolute absence of that trait can be a drawback when you live in a narcissistic self-serving culture where nearly everyone is hustling.

Obsessive suspicion or paranoia can be also a pathological condition, which must be treated pharmacologically with drugs. But the total lack of that trait creates problems in a human world that is fundamentally predatory. The Roman poet Plautus uttered the ugly truth: *Homo homini lupus* (man is a wolf to man).

If you're too trusting, fear not. Even if trust comes second nature to you, learning appropriate boundaries, revealing personal information at the right time, and having better judgment about who you get close to are skills you can practice and learn. As you get more confident, and as you learn healthier behaviors, you'll also be able to spot when someone's trying to take advantage of your good nature.

Keep in mind these boundaries. Don't be so comfortable that you feel okay about sharing too much. Oversharing might be amusing at times but at times can be embarrassing and discrediting. Even worse, those who overdeliver may be irritating. If you're in a new relationship or have just met someone, take the time to get to know him or her before revealing your deepest concerns, that time you were jailed in college, the state of your most recent yeast infection, or your sexual preferences. You may believe this individual is pleasant and trustworthy, yet there are occasions when less is more. I'm not suggesting you become a closed book, but you shouldn't read aloud every page of your book all at once. Know what you should know. When you're trusting, you give your partner the freedom to come and go, to be himself or herself, and to have privacy. There is an implicit sense of comfort and safety believing in the complete integrity in your relationship. Sometimes, when you're too trusting, you let your partner walk all over you. Even though you are bothered or have experienced some things that have hurt, you stay silent. Your partner takes advantage and may always be gone, and you never know where he or she is. Your partner doesn't check in. Your partner is very secretive, and you turn a blind eye. You even may hear rumors about your partner's scandalous behavior over and over again, but you just brush them off. You fear change or the possibility of being alone. It's not okay to police what your partner does, where he or she goes, and with whom, but it is okay to have an idea of how the person you spend your life with spends time. Don't be blindsided. Be proactive appropriately.

Never believe your significant other can do no wrong. He or she can, and you need to be responsible and call him or her out for his or her own good and for the health of your relationship. It is a responsibility to empower those we care about and love. People do make mistakes, and when they make them, they should be called out. It isn't about criticism. It is about learning not to replicate.

Forgiveness is part of any healthy relationship, but so is making your partner take responsibility for his or her actions. If your partner seems to mess up a lot, and you tend to just buy every excuse, you're probably too trusting. What's worse, you're just enabling bad behavior, which lets your partner continue to make poor choices (and those probably involve treating you badly). It's okay to call your partner out once in a while and to be honest about your feelings. People who are too trusting get taken advantage of a lot, and they can be magnets for people who abuse their good nature. If you look back on your relationship history and see too many examples of how you were screwed over, it could be that the common denominator is you. There is a balancing act between being open and honest and being protective of yourself and your heart. The key word is *balance*. The trust instinct must be accompanied by constant verification.

Slow down; perform a comprehensive, balanced, and unemotional evaluation of all individuals and their potential; and ask for trustworthy outside advice to properly analyze the best next move if you consistently trust the incorrect individuals. It is easy for me to share all these objective analytics that are eye opening and empirically make sense. I get it and recognize it, but I am a giver, and my nature is that I am too trusting myself. I know that and have grown smarter about this, especially having made as many mistakes as I have. However, I still want to trust! I also want to learn to without making grave mistakes. Don't change who you are; just be more aware.

CHAPTER 11

What Happened to the Humans?

OVER THE YEARS, changes in daily life due to automation have resulted in people and their services being replaced by technology in the workforce. What we are talking about is human disintermediation. This, like other kinds of economic upheaval, has certain negative consequences. It eliminates some employment opportunities while creating others. I am certain that, like me, you can remember so many jobs and businesses that existed in the past that either don't exist anymore or have been replaced by nonhuman services. Companies today have two choices: evolve with technology or go extinct.

Disruptive technologies in today's society are those that cause a substantial change in the cost of or access to products or services, as well as a significant shift in how we acquire information, create things, and communicate. They are largely enabled by the dramatic increases in computing capacity and Internet bandwidth that has made their diffusion exponentially faster and able to reach so many more people. The advancements are astounding. However, according to new research, automation may result in the loss of up to 800 million jobs globally by 2030.[70] The study finds that advances in artificial intelligence (AI) and robotics will have a drastic effect on everyday work lives. In the United States, between 39 and 73 million jobs stand to be automated—a third of the workforce.[71] The positive take is that technology destroys jobs but not work. As an example, the invention of the personal computer has led to the creation of 18.5 million new jobs. Clearly, there are pluses and negatives.

There are so many examples of human disintermediation. When was the last time you called the operator and a human answered? Do you remember when tollbooths used to be staffed? When I drove into the Lincoln Tunnel and passed through the staffed toll, I always thought to myself what a boring job these people have, but the positive thing was at least they had a job. Toll collectors still exist on toll roads, but as we progress toward automated alternatives, their days are numbered. The updated system has advanced automatic number plate recognition (ANPR) systems located above each lane, which record each vehicle's license plate as it goes by. Drivers can pay before or up to twenty-four hours after incurring a fee through short messaging service (SMS),

---

[70] BBC, "Robot automation will 'take 800 million jobs by 2030' – report," *BBC.com*, November 29, 2017. https://www.bbc.com/news/world-us-canada-42170100.
[71] Paul Davidson, "Automation could kill 73 million U.S. jobs by 2030," *USA Today*, November 28, 2017. https://www.usatoday.com/story/money/2017/11/29/automation-could-kill-73-million-u-s-jobs-2030/899878001/.

online, in local stores. With some systems, in-vehicle transponders trigger deductions from refillable dedicated accounts. Today, these methods are employed all around the world.

Looking back, we can see what was and is no longer a century ago. In my lifetime, I can think of so many things that no longer exist. Change is accelerating, and as time continues to go by, more jobs will be overtaken.

Let's look back at some examples.

- The steam engine was widely used during the first Industrial Revolution, which began in the 1800s. This movement established the machine as a main mode of production, displacing human and animal labor considerably.
- A century ago, the great majority of the world's population worked on farms. Due to technology creation, a small minority of farmers (2 percent in America) can now produce food for everyone.
- There were millions of employment opportunities linked to the major methods of local transportation at the time: the horse-drawn carriage, just over a century ago. This created occupations such as constructing carriages, making buggy whips, breeding horses, and picking up their feces from city streets.
- The railroad sector employed a little over 3 percent of the US workforce seventy years ago[72], transporting freight and people throughout the country. The railroad sector employs barely 0.1 percent of the workforce today, but it transports roughly three times the quantity of freight throughout the country.
- NASA used to use human computers to determine flight paths that helped us get our spacecraft into the sky fifty years ago.

---

[72] Ryan Ansell, "Employment in rail transportation heads downhill between November 2018 and December 2020," Monthly Labor Review, U.S. Bureau of Labor Statistics, October 2021, https://doi.org/10.21916/mlr.2021.21.

The processing capability of human computing in that period is dwarfed by the gadget in your pocket now.

Will Robots Take My Job?

Based upon a landmark 2014 study by Pew[73], the following list notes marketing and sales roles that most likely will be replaced by robots, bots, and AI within the next few years.

- Telemarketers
- Bookkeeping clerks
- Compensation and benefit managers
- Receptionists
- Couriers
- Proofreaders
- Computer support specialists
- Market research analysts
- Advertising salespeople
- Retail salespeople

Robots and artificially intelligent software programs are predicted to eliminate 6 percent of jobs in the United States by around 2025. Deloitte, a global accounting and professional services network, estimates that 39 percent of jobs in the legal sector could be automated in the next decade.[74] The worldwide artificial intelligence software industry will develop rapidly in the next years, according to market research firm

---

[73] Aaron Smith and Janna Anderson, "AI, Robotics, and the Future of Jobs," Pew Research Center, August 6, 2014. https://www.pewresearch.org/internet/2014/08/06/future-of-jobs/.

[74] Paul Wellener, "Deloitte and The Manufacturing Institute: Big Gains in Perceptions of US Manufacturing as Innovative, Critical and High Tech," Deloitte, March 30, 2022. https://www2.deloitte.com/us/en/pages/about-deloitte/articles/press-releases/deloitte-and-the-manufacturing-institute-big-gains-in-perceptions-of-us-manufacturing-as-innovative-critical-high-tech.html.

Tractica, with revenues rising from about $10 billion in 2018 to $126 billion by 2025.[75]

Ten years ago, we had a nominal sense of what a drone was. Now these devices are common both commercially and militarily. Amazon, Alphabet, and Uber are taking to the skies. In a battle to transport anything from food to gadgets, companies are launching fleets of unmanned planes. Flying robots delivering presents to people's front doors are no longer science fiction. According to reports, United Parcel Service (UPS) received Federal Aviation Administration (FAA) clearance to develop a fleet of autonomous aircraft to carry medical supplies and eventually consumer products. Drone sales for a variety of commercial reasons are expected to increase from 600,000 in 2016 to 2.7 million in the year of this writing, according to the FAA.[76]

AI is also in the nascent stages of retail store allocation. Imagine entering a store and finding no employees. There are no checkout lines or people at registers. Sensors detect what merchandise you pick up and add up your purchases. You just exit and are automatically billed. Once again, jobs are supplanted by AI technology.

Amazon Go is a technologically advanced shop. Amazon is testing out checkout-free technology at big grocery chains like Whole Foods and wants to widely license the cashier-less system.[77] When customers leave

---

[75] Sherril Hanson, "Artificial Intelligence Software Market to Reach $126.0 Billion in Annual Worldwide Revenue by 2025, According to Tractica," *Business Wire*, January 6, 2020. https://www.businesswire.com/news/home/20200106005317/en/Artificial-Intelligence-Software-Market-to-Reach-126.0-Billion-in-Annual-Worldwide-Revenue-by-2025-According-to-Tractica.

[76] Samantha Masanuga, "FAA predicts that 4.3 million hobbyist drones will be sold by 2020," *Los Angeles Times*, March 25, 2016. https://www.latimes.com/business/la-fi-drone-forecast-20160325-htmlstory.html.

[77] Annie Palmer, "Amazon brings its cashierless tech to two Whole Foods stores," *CNBC*, September 8, 2021. https://www.cnbc.com/2021/09/08/amazon-brings-its-cashierless-tech-to-two-whole-foods-stores.html.

the business, their accounts are immediately charged via a smartphone app.

My first question is: What happens if you have a question?

The Surveillance Revolution

Although current modes and technologies of surveillance seem to suggest that surveillance is a product of the twenty-first century, there are countless examples of surveillance activities occurring throughout history. "Spying and surveillance are at least as ancient as civilization itself," writes Keith Laidler in his book, *Surveillance Unlimited: How We've Become the Most Watched People on Earth*. "With the emergence of city-states and empires, each needed to know not just their enemy's disposition and morale but also their own population's allegiance and general sentiment."[78] Surveillance has been referred to as spying or espionage in the past. Surveillance was frequently used to obtain and collect information, particularly to keep track of adversaries. The most common approach was the use of a single human spy or a small group of spies. Surveillance technology became more complex as spyglasses, telescopes, and radios became more advanced, and that pattern has continued to this day.

To trust people is to believe that you can trust them and that they don't need to be watched or policed. There was a time when we just expected individuals to do what they were told. The truth was that we had no way of knowing if they were genuine. However, the infrastructure of the sharing or trust economy is primarily made up of technological advancements that allow us to follow individuals in real time, eliminating the need to trust them. Positively, AI provides customers with new resources. Consider the smartphone software Doggy Logs, which allows a dog owner to track her professional dog walker's exact movements as

---

[78] Keith Laidler, *Surveillance Unlimited: How We've Become the Most Watched People on Earth*, London: Icon Books Ltd, 2009.

her dog is being walked. According to Doggy Logs, the program helps dog walkers "build trust." But it's a strange kind of trust that requires constant monitoring. Tailster, a British firm, characterizes its walkers as "trusted" since they provide digital evidence that the walk has occurred.

In a transparent world, what does it mean to be trusted? With the widespread use of digital monitoring tools, the removal of unmonitored, unaccountable time has become a standard element of company operations. There is no need for trust in the absence of private areas, when life occurs outside our gaze or understanding. Trustworthiness isn't so much a moral characteristic in an open-plan society as it is a condition of not needing to be trusted at all.

Artificial Intelligence (AI): A Game Changer

The Jetsons was a cartoon that I used to watch when I was a kid. It was a narrative set in the future, when everything would be different. The flying vehicles stood out back then, and they still do now. I watched when I was five years old, and I still remember it. Consider what's going on right now: fantasy represented in movies is becoming reality. Okay, we don't have flying vehicles yet, but we are on the verge of developing self-driving automobiles. AI is quickly developing—everything from Siri to self-driving automobiles. While AI is frequently depicted in science fiction as humanoid robots, it may refer to anything from Google's search engines to IBM's Watson to autonomous weaponry. There are several forms of artificial intelligence. Narrow AI (or weak AI) is described as AI that is meant to fulfill a certain task. Many researchers' long-term objective, however, is to develop generic AI (AGI or strong AI). While narrow AI may beat humans in a specialized skill such as playing chess or solving math problems, AGI would surpass humans in almost every cognitive task. Such a superintelligent machine may possibly self-improve indefinitely, resulting in an intelligence explosion and leaving human intelligence in the dust. As a result, the development of powerful AI might be the most significant event in human history.

Can we trust machines?

The "trust paradox," which argues that you cannot trust someone you don't know and that you cannot begin to know someone without first trusting them, applies to the people side of the equation.

Trust is a peer relationship in which the trusting partner trusts any promises made despite not knowing for sure if the promises will be honored. This puts them in a state of vulnerability. In contrast, artificial intelligence (AI) is a collection of system development approaches that enables machines to calculate actions or knowledge from a set of inputs. Only other software development techniques can be peers with AI, and since these do not "trust," no one can actually trust AI.

AI can sift through millions of data points in a nanosecond, using techniques that even people with PhDs can't comprehend. That's incredible. Risk managers, on the other hand, frequently question, "How am I meant to regulate AI when it's so quick and complicated?" Thirty-three percent of respondents in a PwC Pulse Survey cited AI is becoming too complex to explain or control.[79]

If all this sounds scary, it shouldn't. It's possible to reduce AI's bias; improve its reliability and its resistance to cyber and privacy threats; and use it to benefit not just your bottom line but also your employees, customers, and community. Responsible AI can help with regulatory alignment, model validation, auditing, and most importantly, explainability, or simply making AI communicate to you. Explainable AI can explain how it came to its findings and made its judgments in plain English or with basic math. It can also predict how it will behave in the future. It will also allow you to go further into its operations in order to view additional information. When AI can explain itself, it's much simpler to keep an eye out for hackers, privacy risks, and anything else that could keep you awake at night. This understanding of how

---

[79] Anand Rao, "Sizing the Price," PwC. https://www.pwc.com/gx/en/issues/data-and-analytics/publications/artificial-intelligence-study.html.

your AI makes judgments makes it simpler to reduce bias in those decisions—and show regulators, consumers, the board, and workers that your AI is operating properly.

Should we fear AI?

In Stanley Kubrick's 1968 movie *2001: A Space Odyssey*, a computer named HAL 9000 was designed to take a spacecraft to Jupiter. But HAL 9000 was flawed. An interesting anecdote is that the name HAL was really a reference to the IBM company. Each letter in HAL is one letter before each letter in IBM: H/I, A/B, L/M. In the end, HAL chose to value the mission over human life. HAL was a fictional character. Nonetheless, this story speaks to our core fears of being subjugated by some unfeeling AI who is indifferent to humanity.

Even though we are still far from general AI, many tech leaders have voiced concerns about potential AI threats. During an interview, Elon Musk stated that AI might be the greatest threat to humanity: "I think we should be very careful about artificial intelligence. If I had to guess at what our biggest existential threat is, it's probably that. So, we need to be very careful. I'm increasingly inclined to think that there should be some regulatory oversight, maybe at the national and international level, just to make sure we don't do something foolish."[80] Bill Gates has talked on the dangers of artificial intelligence in the future. "First the machines will do a lot of jobs for us and not be super intelligent. That should be positive if we manage it well. A few decades after that though the intelligence will be strong enough to be a concern."[81]

---

[80] Aratrika Dutta, "AI, the Biggest Existential Threat to Humankind Says Elon Musk," *Analytics Insight*, July 14, 2021. https://www.analyticsinsight.net/ai-the-biggest-existential-threat-to-humankind-says-elon-musk/.

[81] Peter Holley, "Bill Gates on dangers of artificial intelligence: 'I don't understand why some people are not concerned'," *The Washington Post*, January 19, 2015. https://www.washingtonpost.com/news/the-switch/wp/2015/01/28/bill-gates-on-dangers-of-artificial-intelligence-dont-understand-why-some-people-are-not-concerned/.

What can go wrong?

AI systems can be programmed to be destructive, and autonomous weapons are AI systems programmed to kill. The deployment of these weapons could potentially result in a high number of fatalities if they fall into the wrong hands. Furthermore, an AI arms race might unintentionally lead to an AI war with a huge number of deaths. To prevent being stopped by the adversary, these weapons would be engineered to be exceedingly difficult to simply "switch off," removing any control from humans. This danger exists even with relatively unsophisticated AI, but it rises as AI intelligence and autonomy develop.

Let's say that AI is trained to perform something good, but it creates a harmful means of accomplishing its purpose. This can happen if we don't properly match AI's goals with our own, which is a challenging task. If you order an obedient intelligent automobile to drive you to the airport as quickly as possible, it may get you there pursued by helicopters and covered in vomit, doing exactly what you asked for. If a superintelligent machine is charged with a large-scale geoengineering project, it may cause chaos in our environment as a side consequence and see human attempts to halt it as a danger that must be defeated.

So far, there is still the risk that AI will be biased by the humans who build it. If there is bias in the data sets that AI is trained from, that bias will affect AI action. Fears of AI are common among millennials. Millennials aren't simply the largest consumer demographic; they're also the most influential. They are currently the majority of the workforce. This implies that, just as their parents and grandparents were concerned about machines and computers taking their employment, millennials are concerned about artificial intelligence. In fact, 81 percent are concerned that AI technology will take over all or part of their job responsibilities.[82]

---

[82] Anne Fisher, "Workers Are Worried Robots Will Steal Their Jobs. Here's How to Calm Their Fears," *Fortune*, November 9, 2019. https://fortune.com/2019/11/09/workplace-employee-fears-robots-artificial-intelligence/.

Another issue that millennials are concerned about is how AI collects, keeps, and uses data. AI has already been demonstrated to be used to collect social media data, build bots in the form of social media profiles, and target people with misleading and manipulative material in order to influence elections, according to intelligence agencies.

According to a *New York Times Magazine* cover story by Charles Duhigg, the retailer Target broke through to a new level of consumer tracking with the aid of statistical genius Andrew Pole.[83] Pole discovered twenty-five items that, when purchased together, suggest that a lady is most likely pregnant. Target could then give the pregnant lady coupons during a costly and habit-forming time in her life. After hearing its name on television, Amazon's Alexa began purchasing dollhouses for individuals. When a six-year-old girl in Dallas, Texas, requested her family's new Amazon Echo, "Can you play dollhouse with me and buy me a dollhouse?" The gadget quickly processed the information and placed an order for a KidKraft Sparkle Mansion dollhouse and four pounds of cookies. The parents soon understood what had occurred and have subsequently inserted a purchasing code into their Amazon account. There's real fear that AI will be used to exploit information in far graver ways. This isn't speculative. Ninety-one percent of cybersecurity professionals say that AI can be used to compromise a company's or consumer's data.[84] When data is collected by AI bots or other technologies, it becomes not only predictable but ripe for hackers to access.

Despite some legitimate worries about the technology, millennials are generally favorable about its applications. They are familiar with AI and have used it before, at least in the context of bots. They are likely

---

[83] Charles Duhigg, "How Companies Learn Your Secrets," The New York Times Magazine, February 16, 2012. https://www.nytimes.com/2012/02/19/magazine/shopping-habits.html.

[84] Alison DeNisco Rayome, "91% of cybersecurity pros fear hackers will use AI to attack their company," *TechRepublic*, December 14, 2017. https://www.techrepublic.com/article/91-of-cybersecurity-pros-fear-hackers-will-use-ai-to-attack-their-company/.

to use AI technology in the form of physical IoT in the future, as long as their security and data ownership issues are addressed. There is no question that AI technology will bring to the forefront amazing advances. Recently, I learned of one from a friend who holds some patents relative to the technology. Vision Jet has developed a technology called Vision Jet Safe Return: Emergency Autoland. The system could change personal aviation forever. With the Safe Return safety system, if an airline pilot is incapacitated for any reason, a passenger can land the aircraft with just the touch of a button. Once the button is touched, the Vision Jet turns into an autonomous vehicle that will land the plane at the nearest airport.

NEON is the name of Samsung's artificial human project. The company is developing realistic human avatars for entertainment and business, such as receptionists and other roles. Imagine how, as human avatar technology improves, they will be able to remove conflicts and even divorce. I suppose the chapter's title is accurate.

Then there's MarsCat, a robotic cat with plenty of love to offer and plenty of capacity to expand. This robot pet is a self-contained companion that responds to touch, speech, and can even engage in toy play. After spending even a little period of time with MarsCat, it's impossible not to fall in love with it. The greatest thing is that there is no need for kitty litter, and MarsCat is allergy-free.

What's next?

CHAPTER 12

How Can We Believe the Numbers?

I WAS SPEAKING WITH my friend Aaron Spool. He is an outsourced CFO for forty different companies. While I was writing this book, I sent him some chapters to read. He then called me and asked if he could write a chapter. I asked what he wanted to write about. He said, "You have no idea the amount of fraud and misrepresentations there is in financial statements both nonpublic and public companies. I would like to share what to look for." And so he did.

According to the Public Company Accounting Oversight Board (PCAOB), an audit firm's approval of a company's financials is inaccurate 25 percent of the time because the auditors never do the work required to sign off.[85] So, unless investors like one-in-four odds in financial roulette, they cannot place implicit faith in a company's reported accounting because more often than anyone would like, audit firms seem to be making up stuff.

What's more, certified public accountant (CPA) audits are not cheap, and these audits are not always effective in rooting out financial reporting fraud by managers. Likewise, there are many cases in which CPA auditors have failed to detect serious long-term financial fraud that has been going on right under their auditing noses for years. Cleverly

---

[85] David S. Hilzenrath and Nicholas Trevino, "How an Agency You've Never Heard of Is Leaving the Economy at Risk," Pogo, September 5, 2019. https://www.pogo.org/investigation/2019/09/how-an-agency-youve-never-heard-of-is-leaving-the-economy-at-risk.

concealed fraud is very difficult to uncover unless you stumble over it by accident.

With so much emphasis on income production, it's easy to overlook the value of intangible assets like ethics, social awareness, and most importantly, trust. In a world that is becoming more complex and competitive by the day, trust in numbers, processes, and people is critical to maintaining long-term value. In that sense, I am pleased to be able to reprint the following excerpt with the author's permission, an expert financial counselor and watchdog.

Can you Believe Your Financial Statements?

Managing Director / Eventus Advisory Group

Financial statements hold a lot of uses, data, and insights for consumers. They can be complex and have hundreds of pages or simple and only a few pages. What they contain may be factually correct but designed to obscure certain information that would drastically change your view of the company they purport to represent.

Before you start wondering if you can trust something, it's important to define what you are looking at and what you are asking of it. Then figure out if you can trust it will fall into specific categories. Financial statements are no different. So, before we start to look at whether we can trust them or not, let's do some background work as to what they are and why they exist.

Fundamental Purpose

The fundamental purpose of financial statements is to provide the investor or potential investor with a view into the company. At their best, they show the true financial position of a company, its pros and cons, where it is making or losing money, where it is strong and where it can improve, and how it compares to its peer set (other companies in its industry). At its worst, it deceives an investor to thinking it's stronger or weaker than it is with the purpose of getting the investor to act in the company's best interest, not the investor's. From a content perspective, financial statements have three major sections: an income statement, balance sheet, and statement of cash flows. These are the basic three statements. There is plenty more information in a financial statement, especially for large public companies, but these are the main ones. An income statement shows the amount of money made (revenue) and spent (expenses) in a time frame. A balance sheet shows what the company owns (assets) and owes (liabilities) and what the shareholders own (equity). A statement of cash flow shows the sources and uses of cash in a given period.

Accounting standards exist to ensure financial statement accuracy. They are not perfect and can be twisted or broken; however, they are the major defense in trustworthiness. In the United States, generally accepted accounting standards (GAAP) is the standard while most non-US companies follow International Financial Reporting Standards (IFRS). The purpose of both is to ensure trustworthiness.

Having every financial statement follow a specific standard allows for comparability, which means you can take multiple companies from the same or different industries and can look at their financial performance side by side. You can then look at a company and see how it is performing compared to its peers.

Analysis would be close to impossible without standards. How would you be able to evaluate something if it used a different measure than you thought? If you are trying to understand how easy a company can meet its short-term obligations, you'll want to measure liquidity. But if a company doesn't define a short-term obligation the same way you define it, the conclusions from your analysis will be wrong. Standards attempt to solve this problem.

The most important and basic concept to understand when using GAAP and looking at financial statements is the matching principle. GAAP uses accrual accounting, which, in its basic form, tries to link revenue with its related expenses. Here's an easy example. You spend $1,000 in one month to fulfill a $2,000 customer order and then collect the money for that order in another month. If you follow cash basis accounting, one month will show a loss of $1,000, and the money you collect the following month will show a gain of $2,000. It will not be readily apparent that the company had $1,000 of profit ($1,000 cost for a $2,000 sale). Matching the expense and revenue in the same month would show that profit (the intricacies of accrual accounting are important but won't be explained in this book).

Now that we've explained at a high level what financial statements are (their content), their purpose (investor focused), and the language they are written in (accounting standards), you'll have a general idea of what you are looking at when you view them. Understanding the "what" of something is critical when making assumptions, which is the basis of questions or conclusions. And defining "what" something is, and the rules that govern it, form the system to establish trust. What does it mean to "trust" financial statements? At its essence, trusting financial statements means assuming that what you see is actually true. In other words, are the statements you are looking at fraudulent? Sometimes, fraud is easy to spot since things don't necessarily add up; more to come on this. Other times, fraud is so well hidden and so well managed it could be years before someone uncovers it, if ever. The other issue, and one much more relevant to everyday investors, is that, while the financial statements might be GAAP compliant, they might not fully represent the actual financial status of the company. Luckily, the methods it takes to suss out fraud are the same as those used to see if the financial statements clearly represent the company's financial health.

What motivates companies to "adjust" the presentation of their financial statements? Understanding some of the various motives will put you in the mindset of a company. The more you think in terms of the motivations of a company, the easier it will be to spot their techniques to make the numbers more favorable to the story they want to tell.

Here are three classic motivations:

1. Tax considerations. Usually, this means lowering the current year's tax burden and either accelerating

costs or pushing out, recognizing revenue into a later year. The general thought is that the lower your current tax bill the better.
2. Valuation considerations. When a company strives to sell itself or get an investor, like anyone, it will want the best terms. Companies will want the highest gross margins, net margins, revenue growth, and lowest expenses possible.
3. Internal considerations. Many senior executives are compensated explicitly on financial deliverables and implicitly on stock price (for example, if they have shares or options, the higher the stock price, the more money they make). Executives may go to great lengths operationally and accounting-wise to have the financials reflect their deliverables or whatever will increase the stock price.

Famous Accounting Frauds

Actual planned and organized fraud is tough to spot. There are entire government institutions whose job it is to ensure the truth and veracity of financial figures. However, if someone is trying to deliberately lie to you and others, it can be difficult to spot. On the financial side, think of Madoff, Enron, WorldCom, Tyco, or HealthSouth. Each had some if not all the following:

- Some flavor of CEO-led fraud.
- Outside people who pointed out that the story was "too good to be true," and who were ignored.
- Internal whistleblowers who were ignored.
- The majority of the information was actually disclosed in the financial statements but buried in footnotes or a flood of information, so it wasn't

easily spotted. The techniques of fraud and the situations may differ, but a lot have these same four elements. As you become more sensitized to how financials can be manipulated, you'll more likely be able to spot something.

Methods Companies Employ to "Juice" Their Numbers

Companies employ a variety of accounting techniques to put their financials in the most favorable light. Depending on the situation, a company might want to recognize a larger loss or a lower amount of revenue to achieve more favorable tax ramifications. Sometimes, companies want to show a significant amount of revenue or profit in a particular period, especially if there is a valuation involved. Some companies spend countless hours and money on accounting techniques to show their financials in the best light. And sophisticated investors spend a similar amount of time undoing those accounting techniques to get at a more realistic view of the company. There are many techniques a company can use to change their financials. Here are a few of the more classic ones.

- Big bath. When a company has a number of expenses coming up, especially a large onetime charge, they may "save up" all the expenses and report them all at the same time. If the company can make a plausible story for the largest expense, the other expenses, which may indicate problems with the company, could get lost in the noise.
- Restructuring/below the line. When something happens that a company classifies as "non-core" to the business, such as a restructuring, sale of a

business line, or a large onetime and supposedly nonrecurring event, the expense and revenue associated with that can be moved to a noncore income and expense section, which is "below" the ongoing net income (profit) line. On a positive side, the company does this so the investor knows that these expenses and revenue, while completely real, are not a part of the normal running of the business and should not recur.

A savvy investor should look at the disclosures for these below-the-line expenses and understand the following. Are there future financial implications from these "noncore" events (lower future income, additional future expenses, etc.)? This is a two-parter. Will there be more "below the line" activity from this event next reporting cycle (sometimes it takes more than one-quarter to go through the entire event)? What historical action (mostly revenue) is unlikely to repeat itself in the future? You might perceive a sale as "below the line" if a business had an operation and subsequently sold it, but chances are the company hasn't restated prior financials to indicate what the company would look like without this segment. You'll have to do your own investigation. Are these events really "onetime"? Even though GAAP accepts the below-the-line categorization, if a firm has a history of restructuring every few years, these costs aren't truly "onetime." Why did this happen? Selling off a poorly performing business is painful, especially if you sell it pennies on the dollar, but if the company couldn't make the division work for them, it makes sense to unload it. However, many companies run into cash issues (especially during a financial crisis when the capital markets might be closed to them). If this happens, sometimes a company is forced to sell its best divisions to get the cash it needs to continue the current operation. If that happens, you might be left with a company without a glowing future.

- Revenue/earnings "smoothing." Most investors like predictability and "upward trends." A company that has "bumpy" revenue is harder to predict. But most businesses are like that. There will be excellent months and quiet months. You may get a new customer from time to time, but you may also lose one. The more difficult something is to anticipate, however, the less appealing it is as a conventional investment. Ask people you know who do very well financially but don't have standard salaries, like a commissions-based salesperson. There are many people who have high incomes but do not qualify for mortgages that would reflect that income since it is variable (commission) and not fixed (salary). The same happens with investing in companies. If you don't have predictable revenue, you might get a lower valuation. Therefore, it is in the company's interest to use revenue recognition techniques to "smooth out" the revenue instead of recognizing it all at once. However, a company might be recognizing revenue for quite a while, but that company collected the cash for that revenue in the past. Savvy investors spend a lot of time assessing revenue quality and the cash associated with the revenue.
- Capitalization games. Spreading out the expense of a purchase over a longer period is one approach to achieve "smoother earnings." This is usually accomplished using capitalization. Essentially, a corporation will purchase anything it considers an asset, which means the item will have a longer useful life than the period in which it was purchased.

Think of taking a business trip on an airplane versus buying a computer. The airplane flight happens once, and it is over, so the expense happens when you take the flight. However, the computer isn't just a onetime use. Odds are you may use it for three years or more. Therefore, you would take the entire expense of the computer and recognize a piece of the expense each month through the computer's useful life. In the short run, this allows you to spread large expenditures over a period of time, thus lowering the expense, even if the cash was paid up front. What can you do to know if the financial statements are correct?

So, we've covered what financial statements are, motivations of companies to adjust their financials to their benefit and gone through some of the tools companies can use to adjust the financials. It might seem daunting when faced with this, but don't lose hope. There are plenty of techniques an average investor can use to suss out the truth. Read the footnotes. Companies are required by GAAP to disclose their major accounting treatments in the footnotes. You should be able to see what decisions they made were on capitalization, depreciation, revenue recognition, and onetime expenses. All accounting procedures used to make a company's financials appear good should be revealed. Examine each one to determine if it is logical. For instance, if they say the useful life of a newly purchased asset is fifteen years, but you think it is only five, then you know two things: the future expenses are understated for the next few years, and the company will probably have to do another purchase in five years and not fifteen (thus, more cash out the door in five years). Follow the money. The statement of cash flows can unearth a lot of issues in the income statement.

Companies have leeway in how they recognize revenue and expenses but very little when it comes to recognizing cash.

Here is a quick example. If you see a lot of revenue but little in the way of inflows from cash from operations, the odds are the company hasn't collected the cash or collected it in the past. Check out the accounts receivable balance and the previous cash flow statements. You can probably spot if the cash came in or not. Do your best to match up large expenses and revenue to the cash. If you don't see the cash, adjust your future forecast to assume a large cash outlay (for a big expense), or possibly a lack of cash collection (for the revenue recognized but no cash received).

- Industry comparisons. One way to probe the financials is to see how they compare to others in the industry. If the profit margins are drastically better, then you need to have a very good reason that is the case before you should believe it. If there is no direct competitor, then find a company that does something similar and compare. If the story is too good to be true, then as the old adage goes, it probably is.
- Triangulation. It's decently easy to tell a story if you point to one source. The goal with triangulation is to find multiple sources to prove a story. For instance, if a company has record revenues, find out why. Something may be questionable if nothing is indicated in the investor report, disclosures, or footnotes. Does the customer a firm mentions verify the transaction if it claims to have secured a significant new client? You may not get the deal's specifics, but you may notice the consequences of

one company's huge sale in the financials of its clients as a large expenditure.
- Mosaic theory. This is similar to triangulation but with a different twist. The goal is to take a whole bunch of different data sources and weave together a story. For instance, if you see articles on tariffs going up and warehouse fees rising as well, it may feed into a larger story that a company might have their profit margins squeezed on multiple fronts. Industry experts track multiple facets of the companies they monitor, from weather to new legislation. Piecing all these different data points together can create an image that wasn't visible from a single point, just like a mosaic is an image made up of small tiles. The most important principle is, does it make sense? Always ask this question whenever you see something important or unexpected. Large spike in revenue or profit? Company 20 percent more profitable than its competition? All this sounds great, but does it make sense? Are the answers the company gives plausible? A good attitude to take with any financial statement is one of healthy skepticism. They probably are not fraudulent but were put together to show the company in its best light. Probe the statements with the tools mentioned here and do your best to verify what you see. If something doesn't make sense or looks too good to be true, it probably is. If you can't explain the good fortune a company is reporting, and you do not understand the company's explanation, then it might make sense not to invest.

CHAPTER 13

Political and Judicial System Trust: What an Oxymoron

IT IS UNFORTUNATE that the reality of our political system is a lot less than what we expect. We as voters want to believe in the individuals we elect. In the ideal world, we vote politicians of integrity into power, and they take the position of leadership to do the right things for their constituencies. It isn't about personal benefit or ego. It is supposed to be a self-sacrificing job without a personal agenda. Instead, the process is filled with theatrics and disingenuous rhetoric. It should be implicit that we have respect and belief in what we are told, but how do we look up to these figureheads?

There have been many examples of political malfeasance throughout history. Watergate stands out, but going back in time, there were many improprieties. Do you remember learning about the Teapot Dome scandal?

Improper Leaders

President Warren G. Harding's secretary of the interior, Albert Fall, secretly accepted hundreds of thousands of dollars in liberty bonds in exchange for leasing former navy oil reserves in Wyoming known as Teapot Dome to a private company.[86] He became the first cabinet

---

[86] Olivia B. Waxman, "What Was the Biggest Political Scandal in American History? 7 Historians Make Their Picks," *TIME*, April 18, 2019. https://time.com/5569221/biggest-american-political-scandals/.

secretary to go to prison because of his actions on the job. Unfortunately, there are things that happen that aren't viewed as illegal but still could be considered improper.

There are many stories about how the system condones financial abuse. I have a residence in New York City where I was born and raised. I have seen many mayors come and go. De Blasio is probably one of the greatest examples of someone who makes decisions that are blatantly self-serving. The *New York Post* on February 20, 2020, ran a story with this headline: "New de Blasio Low: Using City Hall for Chirlane McCray to Gain Office."[87]

The story is eye-opening as to de Blasio's self-fulfilling agendas. Also revealed in the story was the abuse of using taxpayers' funds to pay $358,000 for his security bill during his absurd short-term presidential bid. Less meaningful but somewhat annoying was his $490 tab for seven cops to tag along as the mayor watched his beloved Boston Red Sox play the Angels while he was in Los Angeles taping a political podcast shortly before he folded his presidential campaign. The additional absurdity is that de Blasio raised $1.3 million from big donors for his campaign, clearly hoping for favors from city government. When is it improper to grease the wheels and take advantage of who you know?

Take a moment to search *oldps64.com*. This story is an extreme example of political corruption and malfeasance during the de Blasio administration. Greg Singer bought this vacant school building from NYC in 1998, and the zoning allowed him to build a dormitory. After obtaining signed leases from various local schools, he was denied a permit to commence construction. The reason has nothing to do with the property or the legal rights Gregg has. It is all about big-dollar influence. Litigation is ongoing and it will likely take a few more

---

[87] Post Editorial Board, "New de Blasio low: Using City Hall for Chirlane McCray to gain office," *New York Post*, February 20, 2020. https://nypost.com/2020/02/20/new-de-blasio-low-using-city-hall-for-chirlane-mccray-to-gain-office/.

years for a resolution. Greg is a good friend, and I am sickened by this injustice.

There is a fine line between just plain crooked politicians and politicians who are raising money to promote their own agendas. Both cases are telling, and one is more extreme than the other. There is a word that describes the extreme circumstances that actually happens: *kleptocracy*.

Sorting through Entertainment and Education, Ambition and Altruism

Kleptocracy, literally meaning "the rule by thieves," is a form of political corruption in which the ruling government seeks personal gain and status at the expense of the governed. Through graft and embezzlement of state funds, corrupt leaders amass tremendous wealth at the expense of the broader populace. Some of the most egregious examples have occurred in countries with very high rates of poverty. The inherent challenge for corrupt leaders is covertly expatriating and holding money in secure locations where it can be accessed in the future. Generally, that requires international movement of funds. When transfers occur in US dollars or transit the US banking system, federal money laundering jurisdiction is established. The FBI initiates money-laundering investigations to trace the international movement of assets and in conjunction with foreign partners, forfeits and repatriates assets back to legitimate authorities in victim countries.

There have been so many great movies and television shows about politicians. Some of them were very inspiring, and others were very disturbing.

One of my favorite positive movies was *The American President* with Michael Douglas in 1995. Richard Dreyfus played his political opponent who said and did whatever he could to debase the president. He attacked his personal life and inferred his decisions were biased because of his personal relationship. The president wouldn't lower himself to respond or banter with him. His ratings in the polls began to drop. His advisers pushed him to step up to the slander and abuse. Finally, during a presidential speech, he responded with dignity and facts, and that completely discredited his opponent. The president simply told the truth.

The movie was great. I actually felt proud being an American because of the character demonstrated by Michael Douglas's portrayal of the president, but the story was a fiction.

Unfortunately, the very nature of politics and what is pontificated is infused with falsehoods and half-truths. The dissemination and promotion of this information is exacerbated by the power, the influence, and the breadth of media coverage. Politicians want votes, and media wants to sell coverage and capture audience.

All the President's Men, another great political movie, was filmed in 1976 and starred Robert Redford and Dustin Hoffman. It is the story of the break-in into the Democratic headquarters in the middle of the night at Watergate Towers authorized by the attorney general, John Mitchell, to bug and burglarize their offices for political espionage and sabotage of Nixon's opponents. This story wasn't fiction; the actual events ultimately led to the resignation of President Nixon.

So, what is the real truth about people wanting to become politicians representing their constituents? Is it about fame? Is it about power? Is it about attracting wealth? Do these people put their followers first before their own self-interests? What do you think?

Most people go into politics initially because they aspire to change things, influence the course of governance, help their constituency, and make a career. At least that is what we believe is the reason.

To be a politician is a very hard job, which demands a lot of sacrifices by those who are sincere. Good politicians can moves things if they possess good communication skills, commitment, personal responsibility, high motivation, enforcement capacity, and a secure and convincing manner. Just having a noble aim is not enough. People are not suited to pursue a career in politics if they don't have the needed self-confidence, charisma, enduring power of self-assertiveness, and most importantly, passion.

This was reported by the *Washington Examiner* in January of 2020:

> During his speech, President Obama indicated that Americans needed to trust the system of government.
>
> "If people can't trust not only the executive branch but also don't trust Congress, and don't trust federal judges, to make sure that we're abiding by the Constitution with due process and rule of law, then were going to have some problems here."[88]

President Obama was so profound, and his thoughts were just words falling on deaf ears. The fact is that the problem is manifested by what happens over and over again. How can we trust politicians? The rhetoric and reasons for being a politician seem to have been for personal agendas. There are, of course, many exceptions. Michael Bloomberg comes to mind. He is worth sixty billion dollars. Why would he want to become the mayor of New York City, no less president, if his intentions weren't sincere?

The political election machine is a defined process.

At the heart of our ad-saturated democratic process is a moral paradox. Politicians raise and spend billions of dollars promoting themselves to convince us to trust them with the responsibility of governing us. But

---

[88] David Boaz, "Trust in Government?" Cato Institute, July/August 2013. https://www.cato.org/policy-report/july/august-2013/trust-government.

the fevered competition for votes virtually compels them to lie to us. As bad as that is, watching the slugfest is entertaining but really disturbing. Here you have all the candidates on a dais televised slamming and disparaging one another to curry the favor of viewers. It is the definition of ineptitude and a total breakdown of the authenticity of those who desire to govern. When they do this and we know it, we obviously become skeptical and cynical.

The word *integrity* originates from the Latin word *integritatem*, meaning "soundness, wholeness, completeness." Figuratively, it means "purity, correctness, and/or blamelessness." However, there is more to the word than simply suggesting wholeness or purity. In only a circumstance or two, it suggests that the person is consistently integral. In this sense, those who are consistent are said to be standing firm after taking a position; they do not cease or bend. The word *integrity* has the same core meaning as *integer*, meaning "intact, whole, and/or complete," while figuratively it means "untainted and/or upright."

Yes, a politician should have integrity, but it is much more difficult to say this than it is for the mass public to believe it. For politicians to be integral, they must be consistent in their higher moral or ethical stance; they must not differentiate or sway on that standing dictated by the situation. In the movie *The American President*, the Michael Douglas character would not sway on what he knew was right to influence the polls. Unfortunately, many people who claim the title of being politically minded, whether laymen or politicians, vary on their so-called principled stance depending on the situations they find themselves in and their own agendas.

The flip side of the movie *The American President* is the television series *House of Cards*.

House of Cards, the fictional Netflix series, is the story of US representative Francis Underwood of South Carolina who is a ruthless politician seeking revenge. The chicanery and self-serving nature of politicians in the show exemplify an extreme.

The results of lying inevitably undermine trust, including citizens' trust in their leaders and in government. We really have cause to worry about the increasing dishonesty and falsehoods of political campaigns. This series creates an awareness of the extreme possibilities that result when we appoint the wrong candidates to represent us. This series is fictional, but it also may not be so far from reality.

Normal day-to-day politics requires communication with the public, which is broadcasted and criticized. How many politicians are like the character in the movie *The American President*? My guess, in today's world, is none.

In politics, lying by distorting facts or not answering questions that are asked (paltering) takes many forms. A common tactic is to pull a remark out of its original context and depict it as meaning something the speaker never intended or to answer a question with an information that has nothing to do with the question.

There are, of course, numerous other ways to misrepresent the facts, and politicians, particularly when running for office, find it hard to resist them. It is a skill.

All kinds of lies are attempts to manipulate people's beliefs and their confidence to induce them to accept the claims pontificated for the manipulator's purposes (for example, winning votes). Liars don't care if what they say is not true or supportable by sound reasons. Manipulators try to deceive their listeners into thinking their intentions are true or well-grounded. They insist that their ideas should be believed and supported, when in fact they shouldn't, at least not for the reasons offered by the manipulator.

In today's world, we are living this every day.

A *Washington Post* article in October 2019 read, "President Trump has made 13,435 false or misleading claims over 993 days. The president's constant Twitter barrage also adds to his totals. Nearly 20 percent of the false and misleading statements stemmed from his itchy Twitter finger."[89]

Political leaders who trade in misrepresentation and half-truths seem to ignore the fact and are careless. They refuse to believe that lying to the people they serve—or seek to serve—violates the common moral principle that deceiving others is wrong. They don't care, and that is the unfortunate truth. Politics in today's world is truly driven by self-agendas.

From a moral point of view, what's obviously wrong with deception is that it is a betrayal of trust. It is a lie. You cannot deceive people unless they trust you, believing you are being truthful to them.

There are some very disturbing reflections we can infer from this political process and the way political figures view the public, the voters, and those who elect them. Those who are representatives—our so-called tribunes who supposedly implement our aspirations—believe in and bank on our gullibility. The masses are perceived to be easy to seduce and manipulate. In the eyes of politicians, we are easily deceived and are prey to believe a skilled orator who can magnify our fears and make us believe their promises to achieve our aspirations. These people proselytize their listeners to win their vote. That is why many people running for the Senate and Congress hire advertising firms to design and strategize their campaigns. The propaganda is delivered with colorful flamboyant posters and disingenuous promises. It is essentially a sales job, and the target is the buying public. How many politicians do you

---

[89] Glenn Kessler, Salvador Rizzo and Meg Kelly, "President Trump has made 13,435 false or misleading claims over 993 days," *The Washington Post*, October 14, 2019. https://www.washingtonpost.com/politics/2019/10/14/president-trump-has-made-false-or-misleading-claims-over-days/.

respect and believe? Some of us buy the party differences. Republican or Democrat, clearly on paper, have different motives and ideals.

Politics cannot blossom without mania. It is the exuberance and effervescence that makes what looks like, at first, an ideological debate become an emotional and romantic affair. These days, debates and campaigns are insulting slugfests that result in some irrational moments in which candidates lose their composure.

We, the people, want to believe and support our representatives. Many of us become convinced that we are backing the right person, and those who back the other candidate are just wrong and stupid. This is one of the reasons I never talk politics with people. I have been party to heated arguments that sometimes have denigrated to insults between those engaged in the discussion. I absolutely avoid political conversations. You can't win!

Physical appearance can greatly influence outcomes. This was exemplified in the famous televised debate between US Presidential candidates Kennedy and Nixon in 1960. Both refused to use makeup, but Kennedy was tanned. Nixon looked pale, and the studio lights amplified the appearance of the stubble on his face. The contrast might seem petty, but television viewers tended to agree that Nixon lost the debate. Radio listeners, on the other hand, thought Nixon did very well. That debate changed the attitude of many viewers and media people about the role of physical appearance in influencing voting.

It seems that every election becomes a nonending show. Media blows up every statement, and positions and opinions capture news cycles. It is a three-ring circus because the campaigns can be a form of entertainment for the masses with parades, balloons, cheerleaders, and music and movie celebrities. Then the debates top it all off; people love to watch candidates try to make themselves look better by degrading competing candidates.

All media love it. A fever reaches hysterical proportions as voting day approaches and radio, TV, newspapers, and Internet sites vibrate to a whirling crescendo that pushes the masses to a point of delirium. Rapture and ecstasy infect members of the voting public, and we realize we are undergoing a form of hypnosis.

That is the American political show. No wonder in the masterpiece film *Network* (1976), a veteran anchorman Howard Beale (brilliantly played by Peter Finch), who could not live the lie anymore, opens the window of his apartment and screams into the night those unforgettable words: "I'm mad as hell, and I'm not going to take it anymore."

The Verge technology news website recently published an article titled "Facebook's decision to allow lies in political ads is coming back to haunt it." The tagline was, "Profiting from misinformation has put the company back on the defensive."[90]

As reported, Facebook had announced that its advertising policies had been changed to exempt politicians and political parties from rules banning misinformation. As a result, candidates are now free to lie in their ads, and some of them are doing so, and I bet you can guess who one of them is.

Facebook is about population, interaction, and views, and that drives revenues and valuation. The company is an influencer and a source of misinformation. Do they care? Are media and communication services solely about fees and income? Is there any integrity? That last question is rhetorical. Should there be a barometer or verifier that drives what is allowed to be marketed to proselytize viewers? Should technology influence outcomes? This, too, is a rhetorical question because we know it does.

---

[90] Casey Newton, "Facebook's revised political advertising policy doubles down on division," *The Verge*, January 10, 2020. https://www.theverge.com/interface/2020/1/10/21058616/facebook-political-ads-targeting-misinformation-polarization.

Elizabeth Warren, currently the senator from Massachusetts, stated, "You're making my point here. It's up to you whether you take money to promote lies. You can be in the disinformation—for-profit business—or you can hold yourself to some standards. In fact, those standards were in your policy. Why the change?"[91]

Mr. Trump's campaign bought ads across social media that accused another Democratic presidential candidate, Joseph Biden Jr., of corruption in the Ukraine. That ad was viewed more than five million times on Facebook. It falsely said that Mr. Biden offered $1 billion to Ukraine officials to remove a prosecutor who was overseeing an investigation of a company associated with Mr. Biden's son, Hunter Biden.

A company Twitter account responded to the senator, noting that various broadcast networks had aired the Trump-Biden ad nearly one thousand times.

Given how much Facebook has invested in what it calls platform integrity, a coordinated effort to rid the site of misinformation, this policy is counterproductive and demoralizing.

Facebook's sophisticated ad-targeting capabilities could make an untruthful political ad even more pernicious than, say, a broadcast TV ad might be. Reach the right low-information voter with the right lie at scale, the argument goes, and you just might tip the country into full-blown idiocracy.

Time after time on tech platforms, we have seen how a posture of neutrality winds up benefiting the worst actors at the expense of everyone else. And there's a real risk of that happening again.

---

[91] Steff Thomas, Sasha Pezenik, and Karma Allen, "2020 candidate Sen. Elizabeth Warren uses false ads to lash out at Facebook CEO," *ABC News*, October 13, 2019. https://abcnews.go.com/Politics/massachusetts-sen-elizabeth-warren-false-ads-lash-facebook/story?id=66229792.

In 2019, Pew Research Center published "Key findings about Americans' declining trust in government and each other," noting: "The world's trust in the United States is a country entering an election year with its impeached and then exonerated President and stirring global alarm over the U.S. killing of an Iranian general, has dropped by more than 50% since 2016, the sharpest drop of any country assessed in the 2020 Best countries report."[92]

As reported in *Forbes*, September 2019, only 4 percent of Europeans trust Donald Trump. Three years into the presidency of Donald Trump, a new survey has found that Europeans have lost trust in the United States as an ally and would like to see a more self-reliant European Union that stands up to America.[93]

Now we have President Biden whose credibility and motives have shattered his ratings. Guilty as charged or maybe not.

Law enforcers at times use their authority inappropriately and make mistakes. Unfortunately, sometimes, these mistakes or actions are egregious. It is a small minority who are culpable, but the victims' lives are seriously negatively impacted.

Law enforcement is a very difficult job. Brave officers put themselves in harm's way as they protect the population from illicit or dangerous acts. I support the police and, in fact, serve on a board that empowers them and what they do for the community. I am very proud to be involved, and I'm proud to say that I respect them.

---

[92] Lee Rainie and Andrew Perrin, "Key findings about Americans' declining trust in government and each other," Pew Research Center, July 22, 2019. https://www.pewresearch.org/fact-tank/2019/07/22/key-findings-about-americans-declining-trust-in-government-and-each-other/.

[93] Dave Keating, "Only 4% Of Europeans Trust Donald Trump," *Forbes*, September 12, 2019. https://www.forbes.com/sites/davekeating/2019/09/12/only-4-of-europeans-trust-donald-trump/?sh=724206856a5f.

However, the assumption that a person is innocent until proven guilty doesn't always prevail. Just because a person is arrested doesn't mean that he or she is guilty, but the public often assumes guilt because of the arrest. We trust the system.

The criminal justice system isn't perfect, and no one expects it to be. The enforcers make arrests, and judges and juries make decisions based on evidence presented. Problems occur when there are flaws in the evidence. These mistakes can cost years of incarceration and steal away normal productive lives

The rate of wrongful convictions in the United States is estimated to be somewhere between 2 percent and 10 percent.[94] That may sound low, but when it is applied to a prison population of 2.3 million, the numbers become staggering. Can there really be 46,000 to 230,000 innocent people locked away?

Millions of defendants are processed through our courts each year. It's nearly impossible to determine how many of them are actually innocent once they've been convicted. There are few resources for examining the cases and backgrounds of those claiming to be wrongfully convicted.

Once people are convicted, it is next to impossible to get them out of prison. Over the past twenty-five years, the Innocence Project has use DNA testing to secure the release of 349 innocent men and women, twenty of whom had been sent to death row. All told, there have been more than two thousand exonerations, including two hundred from

---

[94] Andriana Moskovska, "33 Startling Wrongful Convictions Statistics," *The High Court*, October 13, 2021. https://thehighcourt.co/wrongful-convictions-statistics/#:~:text=1.-,Between%202%25%20and%2010%25%20of%20convicted%20individuals,in%20US%20prisons%20are%20innocent.&text=According%20to%20the%202019%20annual,between%202%25%20and%2010%25.

death row, in the United States during that same period.[95] But that is only scratching the surface.

Someone is arrested in the United States every three seconds. Arrests are the first entryway into a criminal justice system, and most acknowledge it is a system in dire need of reform. We know remarkably little about who is arrested, where, and why. Advocates and legislators have pushed in recent years for policy changes at various points of the justice process, from pretrial to sentencing, but arrests remain one of the largest and least scrutinized contributors to the country's mass incarceration and policing crises.

The Federal Bureau of Investigation (FBI) and Bureau of Justice Statistics collect arrest data from the country's 18,000 law enforcement agencies—but those agencies self-report on a voluntary basis, and there are significant disparities in the information they share. The data, for the most part, remain inaccessible to the broader public, and statistics on crime are isolated from data about the effectiveness of enforcement.

I recently was introduced to Marty Tankleff, who had wrongly been convicted of killing his parents. He shared his story with me. He was coerced to give a false admission of guilt.

Marty Tankleff had just turned seventeen when he was arrested for killing his parents, Seymour and Arlene Tankleff, in their home on Long Island, New York. Based on a dubious, unsigned "confession" extracted from him following hours of interrogation by a detective with a questionable background, Marty was convicted and sentenced to fifty years to life. After seventeen years in prison, Marty's conviction was vacated by the New York State Appellate Division, Second Department, in December of 2007. On July 22, 2008, a judge signed off on a motion by Attorney General Andrew Cuomo to dismiss all charges against Marty. Today, Marty teaches a course at Georgetown University and

---

[95] Innocence Project, "DNA Exonerations in the United States." https://innocenceproject.org/dna-exonerations-in-the-united-states/.

Touro Law Center on criminal justice, and in 2020, Marty passed the bar exam and became a lawyer.

In 1986, the New York State Investigation Commission (SIC) began "an investigation of the Suffolk County District Attorney's Office and Police Department."[96] The investigation was on the order of Governor Mario M. Cuomo, at the request of Suffolk County judge Stuart Namm, based on two high-profile murder trials over which he presided.

"I have witnessed, among other things, such apparent prosecutorial misconduct as perjury, subornation of perjury, intimidation of witnesses, spoliation of evidence, abuse of subpoena power, and the aforesaid attempts to intimidate a sitting judge" (Judge Stuart Namm, SIC Report, 1989).[96]

Following three years of investigation, including sworn testimony and public hearings, the commission issued a report finding "misconduct and mismanagement in homicide investigations and prosecutions," including "over-reliance on confessions," and called Suffolk's confession rate "an astonishingly high figure compared to other jurisdictions, so high, in fact, that in and of itself it provokes skepticism regarding Suffolk County's use of confessions and oral admissions." The report found "[t]he Suffolk County Police Department and District Attorney's Office engaged in and permitted improper practices to occur in homicide prosecutions, including perjury, as well as grossly deficient investigative and management practices. Because of credibility problems with prosecution testimony, including police testimony, and other defects in homicide prosecutions, guilty persons may well have been allowed to go free."[96]

---

[96] State of New York Commission of Investigation, "An Investigation of the Suffolk County District Attorney's Office and Police Department," April 1989. https://nysl.ptfs.com/awweb/pdfopener?sid=CED9B60BF2C2D3D9E7F60D12B1A362CD&did=112422&fl=%2FLibrary1%2Fpdf%2F20027003.pdf.

Either we trust or distrust, by assumption, those who enforce the laws. I guess we should be more mindful and aware that, like everything else, the system isn't perfect.

The matrimonial justice system is broken; there is no divorce by jury, or a pool of peers. Every state has its own laws, and the difference among them can be significant regarding the financial and custodial outcome, but one thing stays consistent no matter where you get divorced: Your case and the multitude of judicial decisions of your divorce is governed by one person and one person only—the judge. This reality can be either good or ugly when it comes to how the judge's opinion of the divorcing parties creates the tenor of the proceedings and affects important issues, such as custody and financial entitlements.

Judges sit higher than everyone else, but they are just people like you and me. That means that, like you and me, they have opinions, biases, and personal issues they deal with on a regular basis. They are also overwhelmed with heavy caseloads and can become inured to the specifics and sensitivities of individual cases. Unfortunately, it is an unpleasant fact that some, maybe most, judges delegate the reading of the motions to a clerk, who then reports back to the judge. Sounds incredible, but it gets worse. A judge makes judgments and decisions based upon demeanor and approach. That being said, they are supposed to be neutral and abide by the law when making decisions about your life, but judges are not machines. If your judge forms a negative opinion about you early in your divorce, you could be in for a long, stressful, and unsatisfactory ride.

Divorce in the hierarchy of bad thing that happen in life is right there at the top. I would argue that, on that list, it falls into the number-two position, with death of a loved one being in the number-one position.

Divorce doesn't have to be that bad, but when it is an all-out battle influenced by a matrimonial attorney's bantering and constant motion practice, it becomes horrific. I metaphorically liken the experience to that of jumping into a giant vat of quicksand. Every day, you keep sinking, unable to move, while being told by your attorney what to do. Unfortunately, I have a jaded view about this entire process based upon my own experiences and what I learned while creating DivorceForce. I attest that matrimonial lawyers, by the very nature of what they do, often have conflicts of interest. Do you recall the story about my ex-wife's first attorney? They are all about charging fees accomplished by motion practice, and the divorcing couple just wants to get the ordeal over with as quickly as possible. Couples have no input because they are uneducated about the laws, the process, and completely reliant upon advice. I have experienced frivolous divorce litigation multiple times. It costs a lot to defend, but those involved have no choice but to pay the bills. I have been told of instances in which opposing matrimonial attorneys confer when the divorcing parties have substantive wealth and plot methodology to generate fees. This is a heinous and unethical reality. Understand that these lawyers all know one another quite well. They constantly sit across from each other in court, and when they are not opposing each other, they are very friendly. I am not exaggerating. I have heard this from friends who are matrimonial attorneys, and I have personally seen it. This is extreme, and I am not suggesting this behavior happens on a regular basis, but it does happen. I do know many honorable attorneys who never would do anything that was improper.

Divorce is overpriced, and the process is flawed, especially when the decision maker, the judge, isn't paying the bills so he or she doesn't care about the financial cost. Talk about absurd litigation.

My divorce agreement provided for a sharing arrangement on investment real estate. I didn't own these properties individually; I was the general partner, and I had a lot of investors. I agreed that, when these investment properties were sold, my ex-wife would receive 50 percent of whatever I received. During the forensic process, which took place in 2006, these properties were appraised. Needless to say, when 2008 rolled around, the valuations changed, and appraised values from 2006 were not worth the paper they were written on. I spent a fortune hiring firms to appraise the properties. We asked the judge prior to hiring these firms if we could get broker opinion letters (BPOs) instead, which would have mitigated the costs substantially, and again the point was that the appraisal values were not actual sale prices. My ex-wife's attorney wouldn't agree to this. We argued that the appraisal valuations didn't matter; the selling price would dictate what our entitlement would be. We had a joint forensic accountant who oversaw the valuation of my business and the real estate assets. These were real estate syndications in which I was the general partner with two other general partners. There were many moving parts, and valuation was, to a great extent, truly indeterminable. The forensic, when asked about doing the formal appraisals, agreed that the values were really difficult to assess, and formal appraisals were inconclusive. He also agreed with my position that, whatever I got on the sale would be split with my ex-wife, which is a fair resolution, so appraisals didn't matter. Regardless, the judge, during a five-minute discussion in court, ordered that I had to do formal appraisals. This decision cost me around $150,000, which was totally wasted money and a depletion of our assets caused by the judge's lack of financial sophistication, and she just didn't care.

Three of the four properties sold over the next several years, and my ex received her share of my share of the proceeds. The appraisals had no significance. Her expectations based on the appraisals were far below what she actually received, which was calculated on the sale prices.

The remaining asset was an old office building in Jersey City, New Jersey, in which we owned a 50 percent interest. In 2006, based upon the appraisal, my economic interest was $1,000,000. If they were right, then upon the sale of the building, my ex-wife would have been entitled to $500,000. In 2007, Jersey City changed the building codes for buildings ten stories or higher. Our building was subject to the revisions. The long and short of it is that the new regulations mandated that we make improvements that would cost at least $4,000,000 before we would be in compliance with the new code. Our original investment was $2,500,000, and the investors had received their investment back twofold by refinances. When 2008 rolled around, everything was in a free fall. The investors were frozen. They had already cashed out, and they didn't want to put any money in to do the improvements mandated by the code changes. In addition, the financing markets were shut down due to the collapse of the economy. My co-general partners and I attempted to fight Jersey City but to no avail. Ultimately, Jersey City wouldn't let us rent space and forced out our existing tenants. The building went into foreclosure, and we lost the property in the beginning of 2012. Clearly, this wasn't a great outcome, but there was nothing we could have done considering the circumstances.

In October 2013, I was served by my ex-wife's new attorney (number 15). The lawsuit alleged that I had intentionally mismanaged the building and let it go into foreclosure solely to avoid paying her the $500,000 according to the 2006 appraisal. You can't make this up.

I was stunned. I couldn't believe any attorney with a modicum of integrity would put his name on such a frivolous lawsuit. I guess a false expectation fueled by a retainer goes a long way. Consider the allegation that I intentionally lost the building to deprive her of $500,000, which simultaneously meant I deprived myself of the same amount. Also, I screwed my investors and co-general partners so she wouldn't get these funds. I was incensed at this stupidity. Needless to say, I had to defend myself against this ridiculous lawsuit and pay my attorney to do so. We went to court, and the judge said there was no need for argument and just dismissed the motion.

The system is the way it is. We just have to be as smart as we can be and recognize that politics isn't going to change. Avoid getting arrested and stay married.

CHAPTER 14

Trust Starts in Childhood

ONE OF THE most beautiful and precious things we can do is watch babies with their parents. It is so cute and touching when babies reach out for attention from their mommies and daddies. The parents' smiles of joy and happiness are heartwarming and demonstrate the greatest degree of true and absolute love. How many times have you smiled when you have seen parents—total strangers—holding or pampering their babies in public? It happens to me all the time. My reaction is always a smile. I typically interact with these little ones. I am always touched. The parents' raison d'être is that baby, and they will do everything they can do to protect their children and live for them. The trust between parents and their children is absolutely implicit. Parents are the guardians from any danger or ill will, and they do everything to protect their children as babies from the outside world.

Unfortunately, that may change as they get older. Parents ultimately lose control, and outside influences can and in some cases do place kids and adolescents in harm's way. Sometimes, terrible things happen.

Imagine living in a culture or country where the rulers or demagogues have so much influence and power that they can draft kids and young teens for bad causes that put them in physical harm's way. Imagine when kids are proselytized by an inculcated philosophy that makes them imbued with hatred and prejudice. Imagine if and when they are deluded, they then sacrifice their lives because of this belief, and they don't know the difference between what they've been taught and verified facts. Sadly, young people have been taken advantage of, and many of them lost their lives or were maimed for life.

The Nazi Party began targeting German adolescents as a specific audience for its propaganda campaigns in the 1920s. The Nazi Party was portrayed as a lively, resilient, forward-thinking, and strong youth organization in these communications. In classrooms and through extracurricular activities, millions of German students were persuaded to support Nazism. The Hitler Youth had just 50,000 members in January 1933, but by the end of the year, that number had risen to almost two million, and then it grew to 5.4 million members by 1936.[97] By the end of the year, it came to an end. Competing youth groups were either outlawed or dissolved by German authorities.

The goal of education in the classroom and in the Hitler Youth movement was to develop race-conscious, obedient, self-sacrificing Germans prepared to die for the führer and the Fatherland. Hitler Youth training included a significant amount of devotion to Adolf Hitler. For membership inductions, German young people honored his birthday (April 20), which was a national holiday. Adolescents in Germany pledged their loyalty to Hitler and promised to serve the country and its commander as future warriors.

Other advantages were available to the Nazis. It not only enabled the Third Reich to indoctrinate children at a young age, but it also enabled the Nazis to shield them from the influence of their parents, some of whom were hostile to the government. Families—private, coherent groupings that aren't generally influenced by politics—were an impediment to the Nazi Party's aims. The Hitler Youth was a tool for instilling Hitler's philosophy in families. Some Hitler Youth members even condemned their parents when they acted in ways that the Reich did not approve of. These children believed in Hitler's philosophy and abandoned their parents who opposed it.

---

[97] Erin Blakemore, "How the Hitler Youth Turned a Generation of Kids Into Nazis," *History*, August 29, 2018. https://www.history.com/news/how-the-hitler-youth-turned-a-generation-of-kids-into-nazis.

By 1939, 90 percent of young people had joined the Nazi Youth movement. Youths who had not enrolled could be sent to reeducation camps, or their parents could face fines or imprisonment.

Everything begins at inception, and the environment children come from has a huge impact on how they develop. Their ideas and actions are shaped by all influences they experience. Because of this, learning to trust starts at infancy. Babies are totally reliant on their caretakers to provide their fundamental requirements for food, shelter, comfort, and love when they are born. If caregivers respond to babies' screams and body language in a consistent, loving manner, the babies will feel comfortable and will be more likely to learn to trust their environment.

Healthy parental relationships and nurturing guidance have proven to be instrumental in laying the foundation for emotionally balanced children. Every healthy connection begins with the ability to trust oneself and others, and you may start establishing your children's sense of trust as early as infancy by being sensitive to their physical and emotional needs. As your children get older, they become more aware of their surroundings, and you can help them trust you by providing a supportive atmosphere in which you listen and keep your promises. Your words and deeds are inviolable.

When you disavow what you say or become inconsistent or contradictory, you impact your children in a very detrimental way. As a parent, you are a beacon. Your words and actions reverberate. By example, I never curse when I speak. Never. Using profanity to express your thoughts is classless and besmirches your perception to those who are listening to your rhetoric. You are also acting as a negative role model and pouring a foundation for the way your children will be and how they express themselves. My son is twenty-three, and my daughter is nineteen, and they never use curse words even when they get upset. Do you remember previously when I spoke about perception of self? What you say and the way you say it make you stand out either positively or negatively. You may say, "I don't care." I am saying you should care. We are influenced by our influencers. The seeds are sown when we are very young and at our most vulnerable. Awareness starts when we are infants and then evolves very quickly. Consider the following development stages per Stanford Children's Health[98]:

- Between seven to nine months of age, awareness of people increases. Babies pay attention to conversation and respond to changes in emotion of others.
- At ten to twelve months of age, babies have preferences for people and are curious and want to explore.
- At eighteen months of age, babies begin to understand the cause-and-effect aspect of relationships.
- At two years of age, children demonstrate independence from parents and may begin to solve problems.
- At three years of age, children remember certain events and understand long sentences.
- At four to five years of age, children understand the difference between fantasy and reality. As they enter school, they may become more attached to parents.
- At six to seven years old, children start to understand concepts and can become jealous of others.
- At eight to twelve years of age, children have established likes. Respect for parents and friends becomes very important.
- At thirteen to eighteen years of age, children develop the ability to think abstractly and want independence from their parents. The notion of the "mirror stage" was coined by French psychiatrist Jacques Lacan to describe the phenomenon of a kid learning to discriminate between "self" and "others."[99] Seeing one's own image in the mirror enables us to understand we are

---

[98] Stanford Children's Health, "The Growing Child: 7 to 9 Months." https://www.stanfordchildrens.org/en/topic/default?id=the-growing-child-7-to-9-months-90-P02168.

[99] Owen Hewitson, "What Does Lacan Say About… The Mirror Stage? – Part I," *Lacan Online*, September 13, 2010. https://www.lacanonline.com/2010/09/what-does-lacan-say-about-the-mirror-stage-part-i/.

independent. Fear and loneliness give rise to the ego. It shapes our identity and distinguishes us from others around us since we were children.

Parents must also demonstrate that they trust their children. Relationships thrive when all parties trust each other, and by recognizing and empathizing with your children, you show them that, no matter what they do, you will always be there for them. Unfortunately, many parents drop the ball and put themselves first, emotionally abandoning their children. This isn't a case of pointing fingers and assigning blame. Adults have their own problems, and many people are self-destructive or have inadequate stress management skills. Unfortunately, they occasionally forsake their children emotionally and physically.

Alex's Story

Alex was eighteen and had to deal with a lot in his life. His parents were divorced and absorbed in their own battles. I knew him through my daughter. He was reluctant to speak to me and share his feelings. One night, he was hanging out with my daughter, and I got him to open up to me. I promised I wouldn't disclose his last name. I'd known him for over ten years, so he felt some degree of comfort. I knew his mother, who was a strict disciplinarian, and I had never met his dad. His father left when Alex was an infant, and Alex never saw him. It was obvious to me that the kid had issues. He was doing poorly in school, dressing poorly, and exhibiting no ambition. His mother was untrusting of him and was very critical of everything he did. Alex had gotten into smoking pot all the time. He told me he didn't care about doing well in school. He had his friends and a girlfriend, whom I think also was dysfunctional. I asked him if he got along with his mother. He wouldn't answer my question. I asked if he was thinking about his future, and he didn't reply. He started to get uncomfortable and didn't want to answer any more questions. He took out a joint and walked out onto my terrace. Since that time, I have been trying to influence him by sending him things to read, and I have told him I am always available to speak to him.

When parents are there for their children, an emotional foundation is formed that provides security and direction in the lives of the children. People in their mid-teens to mid-twenties usually feel a lot of ambiguity regarding their futures. One of life's great ironies is that we spend a lot of our youth worrying about the future, but once we get there, when we get older, we realize how much time we wasted fretting.

Consistently, respect and guidance are catalysts for building trust with young people as well helping them learn to trust others. For a little child, there isn't much thought about trust; it is mostly innate. It is normal for well-intentioned parents to dedicate themselves to their kids. This is an ideal that, in a perfect world, would always occur, but unfortunately, we do not live in a perfect world.

When I was a child, I did feel safe, but I never thought about trust. Maybe at that early stage of life, feeling safe is the same thing as trust. As I got older, my world became dysfunctional because my parents' lives were separate and contentious. I loved them both, but I didn't respect them. I didn't understand what was happening when they moved apart. I felt a sense of discomfort and sadness. I wasn't in any immediate jeopardy, but I saw a big difference between my relationship with my parents and the parent/kid relationships some of my friends enjoyed. As I aged, I sought what I didn't have and didn't even know I was doing so. I used to watch TV shows that were family oriented; I was mesmerized by the stories. Now I realize I was envious of normalcy.

When I became an adolescent, I became my own parent as well as a parent to my parents. This is unquestionably true, and I say this with tears in my eyes.

Things change as children mature and form their own thoughts, opinions, beliefs, and desires. Regardless of a relationship with their parents, children start to be influenced by their peers. Depending on the strength of their relationship with their parents and other influencing circumstances, they can become insensitive, contentious, and reactionary.

If your children begin to question what you tell them they should do, challenge your knowledge, and repel all the pressures to behave, you must recognize that you are now dealing with adolescents. They are undergoing significant biological changes, and your reactions must be modified appropriately. It isn't wise to be dictatorial. However, bad behavior or disrespect must be properly addressed.

Going through a bad divorce, I always took the bullets and wanted to make my children feel secure. I was and am attentive and generous. I always tell them everything and treat them as adults with respect. I push for them to be responsible. I always stay calm. I never raise my voice. I try to rationally explain my position and point of view. If you show your kids respect, I believe you will experience appreciation, and they will, in turn, respect you.

Alternatively, when fractures happen and respect evaporates, damage ensues. Behavior and reactions by both adolescent children and parents take a different turn, and the interactions change. When children feel distrusted or challenged and parents get angry and draw a line in the sand dictating their position, conflict breaks out.

Recalcitrant conduct, slamming doors, shouting voices, suspension of communication, and sullen looks are the outcome. This is how shattered trust and dysfunction appear, and it occurs frequently. For unhappy parents, the kids lie, violate curfew, experiment with drugs and alcohol, or get into problems at school. This is a continuing, very difficult set of circumstances. Parents begin to criticize their children's acquaintances they believe are unsuitable. The children disregard their parents and become retaliatory. Parents strike back with guilt trips, revocation of privileges, and invasions of their children's privacy. Both parties believe their trust has been damaged beyond repair, and an atmosphere of hate develops, exacerbating the separation and inhibiting free communication.

In adolescence, communication between parents and children becomes a major difficulty for both sides. Because teens spend more time with their peers, there are fewer opportunities to engage—and regrettably, when parents and children do contact, they have trouble communicating. Something appears to have gone wrong, and there is no longer any emotional connection. Teenagers become increasingly secretive and associated with their peers while they pull away from their parents. In some severe situations, it's as if the parents and the children are just cohabiting. Your parenting integrity may also be questioned. Respect and esteem may dwindle. As youngsters mature and become more self-sufficient, they begin to observe and inquire more. Around this time, your kid may notice if you follow through on your promises and are consistent, which is an important component in developing trust.

You can't *expect* your children to trust you as a parent. It's a slow process that takes commitment by both parents and children, but it will surely enhance your bond. It will help prepare your youngsters for the future development of good connections. It's important to remember that teens are going through a very intimate period in their life. Personal space becomes extremely essential to them; therefore, a need for privacy does not automatically imply unethical behavior. It's critical to remember this.

Ben's Story

Ben shared his story with me. I include it here in his own words.

> At the age of twenty-three, I have unfortunately been
> in situations in which I overly trusted, and it has hurt

me, or I have fortunately gotten lucky trusting others, and it paid off.

The first example I can think of is my relationship with my mother and father. Most kids trust both their parents implicitly and without hesitation. Unfortunately, my relationship with my mother was filled with lies and greed. She had no regard for me. It was all about herself.

I was about eight when my parents got divorced. No child ever takes that news lightly; neither did I understand the reasons behind their separation. As I grew up, while living with my mother, she used me as a pawn against my father. She looked at me as an asset to leverage me against him to ask him for more money, and if he did not pay her, she would not let either my sister or I see him. I was depressed, and as a result, I became morbidly obese, prediabetic, and was on the verge of fatty liver disease. I decided that I needed to change my lifestyle and moved in with my father. Obviously, he was pushing legally for that to happen. To this day, I believe that was the best decision I have ever made. Being with him changed my life and the direction in which I was heading.

He taught me so much, but more importantly he inspired me to become a better version of myself. I lost over one hundred pounds, got my grades up, and felt a surge of motivation that I had never felt before. I had trusted both my parents to guide me in life. My mother's guidance led down a dark path, while my father showed me what it meant to become motivated, successful, and do the right things.

As I had been in my personal life, I have been overly trustworthy throughout my business career. I started my first company while I was a junior at the University of Miami. The business was a platform to rent out exotic vehicles daily that were underutilized by wealthy individuals in South Beach. Once I proved the model was profitable, I raised capital and bought cars of my own with my partners. The first person I hired was a guy named Joel. He was a tech-savvy twenty-six-year-old who'd had a difficult life up to the point that I met him.

He was a superstar employee. He was great with clients, incorporated systems that expedited the rental process, and seemed like a genuine guy. One day, out of the blue, he went dark. Shortly thereafter, he began to violate my trust. He stole my company's bank information, used our credit cards to buy goods online, and attempted to steal my identity. To this day, I still do not know why he deceived me and my partners. I was really shocked and hurt by what happened. I also learned a lot from this terrible experience. Today, I still want to trust. I just think I have become smarter about it.

Many teenagers do not communicate openly with their parents, so they make bad choices (often with long-term negative consequences), bypassing the benefit of experienced points of view. The result can be tragic for a teen and even more heartbreaking for the adults who did not get a chance to share their insights. This may be exacerbated by bad handling of the aftermath. I can only speak for myself, and I am so lucky for having the relationship I do with my kids. Both of them experienced a terrible divorce, which could have very adversely affected them. I always set out to do the right things for them; I treated them as young adults at an early age. I respected them and spoke to them very openly about everything that was going on. Some people disagreed with my openness. I wanted them to know things, and I respected their opinions, feelings, and thoughts. I didn't want them to grow up feeling as if I was hiding the truth. I also wanted them to see that I was vulnerable just like them. Today, my son is twenty-three and is my partner in a couple of businesses, and my daughter is a sophomore at University of Southern California business school and straight-A student. I never had any bad experiences with them. I suppose I may have been smart in the way I brought them up, but I also realize that I was lucky. It could have gone the other way. They came from a dysfunctional childhood, yet they still are excelling. There is an expression that I sincerely believe in: "Out of adversity, you build strength." I know I have. Oh, by the way, Ben is my son.

Trusting Youth

Before the twentieth century, many parents believed that "children should be seen and not heard." Children were told what to do and didn't have a vote. Engaging young people in decision making or forming an opinion was beyond comprehension for most adults of past generations. In general, adults recognized the opinions of only people who had reached the age of eighteen or even twenty-one. Kids were told that they just had to listen. Many of them rebelled or became dismissive and ultimately self-destructive.

How hard is it to be young? What are the pressures? Many of us who aren't young may not even consider or think about this anymore. In fact, too many young people become victims of insecurity, competition, and uncertainty. They lack the fortitude of trusting those relationships in their lives that can support them. Sadly, they may unravel and do things that forsake good judgment. If a parent is unavailable when a child or teenager needs him or her the most, the young person may begin to believe that the parent cannot be trusted. Most of the time, a parent is present to keep things in check. The flip side is that, out of adversity, we build strength. I personally can relate to this aphorism. I realized in my teens that I was responsible for myself and became very motivated to achieve. I didn't respect my parents because of the way they were.

It can be difficult to trust teens to make smart judgments as they begin to take more responsibility for themselves. Surprisingly, if we don't allow teens to take charge of their own lives, they are more inclined to revolt. It's difficult to get the balance just right.

Rules are an integral part of trust. Rules are the boundaries you establish within your family and with your adolescents to ensure their safety and to maintain your family's values. When teens strive to think like adults, they must make judgments and determine if something is appropriate, safe, and acceptable to them. But teens don't think like adults. They are:

- more likely to be persuaded by peer pressure
- less likely to think about the future
- more likely to be impulsive
- less likely to weigh risks

So, they need guidance—and you must provide it without preaching. Youth by definition represents the time between childhood and adulthood. It is also the time we are influenced in how we think and feel. It is the genesis of our adult behavior and style of reaction. Things often happen in our youth that affect us in all aspects of our lives and particularly our emotional development. Trust and a sense of the confidence in our beliefs are constructed and occur at this stage of our lives. Aberrations, inconsistencies, and emotional disruptions, like parents getting divorced, can impact adolescents and children emotionally. It is a sober fact that kids who come from broken homes are more likely to get divorced than children who grew up with parents who were happily married. I am an example of this statistic. The formative years are so impactful and directing. While living through our youth, we don't realize that our parents are the primary sources and influencers of our construct of reality.

According to a 2019 survey by the Pew Research Center, "Young Americans are less trusting of other people—and key institutions—than their elders."[100] Author John Gramlich distinguishes that about three-quarters (73 percent) of US individuals under thirty feel that people "simply look out for themselves" the majority of the time. A comparable percentage (71 percent) believes that most individuals "would try to take advantage of you if they had the opportunity." Six out of ten respondents believe that most people can't be trusted. Adults under thirty are much more likely than their older counterparts to have a negative opinion about their fellow Americans in all three of these questions.

Your youngster may notice if you follow through on what you say you'll do, which is an important component in developing trust. You can't merely *expect* your children to trust you as a parent. It's a slow process that takes commitments from both of you, but it will surely enhance your bond. It will help prepare your youngster for developing good connections the future. Teenagers are going through a very intimate period in their lives. They value personal space; thus, a need for privacy does not automatically imply unethical behavior. That is crucial to remember.

Jen Babakhan, an author and educator, wrote a fantastic piece for *Reader's Digest* called "11 Things Parents Say That Ruin Their Kids' Trust."[101] Here are a few of her thoughts. Kids are very intuitive and have a great sense of how far they can go manipulating parents. Ridiculous ultimatums like, "You will be grounded forever," are worthless because everyone knows that is never going to happen. Alternatively, it is essential to set practical boundaries as consequences that can be enforced. For

---

[100] John Gramlich, "Young Americans are less trusting of other people – and key institutions – than their elders," Pew Research Center, August 6, 2019. https://www.pewresearch.org/fact-tank/2019/08/06/young-americans-are-less-trusting-of-other-people-and-key-institutions-than-their-elders/.

[101] Jen Babakhan, "11 Things Parents Say that Ruin Their Kids' Trust," *Reader's Digest*, June 7, 2022. https://www.rd.com/list/parents-kids-trust/.

a teenager, taking away privileges or access to social media could be effective. Follow through with the consequence so it's not an empty threat. Children need to trust that their parents mean what they say. Some parents want their children to be contrite; they want a confession of undesirable behavior. This in a certain way is an attempt to embarrass the child and create an awareness not to repeat the same mistakes again.

Parents have a front-row seat and are the architects of the emotional and social growth of their children.

Children inherently want to please parents and are compelled to make parents proud of them. Parents need to be sensitive to boundaries and not probe too much into private emotional or behavioral experiences. Offer them respect and forgiveness, which will be appreciated and will enhance trust.

"It's critical that parents understand that how they say things to their children or teenagers, not just what they say, may create or destroy trust," Babakhan writes.[101] Children need to feel that their parents appreciate their strengths and understand their limitations. Respect is essential, and repeating bad incidents from the past alienates. Move on and reinforce positivity.

In 2019, I attended Art Basel, the international art fair, in Miami. As I was walking through the exhibits, I saw this piece satirically characterizing Donald Trump. What really struck me was the letter written by the artist hanging below the piece of art. What he said about his dad was impactful.

Children Who Grow Up without Parental Care

According to studies, kids who lose a parent unexpectedly, whether via death, desertion, or extended absence, suffer great anxiety, panic, sadness, melancholy, helplessness, and hopelessness. These youngsters have lost part of their lifeline and, in many cases, their sense of self.

Unfortunately, children's initial line of defense—their parents—can be lost. This can be through abduction, trafficking, migration, living on the street, displacement, induction into the armed forces, health issues, educational reasons, household violence, poverty, death, or stigma. Around the world, there are about 250 million children growing up without fathers in their lives. This is twice the population of Japan. In the United States, 23 percent of children are living in a fatherless home, and they account for 71 percent of high school dropouts, 85 percent of youth in prisons, and 90 percent of runaways. Fatherlessness comes in a lot of forms. For some, it is about divorce or estrangement due to alcohol or drug abuse. For others, it is about lengthy military service. In South Africa, only 37 percent of children are living with their fathers. In Central and South America, half of all kids are born out of wedlock, and most never see their dad.[102]

Fatherhood is vital to a child's development.

When Parent-Child Trust Is Broken

This is a tale of a patient Ben as narrated by his psychotherapist, Stephen Ohayon, with whom I consulted for this book.

> Ben was a thirty-three-year-old Irish American who was raised in Long Island, New York. He was Catholic, but his family did not practice their faith. In his childhood,

---

[102] National Fatherhood Initiative, "The Statistics Don't Lie: Fathers Matter," 2021. https://www.fatherhood.org/father-absence-statistic.

he was impacted by the drinking habits of his mother. She was erratic and unpredictable. Even worse, her behavior was inconsistent and unstable. He experienced a growing sense of insecurity and stopped trusting her.

When he was in his preteens, she insisted on taking him on errands with her. During these travels to the local stores, he felt nervous. He was terrified because she was driving dangerously fast. He recalled her frantically smoking while driving the car carelessly. She'd scream at him for no apparent reason, threatening to lose control and get into an accident. She reminded him that she was in charge of his life and that she could crash the automobile at any time. Ben was scared when he saw his mother acting erratically. He'd sob and urge her to be careful behind the wheel. Her mind, on the other hand, was preoccupied with unseen monsters. One time, while driving to the supermarket with him in the passenger seat, she made a confession. His father, Kevin, wasn't his real father. His real father was Holland, the family friend whom they often visited on weekends in the next town. She demanded from Ben absolute secrecy. He could never tell Kevin, the father who raised him, the truth. Such revelation would destroy Kevin, who in all probability would divorce her. Financial hardship would follow, and that would affect the comfortable life they were enjoying.

The duplicity shattered Ben's innocent soul. He was inconsolable at the reality that his mother had lied to her husband, his father. It disturbed him terribly that she was perpetrating the lie without any prospect of resolution as she didn't intend for the truth to ever emerge. The young boy felt depressed by the lie he was forced to keep concealed. He loved his father, Kevin, who was honorable and decent and treated him with affection and kindness. He felt very badly for his father, who had been tricked by his devious mother. His anger toward his mother unfolded in his heart. He never expressed his discontent to her but rather repressed and sedated his rage. He was furious with his genetic father, Holland, whom he felt was impotent and useless. He had been aware of the duplicity and for many years kept the lie alive. Ben was psychologically broken. He had lost completely the inherent comfort and security that trust generates.

Ben had realized that his mistrust of men and women had injured him greatly. Suspicious and skeptical, he was a serial friend, accumulating male friends and many girlfriends. The relationships lasted weeks or months before they faded away. He could never trust anyone. His world was limited and narrow, his paranoia relentless and vibrant. Depression had darkened his days. Without trust, he couldn't live. One day, he came to his session and confronted the therapist with some disturbing evidence: "Do you know how many individuals in the United States successfully committed suicide in 2014?" He was clearly moved when he asked. "Thirty-eight thousand," he said in response to my query. "Or else," he threatened, "I have to untangle this Gordian knot."

I asked, "What do you think you should do?" He was anxious for an answer.

Both older people and younger people benefit when they share their knowledge and wisdom, according to research and plain sense. Younger people, because a bond of support grows with someone they respect and trust; older people, because they have a sense of purpose

by giving back and helping to influence the future of a young person. They bring the past, present, and future together in a chain of support and understanding that spans generations.

Trust starts at birth. Infants do not experience a sense of uncertainty. Trust is totally implicit. Life advances, and we become ourselves. Our dependence evolves to independence, and we learn to react to our senses that make us trust or not. Unfortunately, there are so many violations in what we believed was sincere. The takeaway is that we do get smarter and hopefully learn.

CHAPTER 15

Beauty Is in the Eye of the Beholder

WE ARE ALL aware that appearances are important. What most of us don't realize is *how* important appearances are—and how tough it is to overlook a person's appearance while making social or economic decisions.

Love partnerships are not only about physical attraction. I'm referring to all our encounters with one another. And I'm not only referring to the "beauty" dimension; I'm also referring to many other aspects of a person's "look." There are many clichés that ring true, but what is certain is that physical attraction is a major force in every realm of life. We all react positively to very attractive people. At least that is the case before we get to know them. On an intimate basis, men will stare and fantasize about the possibility of a sexual encounter. Women will also covet a very handsome man. They will flirt and be very suggestive. They may project the possibilities of a relationship and even try to procure endeavors. In the business world, physicality really can influence success or failure. Achievement can very much be influenced by our appearance.

In politics, the impact of facial appearance has been researched the most. Because many of our social decisions effectively amount to a vote, the voting arena is also an excellent place to examine the impacts of appearance more broadly.

Whom do we hire? Whom do we go out with? Whom can we put our faith in? When we vote for candidates, we want to assume we're evaluating them on their qualities rather than their appearance. But are we there yet?

Attractive people receive advantages and preferential treatment in every field. The halo effect, for example, has significant links to beauty; at first impression, extremely attractive individuals are assumed to have a number of good personality qualities, such as benevolence, stability, and intellect, as if an unseen "halo" were shining down over the beautiful people. People hold them to a higher standard. And they attribute their attractiveness to a variety of good characteristics.

To explain how it might alter perceptions, the phrase "halo effect" employs the concept of a halo. A halo is frequently shown over a saint's head in religious art, representing heavenly light. When you look at people through the halo effect lens, you see them in such a light. Your perception of one trait creates a halo that encompasses all traits similarly. This helps to explain why there is so much discrimination based on looks in the job arena, the dating market, and even the legal system.

In his book *Beauty Pays: Why Attractive People Are More Successful*, economist David Hamermesh demonstrates that handsome individuals are more likely to be employed, to be paid higher salaries, to be accepted for a loan, to negotiate better loan conditions, and to have spouses who are better looking and of higher status. Criminals who are attractive are given more lenient punishments for their crimes (and occasionally, their mug shots go viral, and they end up with fan clubs and modeling contracts).

One of the most prominent biases that is hardly ever discussed or acknowledged is the beauty bias—also known as "lookism." Yet the existence of a beauty premium in the labor market is well recognized. We all have experienced this not just in the work world but even in our youth in school. Our physicality can be an advantage and can foster special treatment and recognition.

In general, the beauty bias refers to the preferential treatment that people receive when they are regarded as more attractive, whether this is done consciously or unconsciously—and few people, let alone employers, confess to preferring to work with others based on their greater levels of attractiveness. There are, of course, certain exceptions. For example, "good looks" are an official criterion for joining the Chinese navy, presumably so that recruits can best represent the country. Even though it appears ridiculous, this is true. Clothing retailer Abercrombie & Fitch was not barred from imposing beauty criteria in its recruiting practices as long as it recruited diverse—but good-looking—candidates, despite being forced into a $50 million settlement for hiring waspy-looking store workers.

Examine the photos that people post on Instagram. Attractive women share sexy photos to attract followers and maybe more. Many "influencers" monetize their number of followers. Jen Selter, a social media phenom, built her following around taking photographs that accentuated her ass. This isn't a joke; it's true. Her ass was the catalyst for accumulating more than twelve million followers on Instagram. Now she markets products branded with her name. There is no question that good looks and physicality are used as marketing tools. Consider Khloe Kardashian. She has 208 million followers on Instagram. A few years ago, she wound up getting backlash for sponsoring detox tea as a meal replacement and a total tummy knockout. She is promoting unhealthy laxatives to young people. She prides herself on staying healthy and looking good by working out but also gets a ton of plastic surgery. The reality is that social media influencers can't be trusted.

Physical looks open doors, make people popular, and in some cases, facilitate success. Many people are obsessed with physicality and appearance; in some cases, this can turn into an illness. I am very conscious about how I look and about my appearance. I am told that I am handsome, and I do like to adorn myself from an attire perspective. I must own at least one hundred pocket squares. I don't want to sound silly, but the way we look really makes us stand out—positively or negatively! Clearly, looking good can be an advantage and even a game changer.

What happens when physicality becomes a primary criteria for recognition? Is that good or bad? Can you trust the recognition as being sincere? How does this affect us emotionally? Do people lose motivation to develop other skill sets because they are physically attractive? What happens as you get older and your looks change? Supermodels' lives are predicated on their appearance and attractiveness. They know it, and that empowers their business success. What about attractive women who aren't supermodels? What are the pluses, and what are the negatives? Historically, attractive women were always a center of attention in the work environment. At my first job on Wall Street, the company employed an adorable, sexy receptionist from Brooklyn. She probably was twenty-two years old. I learned that she was having an affair with the chairman of the company who was in his mid-sixties and married. I am sure that she had to get some fringe benefits. It is fairly obvious that the dimension of that relationship was for a particular purpose. So, the question is, who was using whom?

Things have changed significantly since that first job in the area of company interactions. Today, attractive women face a daunting issue and now a negative prejudice in the workforce on many levels. This change started with Bill Cosby and has escalated to the "Me Too" movement. The extreme of this is being forced to have sex with someone in a position of power to advance one's career. Harvey Weinstein, the movie producer, was found guilty in 2020 of rape in the third degree and a criminal sexual act and has been sentenced to twenty-three years in prison. The obvious discomfort of unwanted flirtation is a lesser level of violation but has always been present. Historically, this has been commonplace and didn't have ramifications. Today, the ramifications are severe to the culpable or accused party.

There are many lawyers who work on contingency to represent accusers claiming sexual abuse. Alleged innuendo is often enough for these ambulance chasers to start a lawsuit. The framework for legal extortion is at an all-time high. Disingenuous claims can deliver a big payday. Andrew Cuomo went from being a potential presidential candidate for his efforts during the coronavirus crisis to being maligned and accused of sexual misconduct .

What happens when the allegations are untrue or exaggerated? Those accused, at the minimum, are embarrassed or, worse, might lose their jobs and then potentially have matrimonial issues because the bar is so low that being accused is just as bad as being guilty.

It is a fact that hiring practices have changed. I know a lot of CEOs, and some have told me they will not hire very attractive women for job positions. This is incredible but true. Let's say you needed to hire a new receptionist. A very attractive woman comes for an interview. Would you hire her? Would you be nervous about the exposure? Can you trust her not to manufacture an accusation for personal benefit?

Unfortunately, in today's world, an owner of a company really has to think about this. The very attractive woman whose physical allure throughout her life has always been an advantage may experience a situation in which her looks become a disadvantage.

A friend of mine shared a story with me that happened a number of years ago. Diane is a very attractive analyst who went for a job interview. Here is her story in her words:

> The director of the clinic was probably in his late thirties, and I was in my late twenties. I had dressed professionally in a suit, and the interview went smoothly for the first hour. Interviews have never been a problem for me as I enjoy telling other professionals about my work experience and schooling because I have found my calling and love the work. My instincts told me after an hour that the interview was going on for longer than I expected, though I had never looked at my watch. I also started to realize that the director wasn't just being nice but was being flirtatious, and my intention was to be friendly with this person. I started to wonder, *Do I continue in this friendly manner?* Is this director being appropriate? He was wearing a wedding ring, and I tried to reassure myself, but ultimately, I didn't like the way the interview was heading.
>
> Well, my instinct was correct because he eventually got around to the question that could land me the job or lose it: "Do you plan on getting pregnant anytime soon?" There it was, one of the most inappropriate, absurd questions. I was confused. How was I to answer? I knew he couldn't legally ask me such a discriminatory

question. But I had just finished my second private school education. I hadn't finished paying off my undergraduate student loans, and I was up to my ears in debt. I really needed the job! While I felt set up, I thought quickly and said that I was in a relationship, but I had just finished graduate school with the intent of working a few years before starting a family. Though I eventually got the job, I left that interview with very mixed feelings about the job probably because I felt neither one of us in that interview could be trusted.

A number of years ago, I was friends with a Major League Baseball pitcher. Aside from being accomplished and well recognized, he was also a very handsome guy. He told me that, when his team was on the road, women he didn't know would show up at his hotel room late at night. Once, after a bad experience that resulted in someone extorting him, he changed his habits. He now has new female acquaintances sign a legal document to protect himself before they pursue any dating or sexual relationships. Talk about getting off on the right foot.

So, we might argue that being attractive is a big advantage, but as we have seen, it can also be a disadvantage. What are the pros and cons?

Pros of being attractive:

- You can strike up a conversation more easily than others.
- You attract more attention than others.
- People like you more.
- You are treated favorably by others.
- You're more likely to be well known or well liked.
- You have an "aura" that permits you to sway the opinions of others.
- You are entitled to additional advantages and privileges.
- You are more likely to get recruited in the workplace.
- Attractive individuals appear to be happier.

- Attractive people may be more self-assured
- Attractive people are more convincing.

Cons of being attractive:

- You frequently attract unwelcome attention.
- It's possible that you won't be taken seriously.
- Some individuals will be envious of you.
- You are branded as self-centered, arrogant, or vain if you express anything nice about yourself.
- You are evaluated far more harshly than others.
- Your priorities may be skewed too far in favor of your looks.
- If you're interviewed by someone of the same gender, you're unlikely to obtain the job.

Some people consider that their looks are their main asset. They trust that outcomes are based on how others react to their attractiveness. What happens when their beauty diminishes with age or for other reasons, and they don't have other skill sets? Well, there's always plastic surgery. But take a moment to Google "Catwoman Jocelyn Wildenstein."

I think the moral of the story is to recognize that looks are only skin deep. The important revelation is that looking good is important on many levels. Recognition for your appearance can be very rewarding both monetarily and personally. However, beauty is only skin deep, and other attributes are so much more important. I am not diminishing attractiveness, but "skin deep" says it all.

CHAPTER 16

Ego: How Dangerous Is It?

YESTERDAY, I WAS brilliant, so I wanted to change the world; today, I am sagacious, so I am changing myself. Turn your ego into your ally. I can't get away from being a word guy.

Do you know what *solipsism* means?

Solipsism: (noun) "the view or theory that self is all that can be known to exist."[103] What is a solipsistic person? It is a person who believes self can know nothing but its own modifications and that self is the only existent thing; it is also extreme egocentrism. From this outlook, the individual cannot get outside of his or her mind to encounter any other

---
[103] Britannica, "solipsism." https://www.britannica.com/topic/solipsism.

objects, including other persons. Other minds are even more removed. The word *ego* is Latin for "I," and in English, it is used to mean the "self" or "identity." It's a belief system that identifies your place in this world. So, what happens when that belief system becomes skewed a little (or a lot), and you find that you've turned into "that guy" or "that girl" whom everybody hates: the egomaniac. Is that really so terrible? Yes, yes, and yes. On multiple levels. Time to rein it in, cowboys and girls, because your ego is going to destroy you.

The Lone Wolf

The *Wolf of Wall Street* is a movie based on a real-life stockbroker whose firm engaged in fraud and corruption. The "wolf" appeared to have it all figured out. However, every big dog has his share of sadness and solitude, and these consequences aren't pretty.

People are drawn to inflated egos, but they are usually the wrong people: egomaniacs and other opportunists. A few years ago, I went to an engagement party in Hallandale, Florida, for a prominent real estate developer's son. It was a fancy event at the Trump International Beach Resort. I knew the developer by name but had not met him previously. He had a reputation for being a show-off. My friend, who had invited me and who knew him, was standing with me during the cocktail portion of the event when the developer walked over to us. My friend introduced me, and as I reached out to shake his hand, the man started bragging to us about the reception and how much money he'd spent on it for his son. Then his son, who was about twenty feet away from where we were standing, strolled by with his fiancée, waving to the attendees. He was rather obese—a younger version of his father. Gil, the father, turned his attention to me and said, "You know he is the luckiest guy in the world. Do you know why?" I thought he was going to tell me he was marrying a great lady. Before I could say anything, he said, "Because he was born after me." He then walked away.

I was stunned. I never forgot this encounter. What an a--hole. People are generally repelled by people who display an overblown ego. They just can't relate, and worse, they can't even stand people who are entirely self-absorbed in their own lives. And that just doesn't work.

Ego can be one of the worst "poisons"; it can be more lethal to our well-being than anything else. Yet we do react to things too often because of our ego. Can we rely on making decisions, deciding what we say, or taking positions because we trust and comply to the direction dictated by our egos? This is a question I guarantee you never thought about or considered. We really don't think about our egos in this context, or for that matter, in any context. We don't think about our egos at all, do we? It just is what it has become.

Pause for moment. How do you perceive your ego? Now ask yourself how you think other people you know perceive you and your ego? Do you think the real estate developer I spoke about earlier has any awareness of his ego and the way be brandishes himself and the way his behavior affects the people with whom he interacts?

A big ego pushes away all those who are subject to this arrogance. People driven by their ego are usually critical of those around them and become trapped and alone in their own selfish opinions. Egocentricity is an unhealthy belief in one's own importance and inflexible views. As others withdraw from these people, these people withdraw into themselves because they can't relate. Everyone around them can't stand them. After all, they no longer share the same interests; the primary interest of egotists is themselves! All that's left are the folks who believe they stand to benefit from a person's perceived superiority.

Your ego isn't the issue; your false sense of self is. We damage ourselves and others by pinning our hopes on an unachievable objective in order to keep our illusion self-satisfied. To defend their ego borders, people are prepared to lie, kill, cheat, hide, or steal. When that "ideal side" is criticized, they take it personally and believe their entire identity is at jeopardy.

We may damage personal connections, business partnerships, and friendships if we let our egos take control. An inflated ego can persuade us to perceive things differently than the way they are. The belief that the universe revolves around us—that all wonderful things that happen were designed for us—is ego at its most extreme. We have a right to it. All the horrible things that occurred were intended to harm us.

I had an open conversation about this with a friend I have known for over twenty years. He opened up to me about how his ego had affected his life. "Personally, ego has had a self-destructive effect on my life. I could not share issues I was going through with others for fear that they would think less of me or think of me as 'weak.' I always wanted to be perceived as powerful and in total control, and that I knew better than everybody else. As a result, I kept everything to myself and felt I was alone. I often thought I 'knew everything' when, in fact, I simply couldn't admit that I knew very little. I ignored others. My ego would not let me concede that their opinions or ideas might be better than mine. The list of the imperfections in my life my ego caused could go on and on."

Ego Is the Enemy, written by Ryan Holiday, is a powerful book. His comments ring true, particularly this one: "Entitlement presumes: This is mine." It's something I've worked hard for. At the same time, entitlement nickels and dimes others since it can't see someone else's time being valued as highly as its own. It makes tirades and proclamations that weary those who work for and with us and who have no option but to comply. It exaggerates our talents in front of others, makes a favorable assessment of our prospects, and sets unrealistic expectations.

Our egos crave safety, predictability, and repetition. We promote an idealized picture of ourselves because it makes us feel at ease. We turn individuals into enemies if they challenge that illusion. That is why egotistical individuals are always fighting. They have to guard the delicate illusion of who they are. The irony is that we struggle to maintain a picture of ourselves that no one else believes. At some time, we will all cave to our egos. It is unavoidable. We're slipping into ego traps more frequently than ever before because of social media, which has made it simpler than ever to deceive ourselves.

What matters is that we do our hardest to detect these traps when we fall into them and then learn how to avoid them in the future because, at the end of the day, humility isn't something you're born with or without; it's something you can cultivate. However, you must strive to keep your ego in control and be intellectually honest in order to remain humble.

At a private event a few years ago, Google founder Larry Page told a rapt audience that he judges new firms and entrepreneurs based on a single metric: whether or not what they're working on has the potential to "transform the world." It's a unique perspective on things as well as a tired stereotype. It's also a little delusional. Confidence, on the other hand, is a wonderful thing, and Larry did revolutionize the search industry.

Everything is made personal by the ego. Making things too personal is a common blunder. When it came to intensifying the Vietnam War, Lyndon B. Johnson made it personal. Johnson personalized the war, not as the United States versus North Vietnam (or Russia and China), but as LBJ against the world, be it the enemy abroad or those inside his administration and throughout the country who criticized the war, as evidenced by tapes of him in the Oval Office.

President Trump, asserts Republican strategist Rick Wilson in his book, *Everything Trump Touches Dies*, is motivated by one thing: his ego. Wilson states, "There are no conservative instincts in this person. There are a few conservative principles that are pulled up behind him from time to time, but this man is driven by his ego, morning tweets, a feeling of notoriety, and a sense of venality."[104]

Great teams tend to follow a trajectory, according to Pat Riley, the famous coach and manager who guided the Los Angeles Lakers and Miami Heat to many championships. A squad is innocent when they first begin—before they have won. When the circumstances are appropriate, they band together, keep an eye out for one another, and cooperate toward a common objective. He refers to this stage as the "innocent climb."[105]

When a team starts to win and the media starts to pay attention to them, the simple connections that bound them together in the beginning begin to dissolve. The importance of each player is calculated by the players themselves. Chests enlarge. Frustrations start to surface. Egos emerge. Riley claims that the "innocent climb" is nearly always followed by the "sickness of myself." It has the ability to "strike any winning squad in any year and at any moment,"[105] and it does so alarmingly frequently.

We have a propensity to move to a mindset of "grabbing what's mine" once we've "made it." Awards and accolades are suddenly important, even if they weren't what brought us to a particular place in the first place. We need the money, the championship, and the media exposure for ourselves, not for the team or the cause. "We've earned it," they say.[105] Entitlement is one of the biggest and most harmful misconceptions that comes with success.

Being "believable," which implies acting with honesty and transparency, is one of the most important aspects of creating trust in a relationship: it isn't only about me. This foundation establishes trustworthiness. It's

---

[104] Rick Wilson, *Everything Trump Touches Dies*, New York, New York: Free Press, February 26, 2019.

[105] Mike Vaccaro, "Loss Would Mark End of Innocence, "Loss Would Mark End of Innocence," *New York Post*, December 17, 2006. https://nypost.com/2006/12/17/loss-would-mark-end-of-innocence/.

also the foundational aspect of trust that suffers the most damage when your ego is uncontrolled and self-serving. An out-of-control ego sends out signals to others that you think you're more important than they are, that you prioritize your interests over theirs, and that they can't be vulnerable with you without being exploited.

Can you think of people you know who have ego issues? I am sure the range of candidates is pretty wide. How about the boss who is demeaning and is full of himself or the friend who always wants to one-up you? The first person who comes to mind for me is Steve. I have known Steve for about twenty years. He is a nice guy and made a lot of money when he sold his business. He always brags about what he has and mostly talks about himself. He complains about whatever girlfriend he is with at any given time. He has never married, and he now is in his late fifties. We have a mutual friend with whom he has business dealings. Apparently, things haven't gone so well. Whenever I see him, he brings this up. He tells me the same stories over and over. I rarely get a chance to share anything about my life. It is apparent that he has no interest in me or my life. He truly is monochromatic. Some people agree he is vainglorious. I metaphorically describe him as someone who lives in a room where all the walls are mirrors.

Steve also happens to be a nice guy. He just doesn't see himself and his ego flexing. An overblown ego reflects insecurity. I should ask him if he trusts his ego. I wonder what that question would evoke. He has no perception of himself as others see him. By the way, I stopped spending time with him a couple of years ago.

Although most of us aren't egomaniacs, ego is at the foundation of nearly every chronic issue and hurdle we encounter, from why we can't win to why we must always win—at the expense of others. We don't normally perceive things in this light. We believe that something or someone other than us is to blame for our troubles. We are the classic "ill man ignorant of his malady," as the ancient Roman poet Lucretius phrased it. Ego is there in every desire and objective, undercutting us on the very trip we've invested so much time and effort into.

Harold Geneen, a pioneering CEO, linked egoism to alcoholism: "The egotist does not stagger around his desk, knocking stuff off. He is neither stuttering nor drooling. Instead, he grows increasingly arrogant, and some others, not understanding what lies underneath such an attitude, mistake his arrogance for power and self-confidence."[106] You might argue that people start to make the same error about themselves, without understanding the sickness they've caught or how it's killing them.

Make a positive difference in your life and career. By keeping an eye on your ego, you may tap into the true strength of your self-assurance. It will be much appreciated by your future self.

Ego Weakness

According to psychoanalytic theory, people who have weak egos experience anxiety and conflicts, use excessive or immature defense mechanisms and are more likely to acquire neurotic symptoms. I asked a friend to become introspective and share his story. He agreed to do it, but it was very difficult for him. We went back and forth about what he wrote, and I kept pushing him to be objective and tell it like it is. He literally wrote his story five times, opening up more with each new version.

> My name is Elijah. I am a forty-eight-year-old male who was controlled by my evil inclination for over twenty years. I have three children, Romi, Dia, and Niel [ages twenty to twenty-six] whom I've not spoken with or

---

[106] Ryan Holiday, "Meet Your Worst Enemy," *Psychology Today*, June 15, 2016. https://www.psychologytoday.com/au/blog/the-obstacle-is-the-way/201606/meet-your-worst-enemy.

seen on a regular basis for numerous years. In addition, I have a one-year-old grandchild whom I have never met and another on the way. As I rewind the tape of my life, I am tormented to recognize that my ego and low self-esteem were the source of the slow disintegration of my existence.

Ego strength, according to Sigmund Freud's psychoanalytic theory of personality, is the ego's ability to deal effectively with the demands of the id, superego, and reality. Those with little ego power are torn between competing demands, while those with much ego strength are inflexible and unyielding. My personal lack of ego strength can be attributed to creating emotional instability and coping abilities relating to internal and external stress throughout much of my lifetime. There are no words that exist in Webster's dictionary that can express my pain as I reminisce about how my weak ego allowed the spiraling succession of multiple failures, including the demise of two marriages and the rupture of my relationship with my children.

Deficient self-respect and lack of self-confidence led my ego down the path of darkness. This is my story.

The onset of my ego's downfall began in the year 2000 when I was forced to sell my family business, putting me in a state of despair. I lost my identity. I had no job, no income, and no way to support my family. I was so fearful and overwhelmed that, at times, I felt frozen and couldn't move. I fell into a state of deep depression, convinced I was a victim of unfortunate circumstances as I lived a life imprisoned by uncertainty with no exit. My self-esteem plummeted to the depths of a lonely and unknown place as I had no courage to face my responsibilities. I contemplated suicide on a daily basis. The default position of my ego chose to opt out of life, forsaking my priorities for opioids. Drugs became the driving force of my ego as my decisions and thinking became overcast with clouds. I was unrecognizable to my wife and children. What had I become? Who was I? What did my children think of me? How could I let everyone down? I saw no gateway on the horizon. I hated myself and had no self-respect.

Simultaneously, I was diagnosed with a rare and painful arthritic condition called ankylosing spondylitis requiring prescription painkillers. Finding solace in opioids and their ability to make me feel invincible, I became a drug addict, which clouded my view and judgment, leading my ego further downward. My marriage and family life were dissolving; my weak ego told me I didn't deserve a relationship with my children and that I was "unworthy" and "less than." The drugs told me I could do whatever I wanted all the time and that nothing mattered.

I would spend days sitting down by the Hudson River fearing the future while studying for the series 7, series 63, and series 55 [securities trader exams given by the Financial Industry Regulatory Authority (FINRA)].

I finally passed my exams and launched a new career in the stock market as a bond broker and then a stockbroker. Subsequently, I failed a drug test and was then let go by the firm. I was getting rejected by potential clients day by day, and my ego couldn't take the debilitating rejection. I next went to work at a day-trading firm where I lost my father's $10,000 investment while my colleagues were making six figures a week day-trading during the golden internet boom.

All these events were incapacitating and brought my fragile ego down to a new low. Instead of picking myself up and brushing myself off with the will and drive to prevail, I kept retreating. I wasn't present for my three young kids or my wife, and life continued to spiral downward. I became extremely attached to my two dogs as they became substitutes for my wife and children, the family I had forsaken. Soon thereafter, I had the opportunity to set up a drug deal for a so-called friend, which resulted in me being set up in a drug bust by thirty-five DEA agents. I was arrested and charged with three A1 felonies. After the judge's ruling, I was sent to an inpatient facility in upstate Rhinebeck, New York, to a place called Daytop for six months and then to a halfway house in Far Rockaway, New York, for another six months.

Why did I create this depressing and terrible life? What did I do wrong? I turned my back on my responsibilities. Because I did not deal with my problems, my ego grew into a monster. I created a movie in which I would hide from the truth, and I created distractions to take me away from dealing with reality. I recognize that the weaknesses in my character created this chapter in my life. The negativity didn't go away; it only got worse. Since this time, many years have passed, and I have successfully been able to transform my weak ego with the help of loving friends, family members, and medical professionals. Looking back knowing what I know now, I would not have trusted myself. I have a strong understanding of my ego, and I now choose the light over darkness.

CHAPTER 17

Ask Yourself These Questions

YOU NOW SHOULD be more aware and thoughtful about your own life and where you place your trust. I hope what I have shared has empowered you and that you will be more mindful. Let's reexamine these core questions of trust.

How can we trust doing business with others?

In an ideal world, there is an implicit trust, and if that trust is broken, the business connection will be terminated, which provides motivation to behave with integrity. Being trustworthy requires a degree of vulnerability; for example, a shop owner who guarantees a money-back exchange for any client who is unsatisfied establishes credibility. Integrity means doing what you say you'll do and then following through.

Do you assume trust?

Just because you have had a long relationship with someone does not mean you should ignore or explain away signs that something may be wrong. You may be blocking out reasonable suspicion. Don't avoid your gut feelings because a day of reckoning may come.

When your gut mistrusts, what do you do? This is a very important question. Don't avoid or kick the can. You must deal with the ramifications of what has happened or is happening. Do it sooner rather than later. Later will prove costly.

Can you be objective about your emotions and how you react? Emotions can make you irrational and cost you objectivity. Here's a personal example: My ex-partner, who is a crook and a sociopath, did terrible things to harm me. His actions forced me to close my company and deal with the antipathy he created among people with whom we did business. Initially, I was reactive, responding to him with animosity. My anger fell on deaf ears. A sociopath is never contrite. As I learned, less said is more said. You can't speak to deaf ears. Now I say nothing, and I just pursue remedies through the legal system. I no longer allow my emotions to control what I do or say.

Step outside yourself and be objective.

How often do you lie?

I confessed that I counted seven white lies in one week. I believe most people don't think about or care if they lie. Do you? Really consider this question. Should others trust you?

How close are you with your family members? The way our family relationships are and the way we think they should be different vary considerably for most of us. We don't pick our families, but there should be implicit trust among family members. The expression "blood is thicker than water" is, unfortunately, just an expression. If you are able, respect and cherish your heritage and go out of your way to nourish the people, circumstances, and surroundings that have always been part of your life. If you are fortunate to have it, cherish it.

Can you rely on what you think and do? Think about that! How you react and what you do may be correct—or possibly not. Be objective! If you want the best outcome, really think about the results of what you say and about how your actions affect others.

Have you learned how to handle betrayals?

My guess is probably not. Violation of trust is so hurtful and disappointing. Aside from experiencing anger and hurt, we often want to be vindictive. These feelings are very hard to control, but they must be. Be smart! Learn from mistakes and move on. Repetition is self-defeating and mostly exacerbates bad conditions.

What do you find hard to talk about with your partner?

Many couples find it difficult to discuss some topics with each other. Others, like myself, shun confrontation and unpleasantness. This is a huge blunder. It's simpler to figure out what the problems are and how to address them if you hash them out. Your spouse's input may appear to be judgmental, but if you want to develop complete trust, you must be welcoming. Never go to bed in the middle of an argument. Stay awake until you've figured out what's wrong. Do you consider your partner to be your best friend?

People don't enjoy being questioned about whether or not they love their spouses and how much their spouses love them. But during my research, I've heard time and time again that being with your best friend is essential for a strong, long-lasting, committed relationship. This isn't the only criterion, but it's the most important one.

Are you conscious of what you write on the Internet?

Do you remember any of the tales I told you? Images that are inappropriate or remarks that are derogatory might bite you in the a— if you post them on the Internet. Conversely, do you believe in what you're being sold? Always double-check! We might be healthy or ill depending on what we consume or put on our bodies.

What kind of buddies do you have?

Don't be fooled. It's critical to know who's on your side and who will be there for you in good times and bad. Which of your memories is the most painful? We all have at least one, if not more. It's a fact of life. Remember to keep these in mind. Take notes from them.

What was the last thing that made you cry?

Crying is a powerful emotion triggered by highly emotional circumstances or feelings, and not just painful ones. Being able to talk about something difficult implies that you have faith in the person with whom you are sharing your sorrow or deep feeling. And that person must have faith in you.

Do you have a hard time addressing your mistakes?

It may be emotionally beneficial to not linger on terrible judgments or individuals who have deceived you, but good judgment comes from experience, and experience comes through bad judgment. Learn by becoming a sponge.

What is one thing about yourself that you would change?

Depending on your response, you'll learn whether you recognize and, more importantly, wish to improve the bad aspects of yourself. At the very least, we all have something.

What would you do if you had only six weeks to live?

At this moment, I am reflecting on something that happened today. My son called me a few hours ago, really upset. He was crying. He had just heard that Kobe Bryant, his favorite athlete, had died in a helicopter crash at the age of forty-one years; one of his daughters died as well. I was stunned, and honestly, tears came to my eyes too. He was one of the greatest athletes—a sports icon, twenty-years a Lakers basketball player—and his life ended in a flash. His success, wealth, and stardom now mean nothing to him.

I have a friend who has Lou Gehrig's disease (ALS). I am watching him atrophy, and I know that it's just a matter of time before the disease overtakes him.

Cherish your life. Be positive. So, the answer to this question for me is…I don't know what I would do if I only had six weeks to live. Hold this question. The response will come for us both.

CHAPTER 18

Conclusion

TWO REASONS THAT we don't trust people:

- We don't know them.
- We know them.

I sit at my desk here at the finale of this book thinking about the breadth of trust and how fundamental it is to everything in life. Writing this book has really been an epiphany for me—and right now, I feel empowered. This experience has been simultaneously cathartic and educative. I have learned so much. Over the year-plus of writing this book, doing a huge amount of research, speaking to everybody about its mission, and getting feedback and content contributions, I have come a long way, especially since I have confessed more than once how foolish I have been in giving away my own trust.

At the earlier stages of the coronavirus pandemic, Bill Ackman, Pershing Square Capital manager, appeared on CNBC and forecasted doomsday, saying that the stock market would continue to crash. At that time, he warned that Hilton worldwide was going to zero and that America could "end as we know it."

What he didn't say was that, earlier in the month, he had made a $27 million bet in a bear-hedged/leveraged transaction; shortly after his interview, his fund made $2.4 billion dollars. Clearly, his interview wasn't the cause of the market collapse, but it exacerbated the selling and losses. Did he say what he said knowing that would enhance his profits in the position he took? Rhetorical question! Maybe we could have trusted him more if, prior to starting his interview, he said, "I just want to fully disclose before I speak that I just placed a bet on a bearish position."

I close with this story simply to point out that the lessons in this book are ongoing, widely applicable, evolving, and urgent. Trust—but do so with great care. And when your trust gets violated, always remember: good judgment comes from experience, and experience comes from bad judgment.

APPENDIX A

The Ten Commandments of Trust

After you finish reading this book, your self-awareness should be at a totally different level. If I have been successful in my work, you are now far more introspective. This was my goal. What follows are some of the edicts that should hereafter influence your thoughts and your trust decisions. These are the key essentials as there are so many more.

1. **Follow your gut feelings carefully.** Your instincts are mostly correct. If you a have bad feeling about someone, do not trust him or her. The likelihood is that you will get hurt doing so. Do not kick the puck into the corner—react promptly. If you are positively predisposed and feel totally confident about your relationship, do not be seduced into letting your guard totally down; this is being too trusting. Be wary and cognizant.
2. **Face the music!** When something *seems* wrong in a relationship, it is. Do not ignore that feeling. If you do, the issue will absolutely not go away and most probably will escalate. You must confront the violation of trust, or it will grow worse, and you will pay a punitive price.
3. **Know by verification what you believe in or buy.** You cannot trust marketing or sale pitches. Do your homework, especially about what you put on or into your body. This discipline is essential for your well-being. Check consumer reports. A friend of mine sold hurricane-proof windows. They were great until the hurricanes hit.
4. **"Et tu, Brute?"** This is a classic aphorism. Caesar was murdered, and his best friend was among the assassins. Always keep your awareness sharp and take nothing for granted. This, again,

refers to trusting too much. Betrayal comes in many forms. Be very careful about sharing personal information with others (and on the Internet). Absolute trust is never absolute. Sadly, I have experienced this. But there's a silver lining: because of my poor judgment, I was inspired to write this book and help others.

5. **Do not always trust what you are told.** You must be leery. Everybody lies. If you say to yourself that you do not lie, then you are lying about never lying. Yes, many of these lies may be "white lies," but it is what it is. Magic is the only honest profession. Magicians promise to deceive you, and they do. Always get references and do research on people you are doing business with. Intimate relationships are more difficult because our hearts are influenced. Look for consistency, vulnerability, and sincerity. A hackneyed expression may say it all: the sizzle is not the steak. If you are loved, you are told the truth, and you feel safe. Good judgment comes from experience. Experience comes from bad judgment. Everybody's past reputation is a biography, and it embodies a history of good and bad.

6. **Trust your decisions!** Do not equivocate! When I got married for the first time, I felt uncertainty. My gut was ambivalent, but I proceeded against my instincts and committed. Thereafter, I went through the worst imaginable divorce, though I also have two wonderful kids.

7. **Do not disclose personal information on social media.** Be aware of the perils of artificial intelligence/hackers. Matrimonial attorneys now scour social media to discover information and evidence. Jealous people will slander self-promoting successful people who share their stories on Instagram or Facebook because they are envious. Craving recognition for achievement can become a vulnerability. Remember Raina Aiube, the journalist from India who was hacked with a deep fake sex video? She was devastated, and her career was almost destroyed. I am very careful about sharing my personal information.

8. **You must be able to trust yourself.** Do you? Most people do not, even though they will say they do. Be honest on both personal and business levels. This commandment is the most important: be honest to yourself and others. Figure out how to trust yourself.
9. **Trust your beliefs but trust knowledge more.** We are products of our environment and of influencers who manipulate our passions and behavior, often based on vulnerability, ignorance, and prejudice.
10. **In the end, do not forsake trust!** Trust is healthy and empowering. Integrity is everything. I will say it again: integrity is everything. I want to trust so much. I really do, and I will continue to want this. It is who I am. I implore you to do the same. If 9/11 happened again, would you embrace a stranger in light of circumstance?

APPENDIX B

Trust 911: Trust Warning Signals

- **"Trust me"**: How many times has someone said to you "Trust me"? Red lights should go off immediately. This statement is supposed to give you a sense of confidence that what you are being told is true. If what a person is saying is true, there would be no need for him or her to convince you. Truth and trust go hand in hand. You will be disappointed almost every time someone says "Trust me" to you. The other catchphrase to be aware of is "I've got your back." More likely, this person has a stiletto in his left hand. My crooked ex-partner used to say that to me regularly.
- **Nonverbal communication warnings**: Someone who doesn't look in your eyes when speaking to you is often signaling untruthfulness. (Also, beware of the person who stares too intently into your eyes as though trying to compensate for something.) Eyes are beacons. In addition, there are four nonverbal behaviors that, when done together, are reliable signals of untrustworthiness: (a) hand fidgeting, (b) face touching, (c) leaning away, and (d) crossing arms.
- **Wishy-washy language**. "I can't promise, but I will try ..." "I believe I did ..." "I thought I told you ..." The way we speak is very telling. If you think about these hedged statements, you will realize that they are signals—and the probability is that you are being lied to or deceived. Do not dismiss these alerts.
- **Uncomfortable conversation**: Conversational intelligence makes you attuned to signals of trust and distrust from people who work for you and the people you work for. Sometimes, the need for distrust is obvious. If you are told something that is untrue or you are asked to do something that you know isn't right, it is time to evaluate your options. Alternatively, if trust has become ingrained,

a person might be able to *seem* at ease when conversing with you, but you might notice signals that indicate cause for distrust. For example, the person might always keep interactions short, avoid personal topics, or avoid providing you with any specifics about how their work is progressing. When people feel trust, conversations are marked by ease and friendliness. If you get the sense that you might not be trusted by the people whom you work for, consider how your conversational style might factor in.

- **Too many questions**: A healthy personal relationship is marked by implicit trust and security. A good marriage is one in which each partner thinks he or she got the better end of the deal. Conversely, if you need to know what your partner is doing all the time, your insecurity is a sign that you don't trust your partner. Constant questioning never feels good on either side, and if this is happening, it may be time to rethink the relationship.
- **Not trusting yourself**: Lack of self-confidence, missed opportunities, loneliness, and even social anxiety are the results of self-sabotage. They indicate a lack of self-trust. It is important to be introspective and honest with yourself to overcome these issues.
- **Trusting too quickly**: Do you trust people too quickly? I have—and I have paid the price. Real trust comes over time and with experience. You're best off starting with an open mind and extending trust to people as they build a track record with you. But don't get lazy. Always verify!
- **Signs that you have trust issues**:
    o You overthink and predict how someone will betray you.
    o You are overly protective.
    o You distance yourself from others.
    o You avoid commitment.
    o You don't forgive the smallest mistakes.
    o You are excessively wary of people.
    o You feel lonely and depressed.
    o Your relationships are shallow or superficial.
    o You fear becoming attached.

APPENDIX C

Trust Triage: How to Recover When Your Trust Is Violated

- Betrayal hurts, especially when it is a personal violation! The impact can cause emotional harm and irrational reactions. Overcoming betrayal may be easier said than done, but don't succumb to self-destructive or vindictive behavior. Take a deep breath. Edify yourself and think about positive things in your life. Be practical about your reactions. Future-forecast and recognize that time does heal all wounds.
- Business dishonesty is commonplace. React promptly and pursue plausible and practical remedies. If you don't trust your boss or supervisor, be objective. Things won't change. You may be better off changing your job. You must mitigate the damage. Take seriously what you've discovered and act constructively.
- Maintain your boundaries. If you are getting divorced and it is ugly, don't make things worse. One implicit rule I implore you to heed is not to use the children as pawns. Control your anger. The violation of infidelity or distrust is horrible, but putting your children in harm's way, physically or emotionally, brings long-term negative consequences. Matrimonial law is an inherent conflict of interest. You want to end the battle, but attorneys are incentivized when you litigate. Go into this process with your eyes open.
- Be realistic about reconciliation. Someone's promise to change his or her behavior will facilitate initial trust recovery. A promise following deception may also be suspect. The meaningfulness of the promise following deception depends on the extent of trustworthy actions taken to restore credibility and trust. Although a promise may play

a significant role in restoring trust for those who were deceived, nothing is as effective as not being deceived in the first place.
- Respect, respond, and learn from a social media disaster. Technological advancements both on a personal and business basis can ignite disasters. Businesses must be very sensitive about social media and must respond immediately and appropriately when something negative circulates. Personal posts can also be dangerous. Be mindful of what can be used against you. Remember some of the stories I shared, particularly the one about matrimonial attorneys.

INDEX

A

abuse, 73, 184, 211, 213, 224
accounting, accrual, 201
Ackman, Bill, 272
addiction, 41, 44, 47, 91
  symptoms of, 125
adolescents, 229–30, 234–35, 240
adults, 233, 235, 238, 240–41
Airbnb, 45–46, 76, 78
  genesis of, 78
All the President's Men, 213
Amazon, 45, 47, 50–51, 190
Amazon Go, 190
American President, The, 212, 215
Americans, x–xi, 3, 52, 74, 107, 214
anger, 82, 147, 155, 246, 268–69, 281
anxiety, 85, 151, 154
artificial intelligence (AI), 50, 117, 187, 189–96, 276
  narrow, 192
Art of War, The (Sun Tzu), x
Ashley Madison, 6, 48
attorney, 5–8, 19, 138, 281
  criminal, 7
  real estate, 19–20
attractiveness, 249–51, 255

B

balance sheet, 200
beauty, 158, 249, 255
Beauty Pays (Hamermesh), 250
betrayal, 87, 276
bias, 3, 108, 131, 193–95, 225
  confirmation, 110
Big Short, The, 11
Blockbuster, 172
Boeing, 61

C

cash flows, statement of, 200, 207
caveman, 29
Chamberlain, Neville, 4
Charmin, 31–33
cheating, 53, 110–11
Chesky, Brian, 78
childhood, 25, 68, 229, 240, 244
China, xii
Churchill, Winston, 4
Citron, Danielle, 115, 117
Cleopatra (Egyptian queen), 4
Coca-Cola, 41–42, 62
collateralized debt obligations (CDOs), 11–12
  synthetic, 11–12
consumers, 33, 35, 45, 49–50, 56–57, 59, 194
Conti, Leonardo, 125
coronavirus, xii–xiii
counterfeiting, 56
credibility, 14, 45–46, 49, 100, 110, 221, 267

D

Dalio, Ray, 169
dark web, 48
death, 148, 181
de Blasio, Bill, 211
deception, 104, 113, 115, 281
deep fake, 116–18
depression, 85, 96, 154, 246
Dillinger, John, 136

disintermediation, 45
  human, 186–87
dissonance, cognitive, 109–10
distrust, 1, 3, 117, 130, 279–81
divorce, 5–7, 16, 136–38, 144, 146–48, 151, 154, 156, 225–26, 244
  risk of, 137
Divorcing Dads Council, 146
Dreyfus, Richard, 212
drugs, 90, 122–23, 125, 265
  effects of, 124

E

eBay, 45–46
ego, 91, 210, 233, 256–59, 261–63
Ego Is the Enemy (Holiday), 259
egomaniacs, 257, 262
Einstein, Albert, 129
emotional intelligence, 100
emotions, 82, 101, 133–34, 152, 180, 268, 270
empathy, 9, 163, 178–79
Enron Corporation, 10, 203
entitlement, 261
Environmental Working Group (EWG), 35, 41
epistemology, 120–21
Epstein, Jeffrey, 97

F

Facebook, 5, 47, 66, 80, 219–20, 276
failure, 15, 65, 98–99, 149, 168
  fear of, 98
  pain of, 99
faith, 38, 60, 65, 68, 174–75, 181
  blind, viii
  lack of, 85
Fakespot, 50–51
family, 30–31, 40, 80, 147, 149, 155, 161, 244
Fauci, Anthony, xii

fear, xi, 29, 87–88, 107, 133, 151, 167, 183, 233
Federal Bureau of Investigation (FBI), 79, 136, 160, 212, 223
Federal Trade Commission (FTC), 53, 55
Financial Industry Regulatory Authority (FINRA), 47
financial statements, 199–203, 207, 209
Food and Drug Administration, 37
fraud, 14, 24, 56, 198, 202, 204, 257
friendship, 68–69, 73, 259

G

Gates, Bill, 194
Geneen, Harold, 263
generally accepted accounting standards (GAAP), 201, 207
Germany, 122–23, 125, 132
God, 79, 179–80
Google, 33, 40, 47, 52
government, xiii, 35, 41, 48, 216
  system of, 214
Great Depression, 169
Great Recession, 10–11, 17
gut, 129, 167, 170, 267, 275–76

H

hackers, 47–48, 193, 196
HAL 9000, 194
halo, 249–50
Hamermesh, David
  Beauty Pays, 250
hara-kiri, 126
Hassan II (king of Morocco), 65
Hastings, Reed, 171
Hawaii, 39, 66–67
Hemingway, Ernest, 16, 86–87
Henriques, Diana
  The Wizard of Lies, 9
heterophily, 68

heuristics, 168
Hitler, Adolf, 4, 62–63, 99, 125, 132, 230
Hitler Youth, 230
Holiday, Ryan
   Ego Is the Enemy, 259, 263
homophily, 68
honesty, x–xi, 149, 261
humiliation, 127

I

income statement, 200, 207
independence, 232, 247
   fear of, 151
injustice, 127, 212
insider trading, 160–61
instincts, 129, 170, 174, 253, 275–76
Internet, 4, 6, 46, 48, 56, 78
intimacy, 162
intuition, 129, 167, 171
investments, 117, 227

J

Japan, 126, 244
jealousy, 68
   signs of, 69
Jersey City, 227–28
Jetsons, The, 192
Jews, 62, 74
Johnson & Johnson, 43–44, 60
judgments, 87, 155, 171, 174, 194, 225
Julius Caesar, 65, 275

K

Kennedy. John F., 218
Key Biscayne, 13
kleptocracy, 212

L

Laidler, Keith
Surveillance Unlimited: How We've Become the Most Watched People on Earth, 191
Langer, Walter, 132
laws, 116, 118, 139, 166, 225–26
Lehrer, Jim, 105–6
liars, 113–15
   pathological, 115
Life Mastery, 39
loans, 11–12, 14, 250
   liar, 12
Lyft, 15, 46

M

Madoff, Bernie, 8–10, 14, 100, 111
Madoff Securities, 14
Mark Antony (Roman general), 4
marketing, 29, 40–41, 189
   millennial, 49
Markopolos, Harry, 14
marriage, 136–38, 148–49, 151, 154, 162–63, 264–65
MarsCat, 197
melanomas, 37
methamphetamine, 125
millennials, 49, 195–96
money, 10–12, 21, 24–26, 57–58, 75, 107–8, 138, 161, 169, 200–201, 203–4, 207, 212, 220, 261–62
Morgan. J. Pierpont, 59–60
Musk, Elon, 194

N

National Aeronautics and Space Association (NASA), 166
Nazi Party, 122, 124, 230
Negotiating the Nonnegotiable (Shapiro), 131
Netflix, 171–72

O

Obama, Barack, 214
opioids, 265
oxybenzone, 36
oxytocin, 130–31

P

Page, Larry, 260
paltering, 104, 106–7, 216
Peace Corps, 75
Pence, Mike, xiii
physicality, 249–51
pistanthrophobia, 133
procrastinator, 112
Procter & Gamble, 31
profits, 15, 52, 62, 111, 204, 272
Public Company Accounting Oversight Board (PCAOB), 198
Purvis, Melvin, 136

R

Ranke, Otto, 124
reputation, 46, 106, 257, 276
robots, 109, 189, 195

S

Santa Claus, 42
Satan, 180
Schmell, Craig
 The Uninvited: How I Crashed My Way into Finding Myself, 91
self-awareness, x, 97, 134, 275
self-confidence, 98, 172, 176, 214, 264, 280
self-deception, 111–12
self-magnification, 111
self-trust, 82, 84–85, 88, 99, 280
sex, 116, 252
shame, 126
Shapiro, Daniel
 Negotiating the Nonnegotiable, 131
Smith, Edward, 59
social media, 4–6, 47, 49, 78, 118, 220, 242, 260, 276, 282
sociopath, 8, 18, 268
solipsism, 256
special-purpose entities (SPEs), 10
special-purpose vehicles (SPVs), 10
suicide, 85, 96, 126
suicide missions, 125, 127
Sundblom, Haddon, 42
sunscreens, 36–38
 spray, 37
Surveillance Unlimited: How We've Become the Most Watched People on Earth (Laidler), 191

T

Tankleff, Marty, 223–24
TaskRabbit, 46, 48
Teapot Dome, 210
technology, 45–47, 78, 116, 186–87, 191, 196–97
Temmler Werke, 124
Tesla, 109
Titanic, 59
toilet paper, 31–32
triangulation, 208–9
trust, v–viii, 1, 84–86, 88–90, 98, 100–101, 158, 174–75, 177–83, 231, 233–34, 240–42, 267–69, 275–77, 279–81
 absolute, 276
 breach of, 24, 64, 160, 181
 chemistry of, 130
 consumer, 36, 63
 degrees of, 3, 25
 foundations of, 14, 77
 marital, 137
 real, viii, 280
trust paradox, 193

U

Uber, 46, 190
Uninvited, The: How I Crashed My Way into Finding Myself (Schmell), 91
United States of America, 4–5, 10, 36–37, 52–53, 63, 90, 221–23, 244, 246, 260
United States Pharmacopeial Convention, 39
UrbanSitter, 78–80

V

Vision Jet, 197
Volkswagen, 53
Volvo, 30–31

W

Wall Street, 10–11, 14, 251, 257
Walters, Barbara, 9
War of the Worlds, The (Welles), 107
Welles, Orson, 107
WeWork, 15
Wizard of Lies, The (Henriques), 9

Z

Zerbe, Leah, 35–36

Made in the USA
Columbia, SC
15 December 2022